MILK & MOCHA

comics collection

Our Little Happiness

Melani Sie

Andrews McMeel
PUBLISHING®

INTRODUCTION

What does happiness mean to you?

Is it the taste of strawberry on top of your cake? Or is it the funny memes you discovered while scrolling online? Or is it waking up next to your loved one and seeing their sleeping face?

Happiness can be the littlest, the simplest, and the silliest things that may seem underwhelming to others, but they can put a smile on your face and keep you going.

This book is for those who love to enjoy all the little things. A little bit of happiness in the form of two bears living life with each other, being there for each other, and sharing joy and sadness with each other. We hope this book can make you giggle and smile and be that one little happiness that you share with your loved ones.

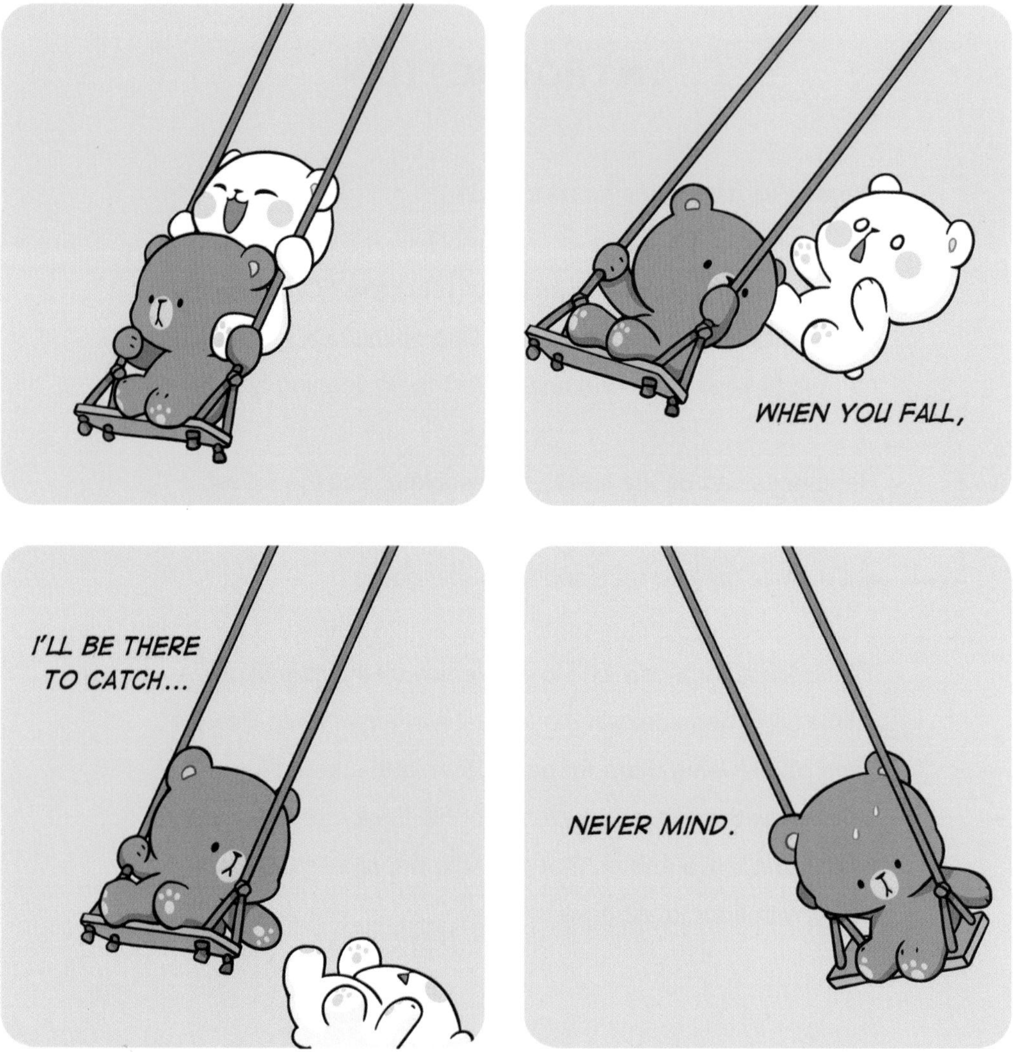

WHEN YOU FALL,
I'LL BE THERE TO CATCH...
NEVER MIND.

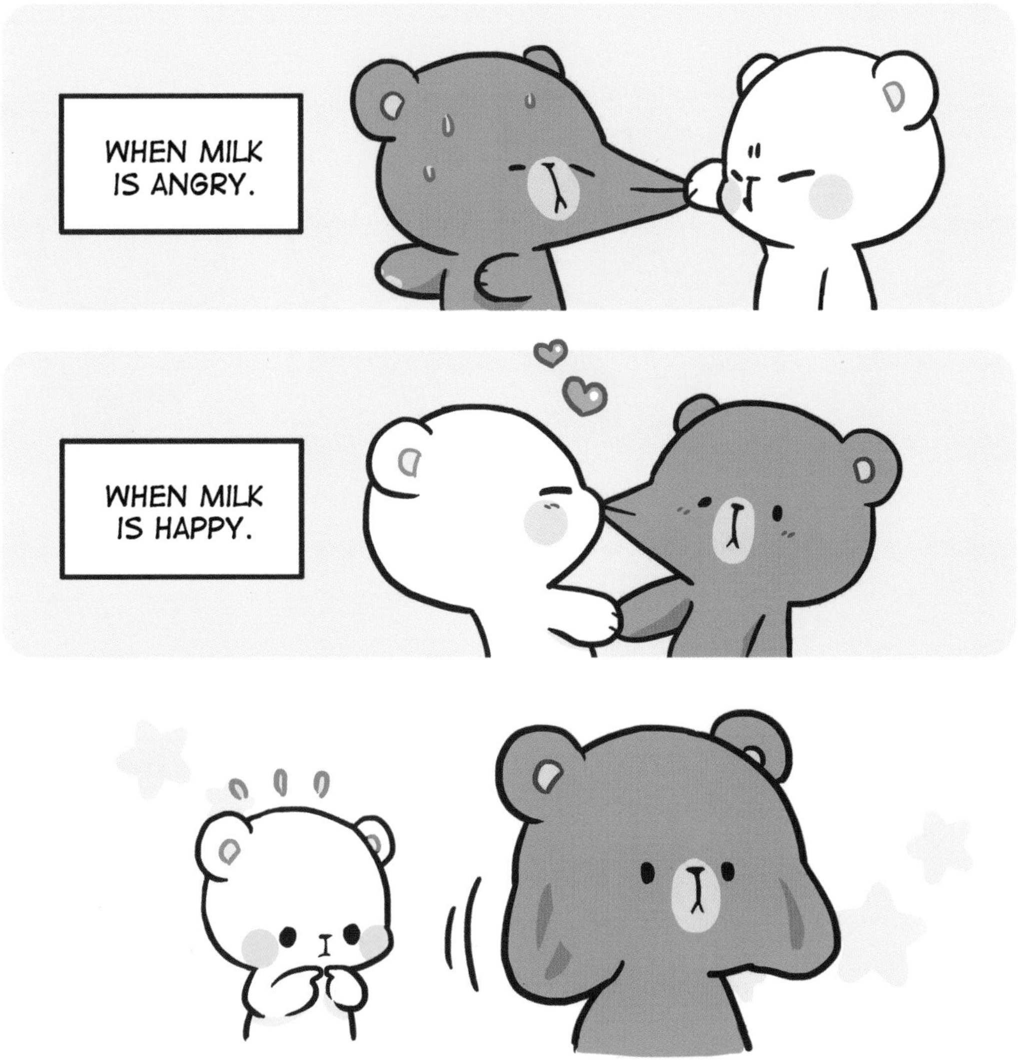
WHEN MILK IS ANGRY.
WHEN MILK IS HAPPY.

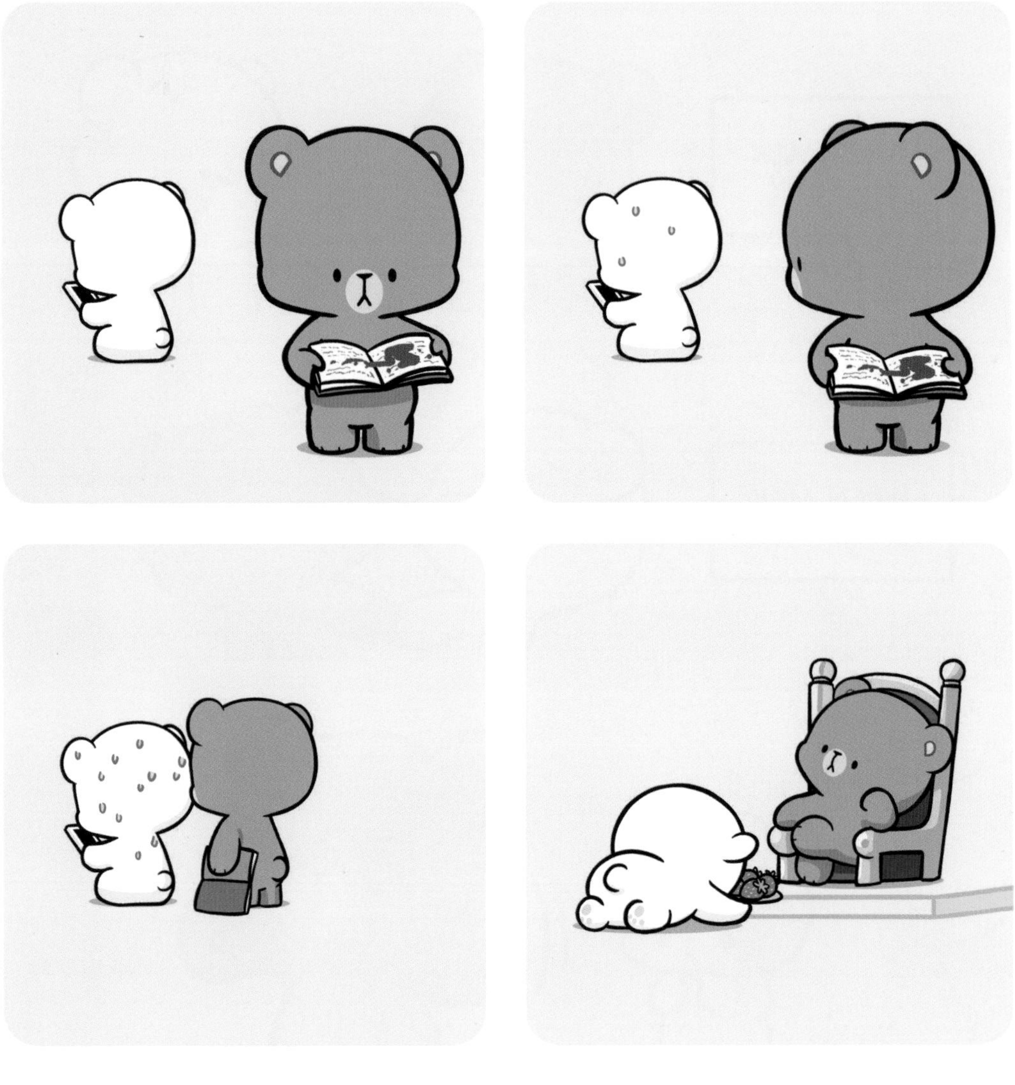

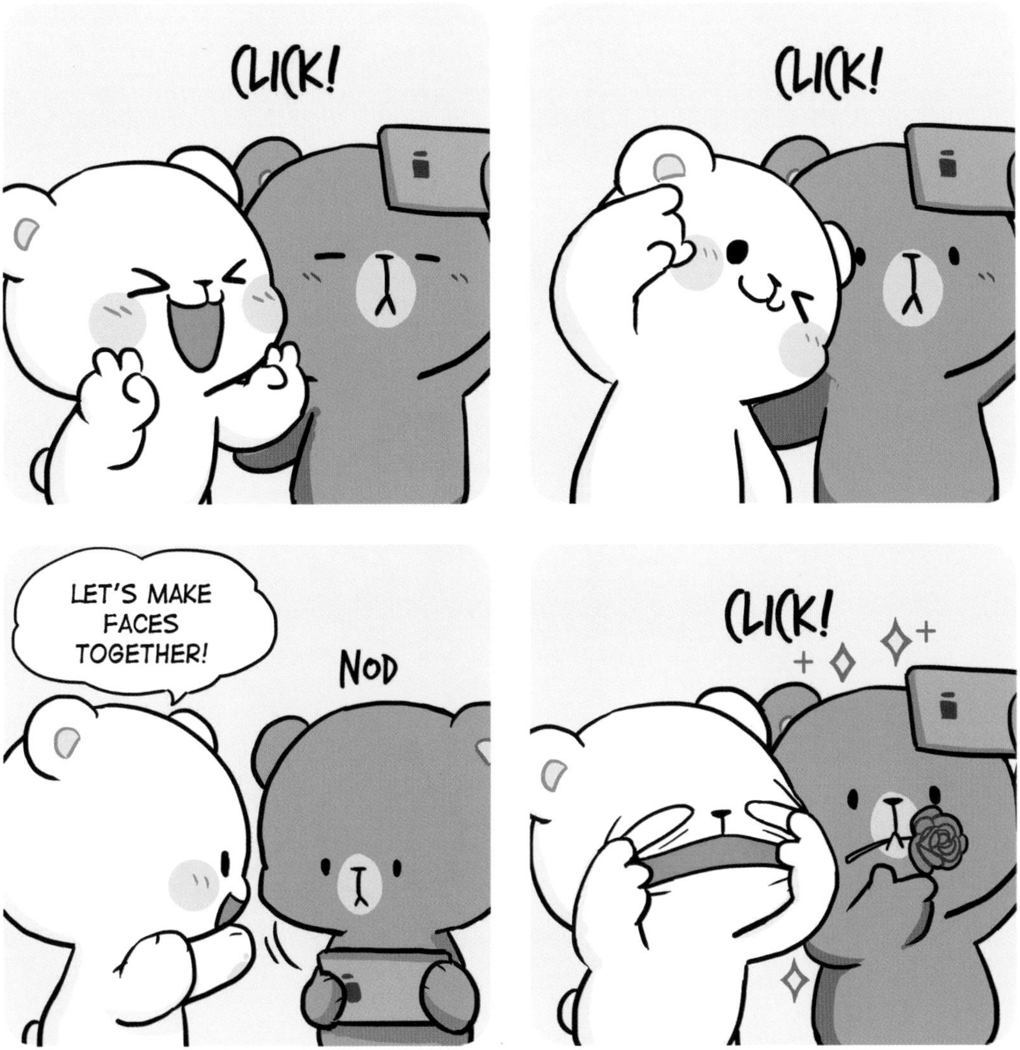
CLICK!
CLICK!
LET'S MAKE FACES TOGETHER!
NOD
CLICK!

Milk & Mocha's Dynamic

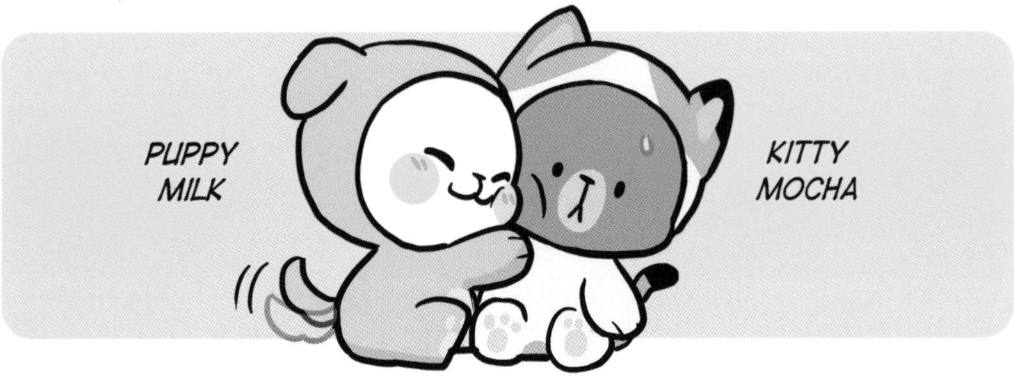
PUPPY
MILK
KITTY
MOCHA

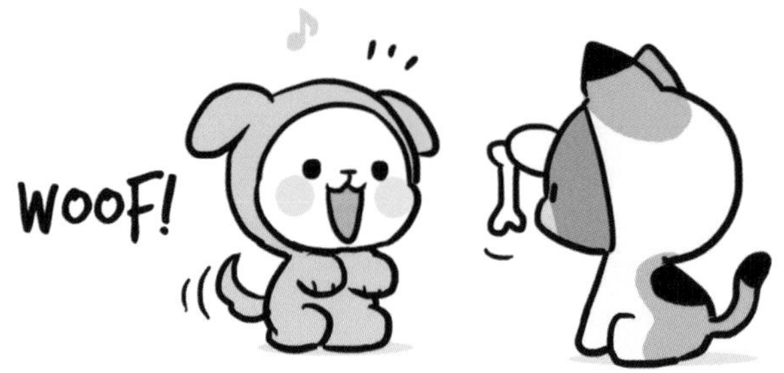
WOOF!

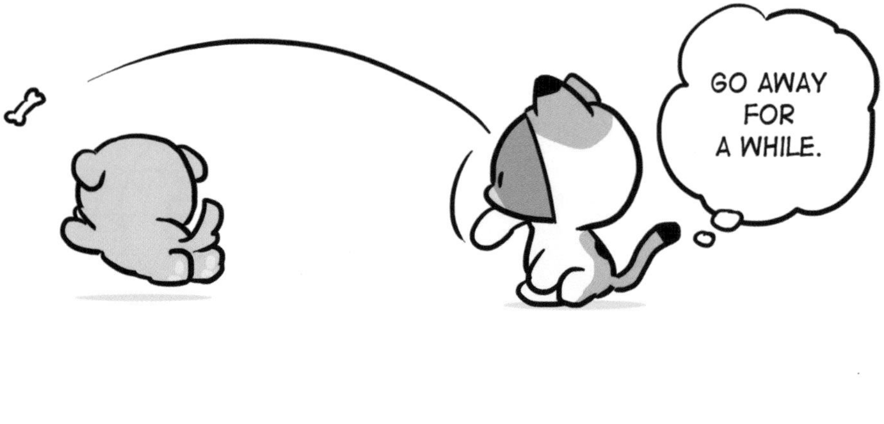
GO AWAY FOR A WHILE.

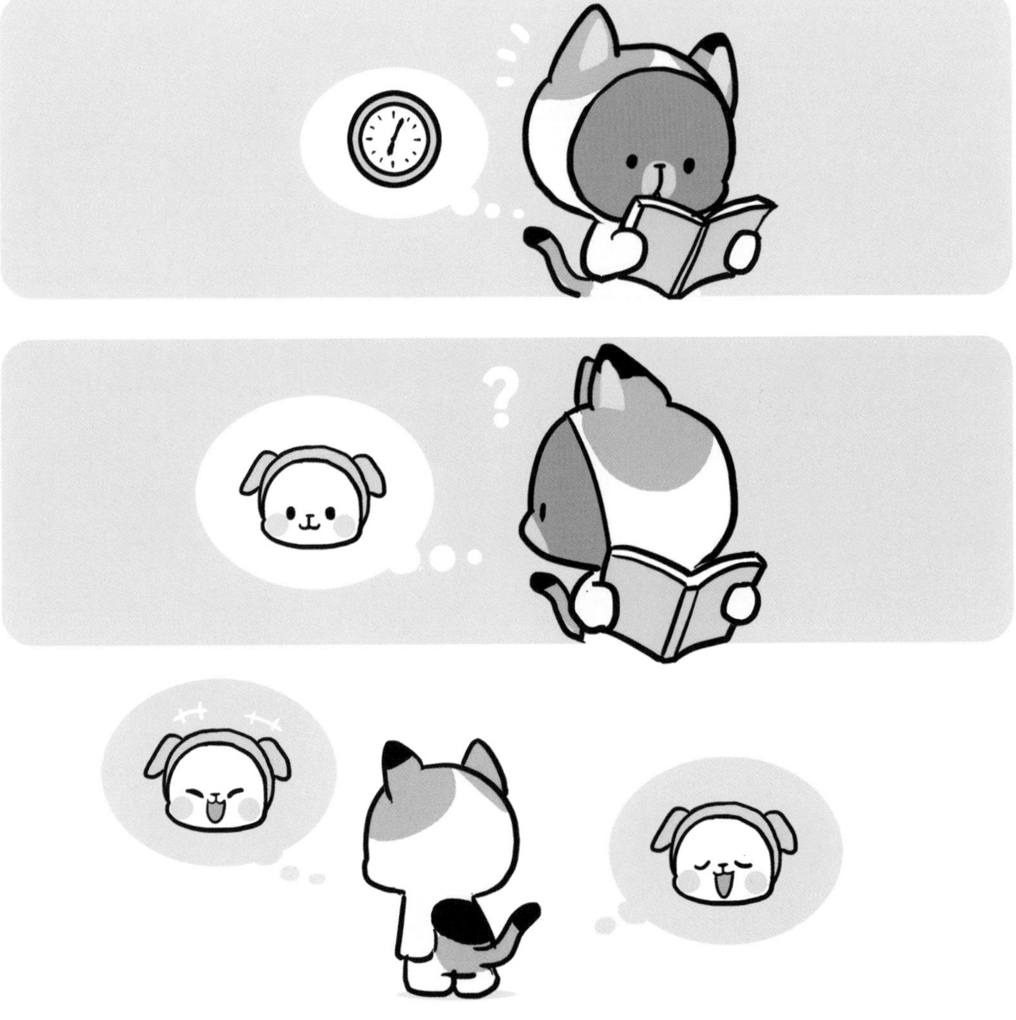

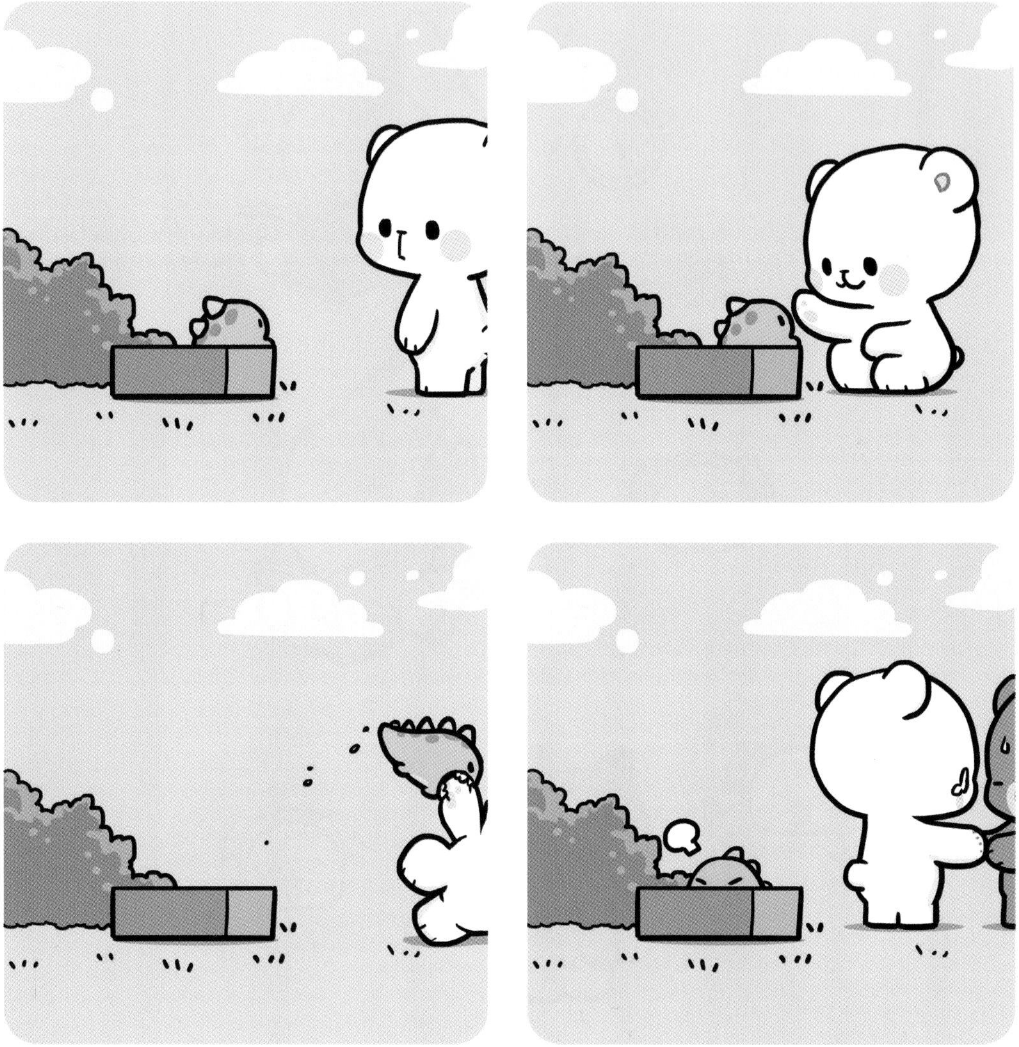

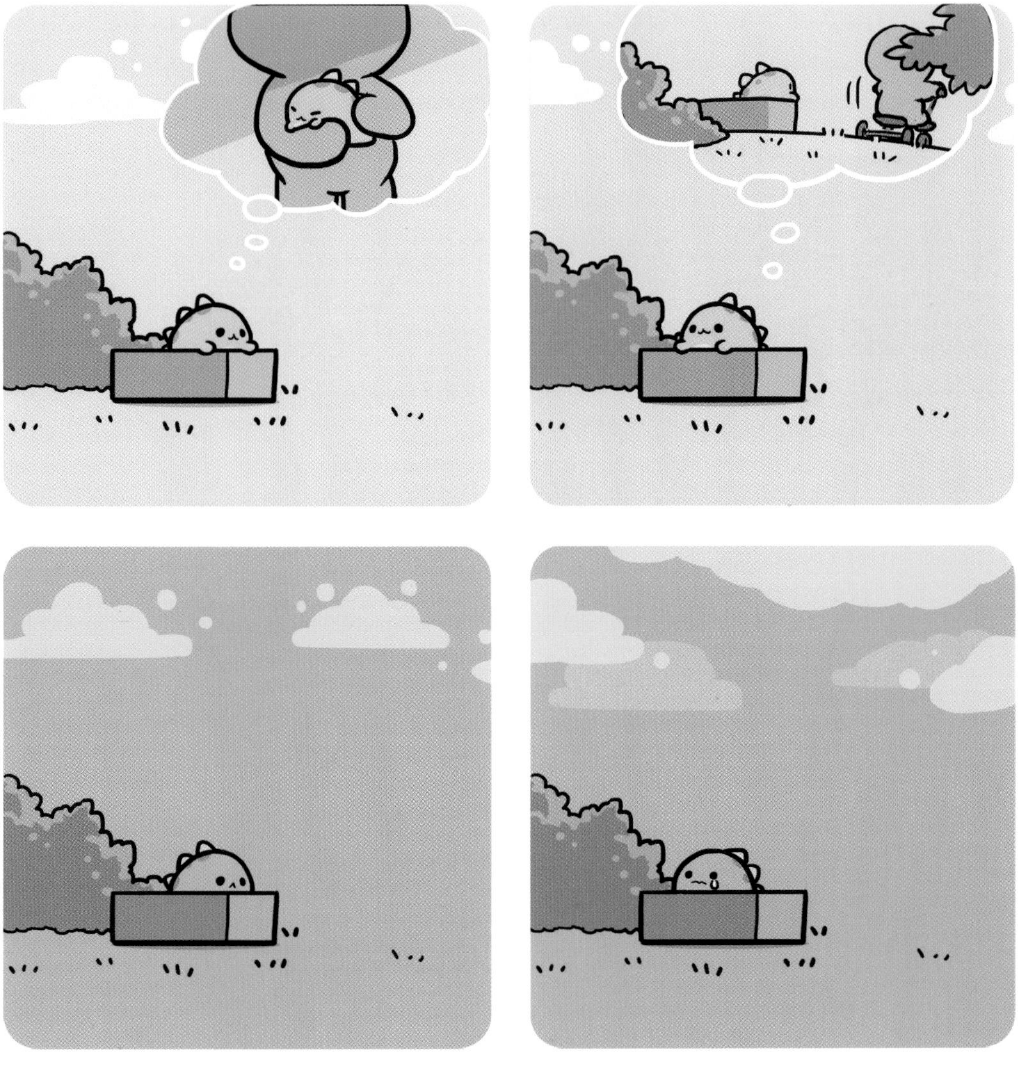

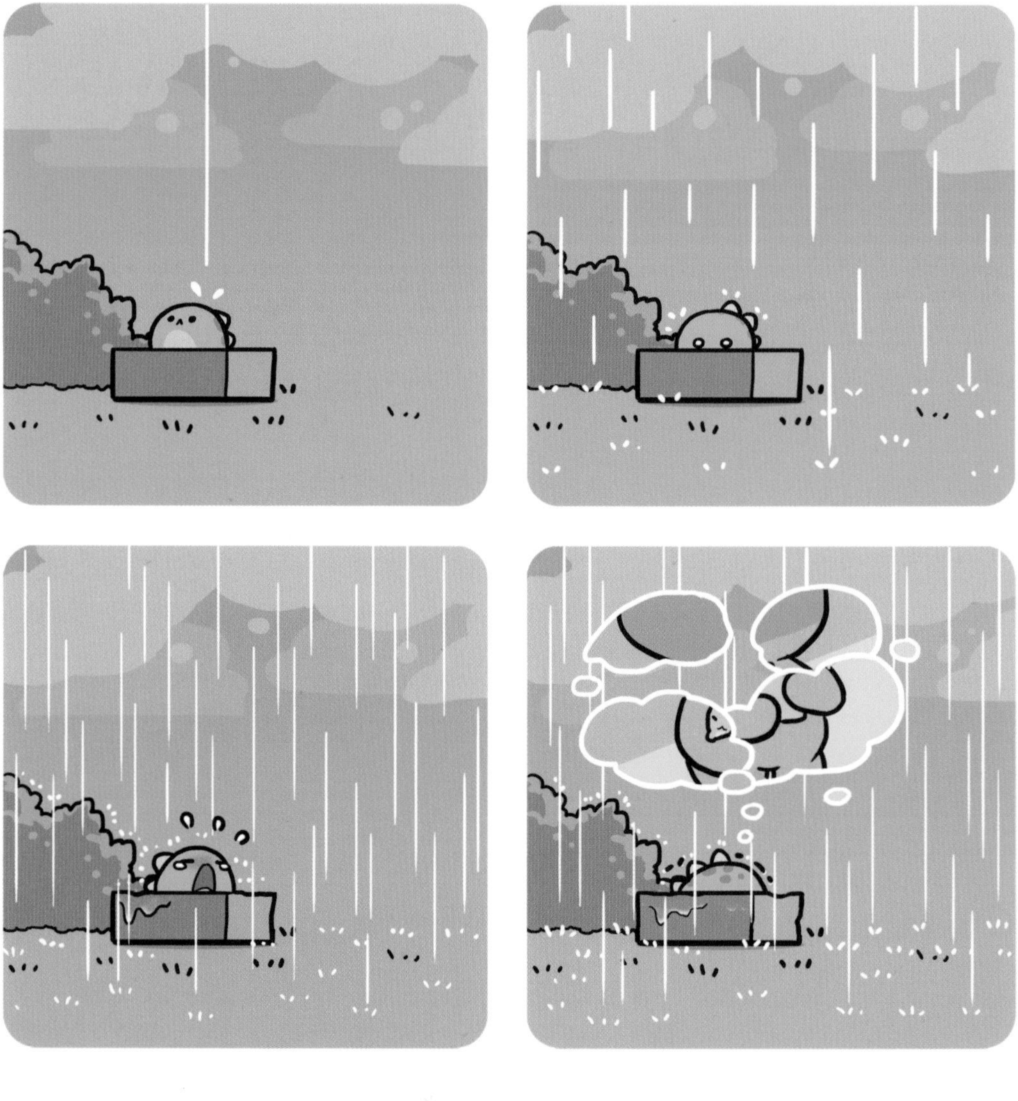

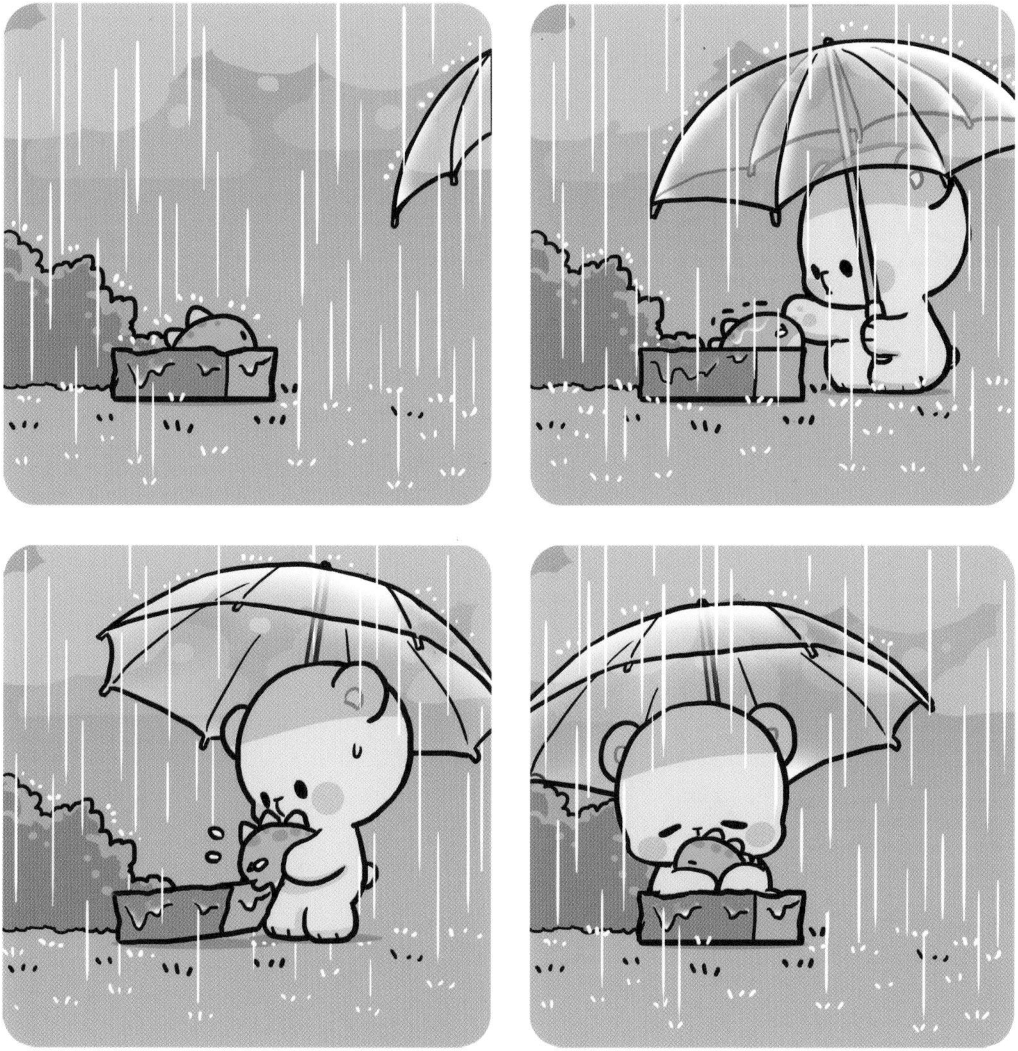

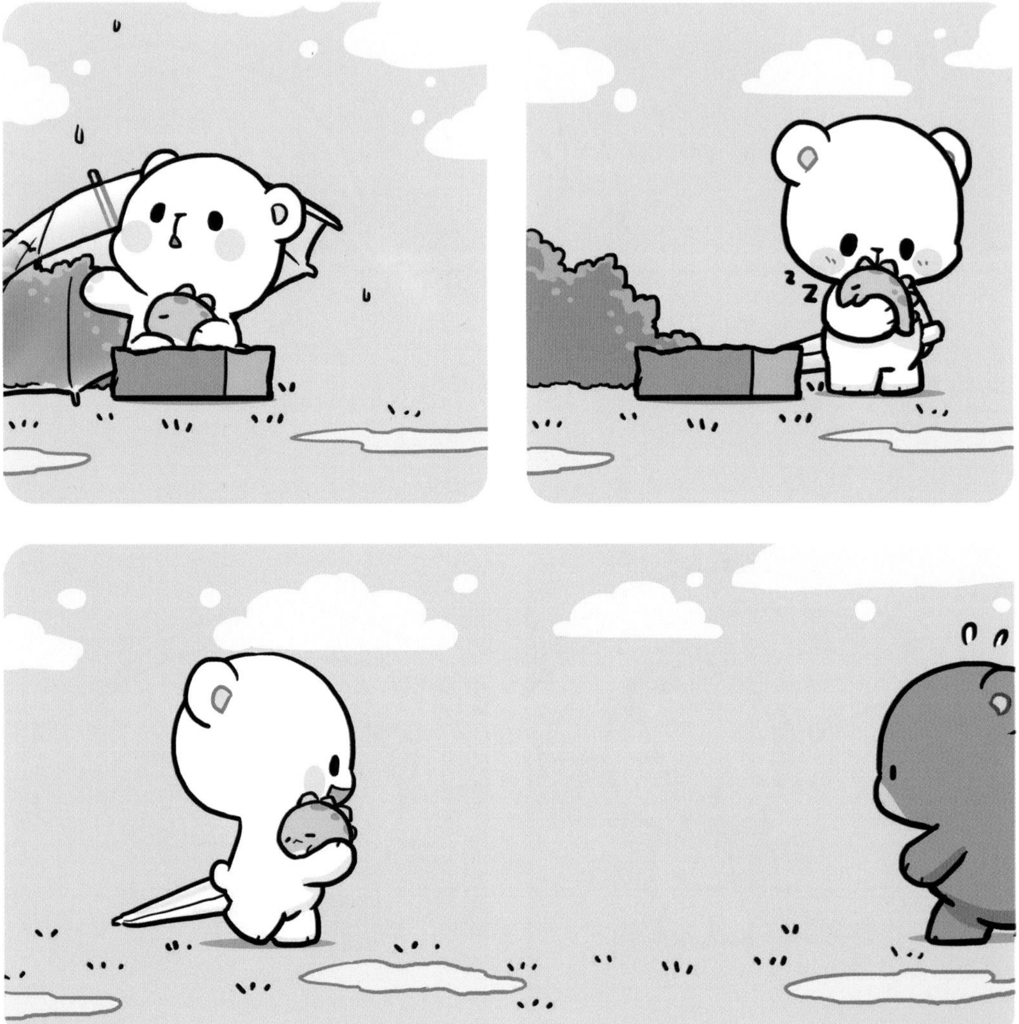

HELLO, MATCHA.

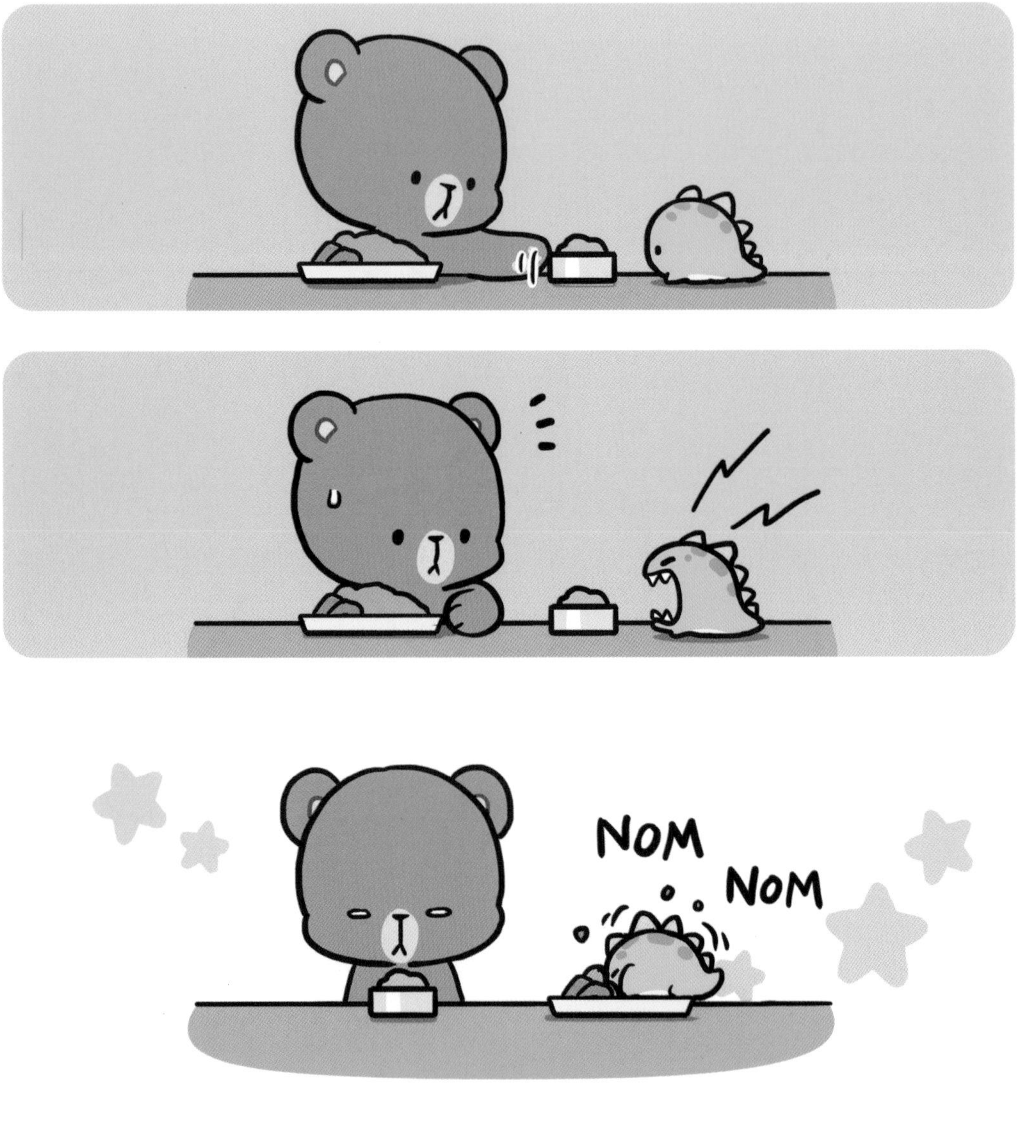
NOM
NOM

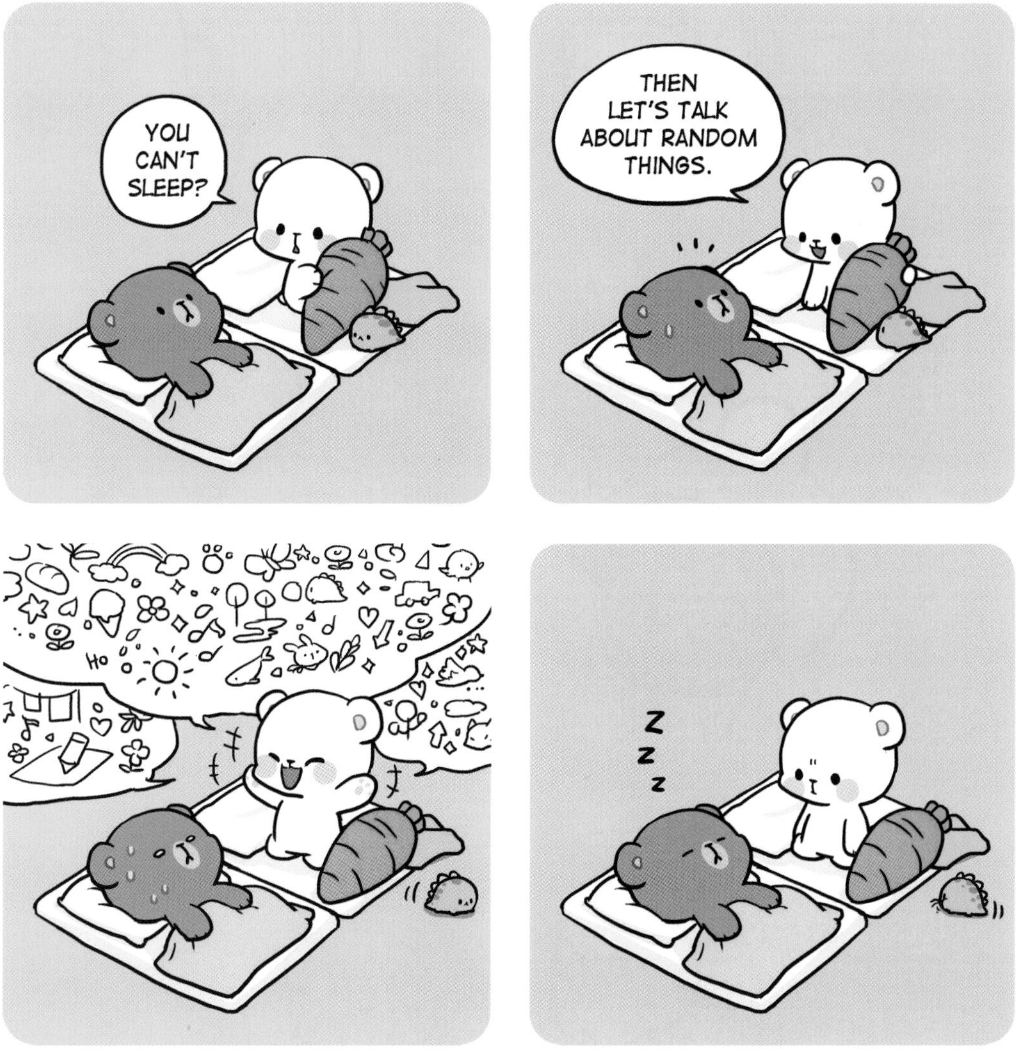
YOU CAN'T SLEEP?
THEN LET'S TALK ABOUT RANDOM THINGS.
HO
Z Z Z

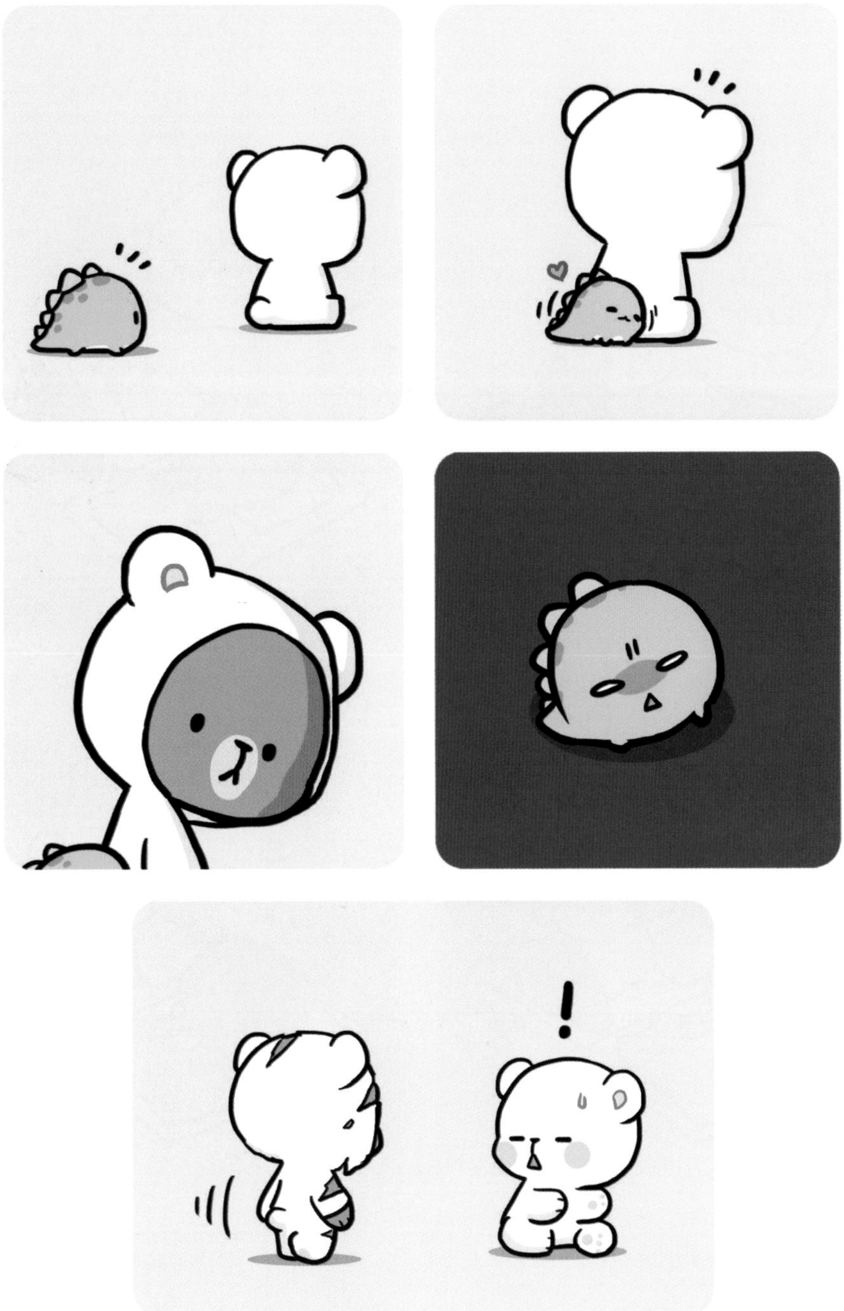

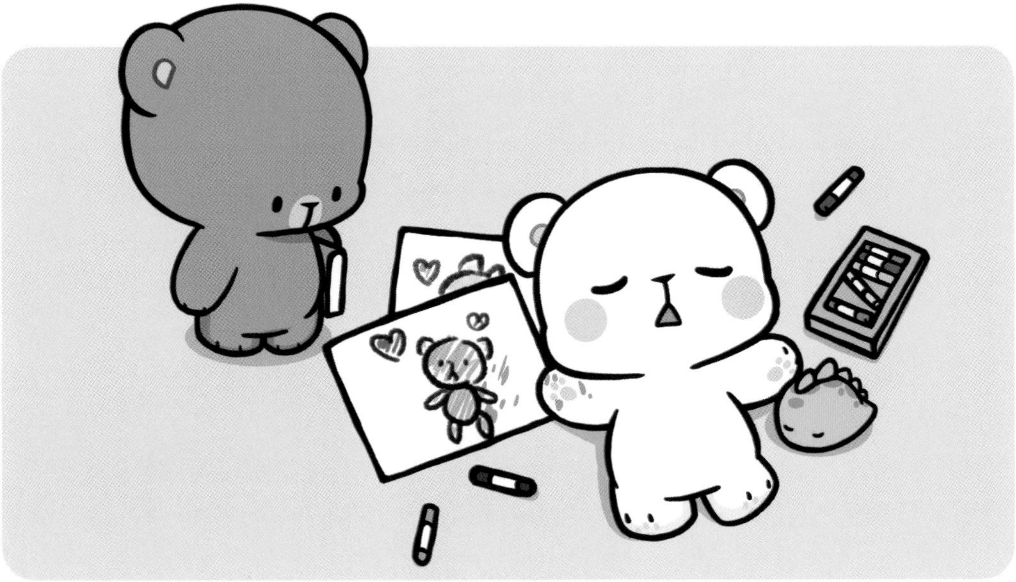

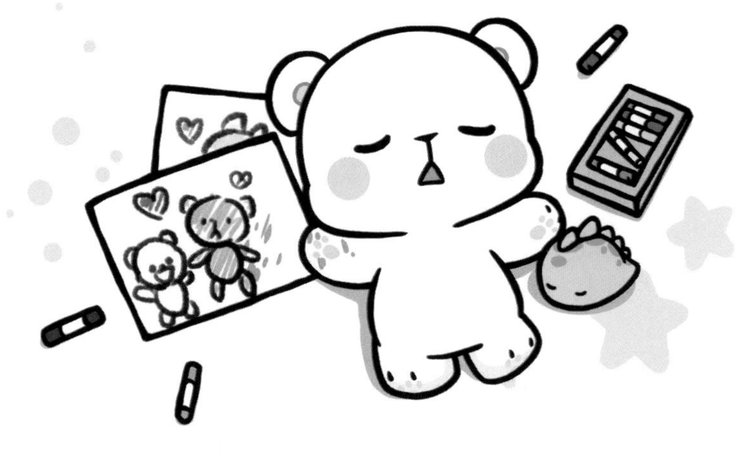

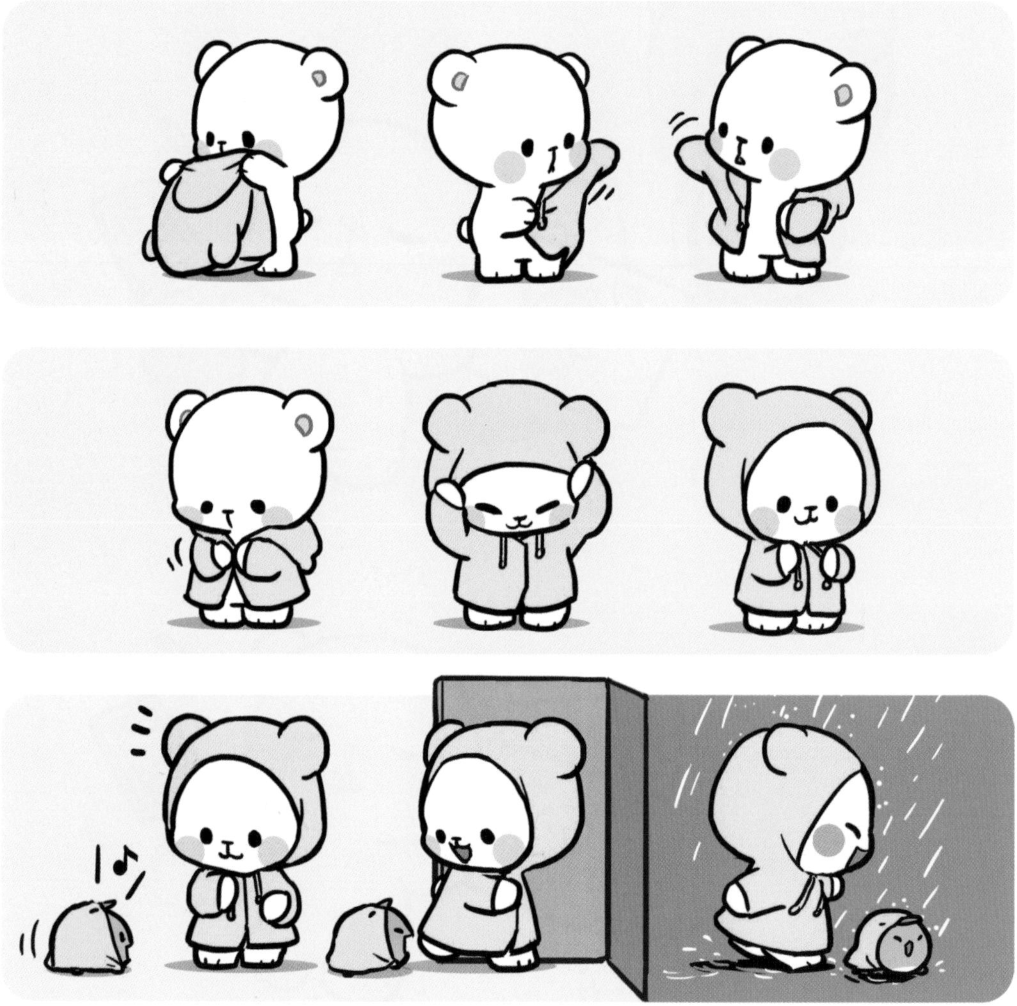

MEANWHILE...

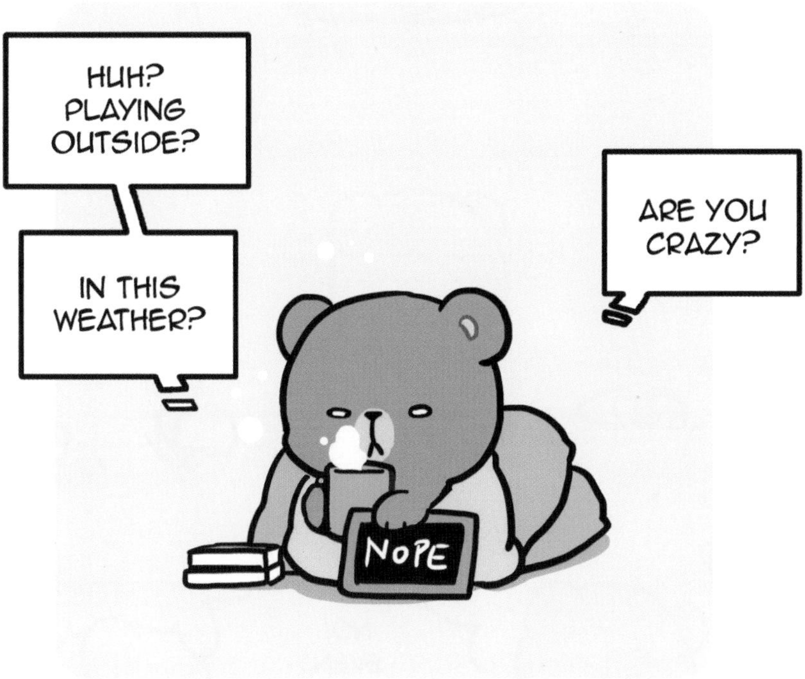
HUH? PLAYING OUTSIDE?
IN THIS WEATHER?
ARE YOU CRAZY?
NOPE

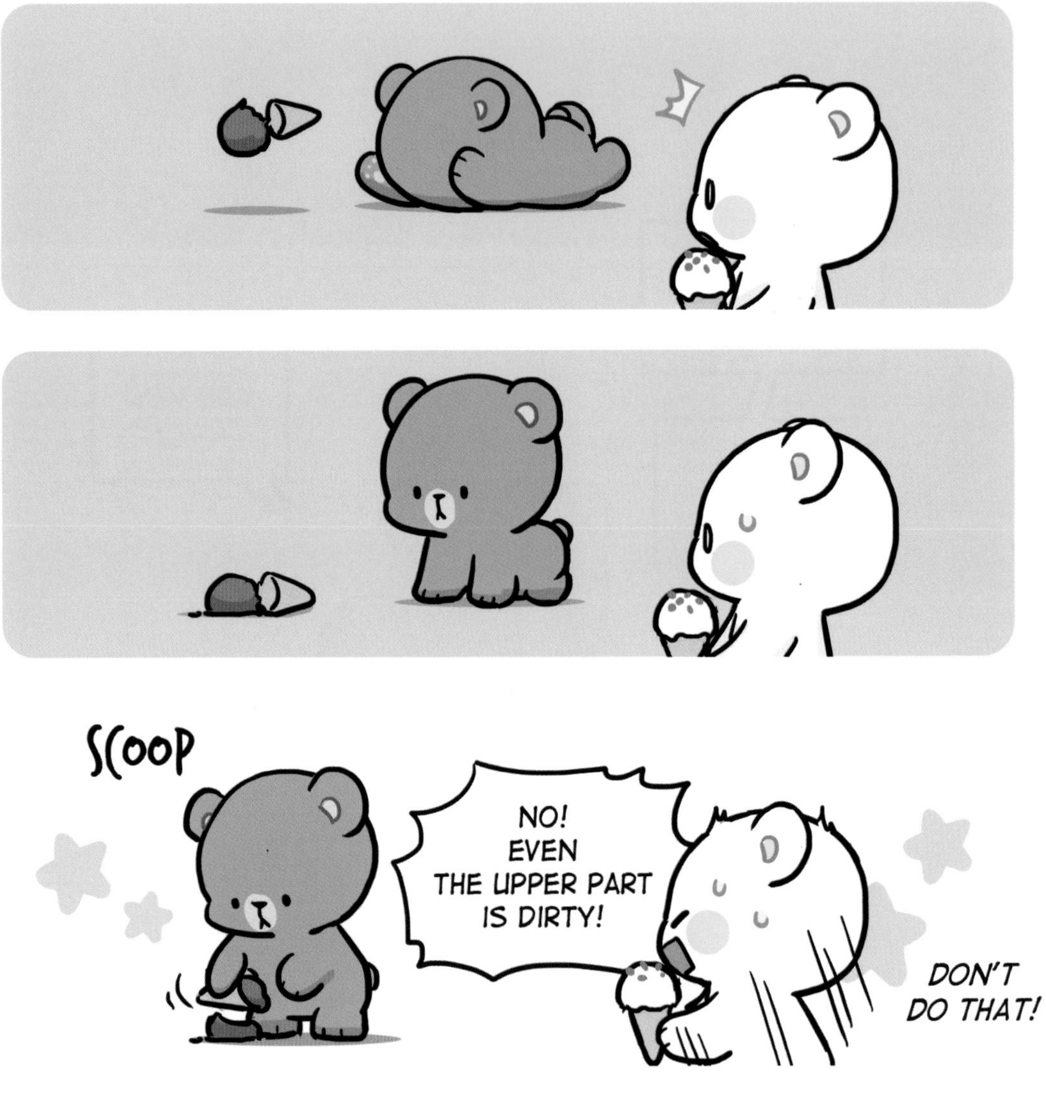
SCOOP
NO! EVEN THE UPPER PART IS DIRTY!
DON'T DO THAT!

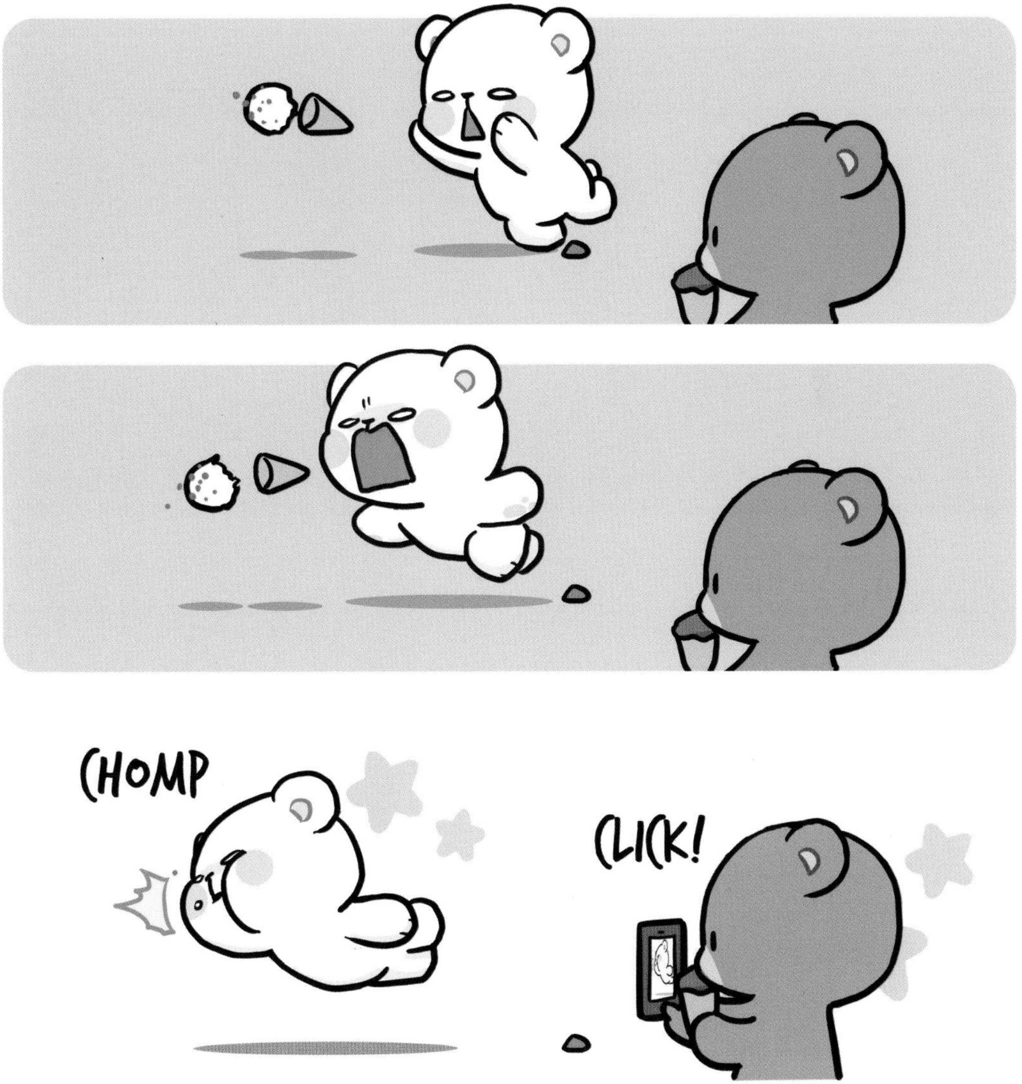
CHOMP
CLICK!

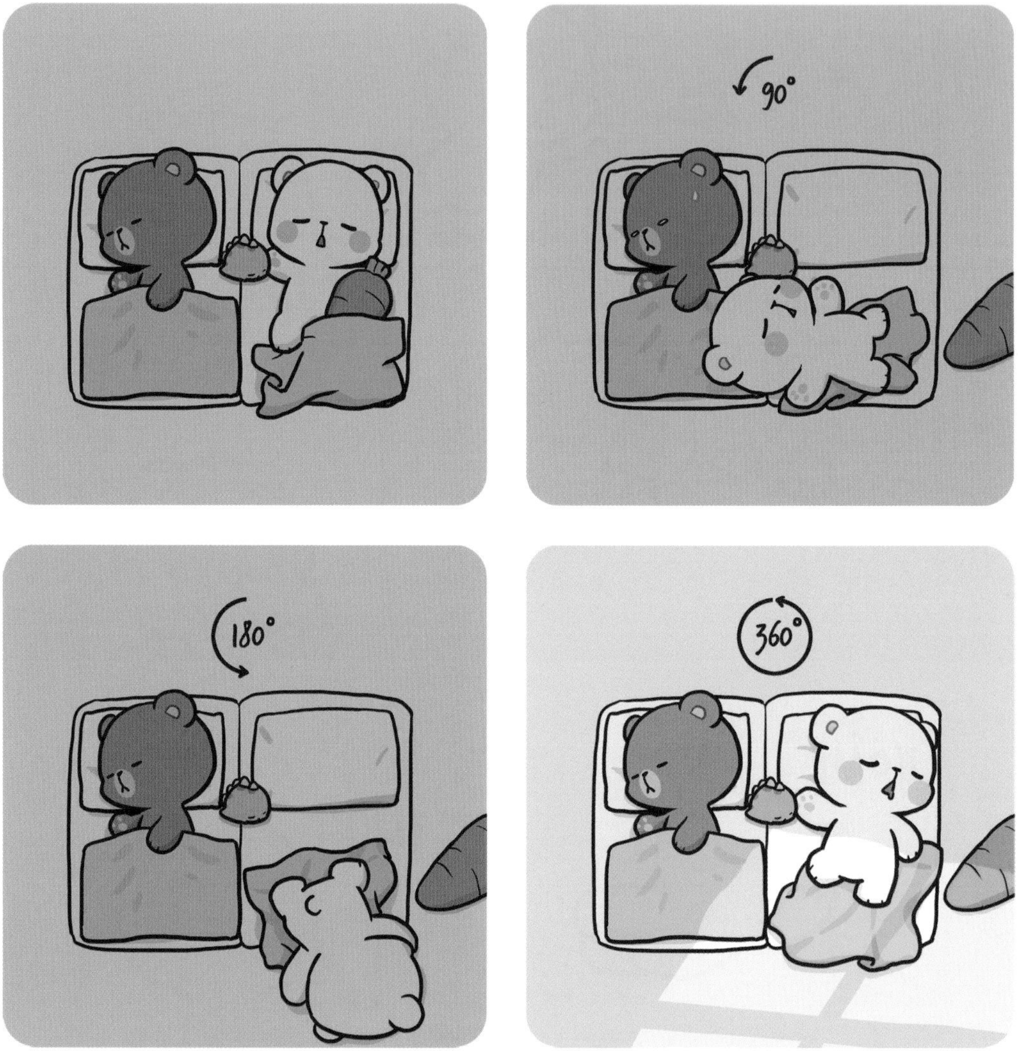
90°
180°
360°

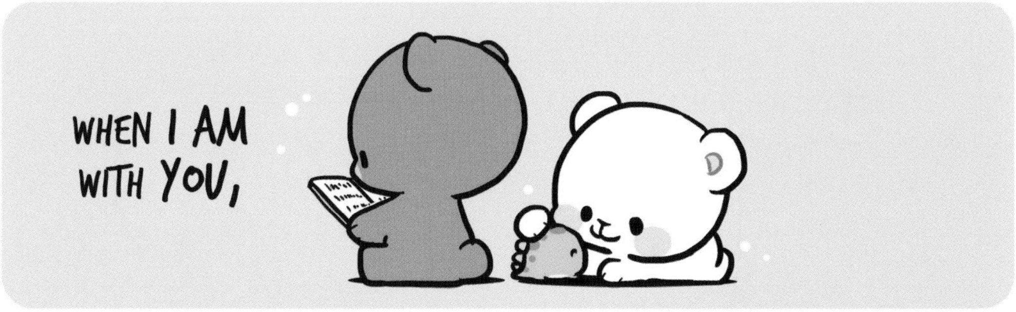
WHEN I AM WITH YOU,

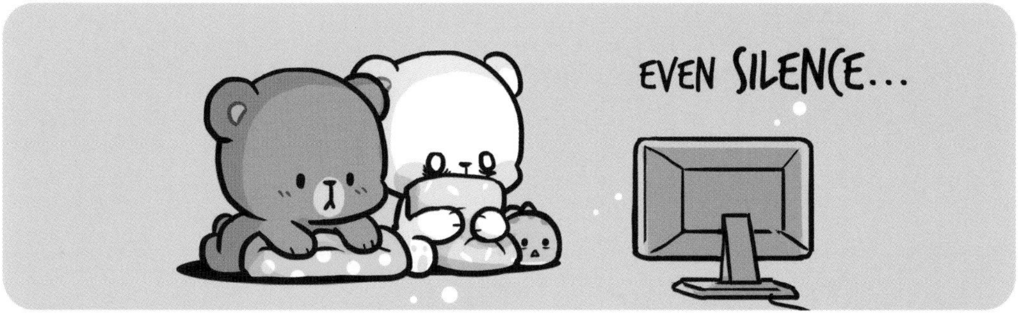
EVEN SILENCE...

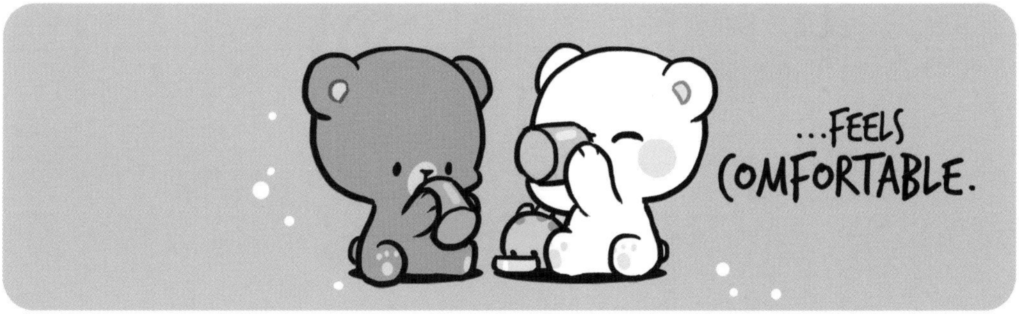
...FEELS COMFORTABLE.

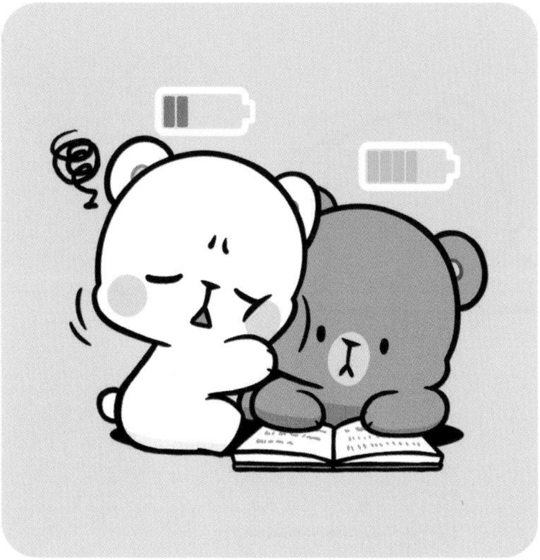

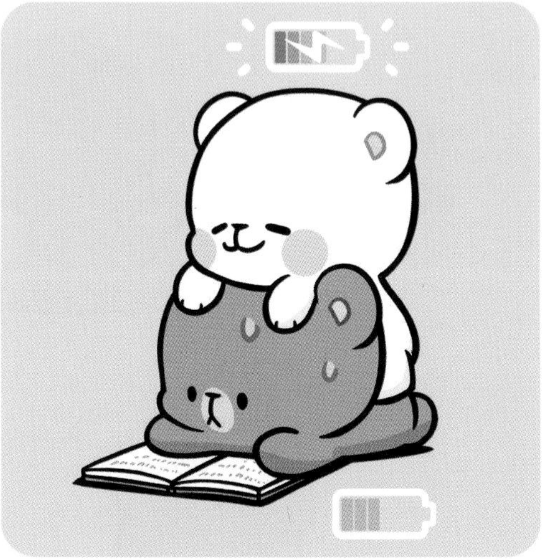

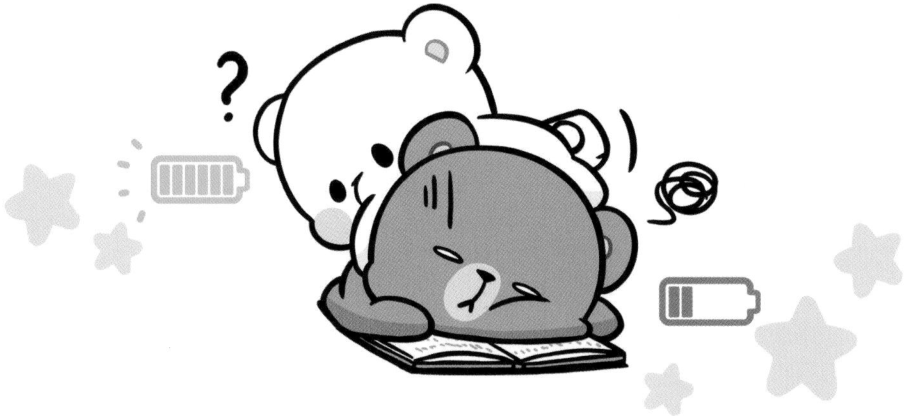

?

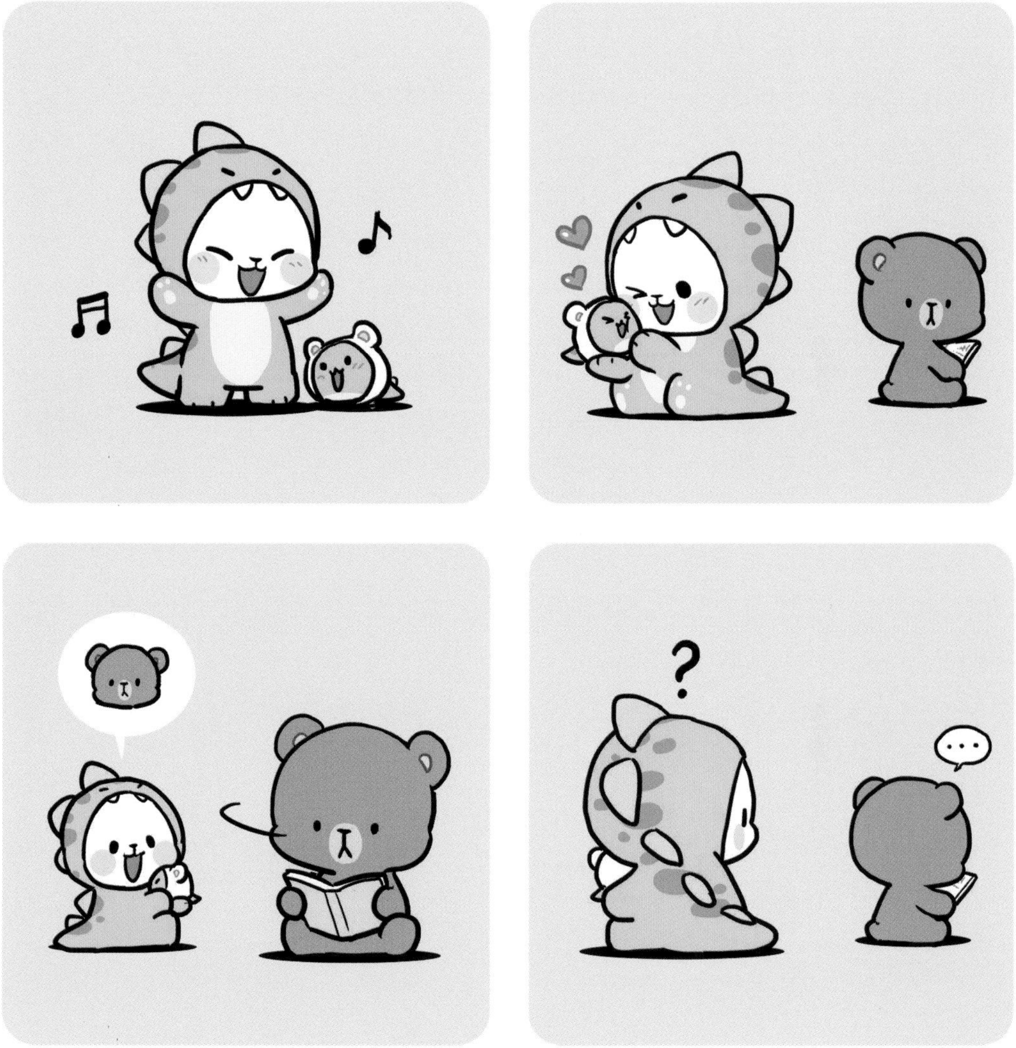
?
...

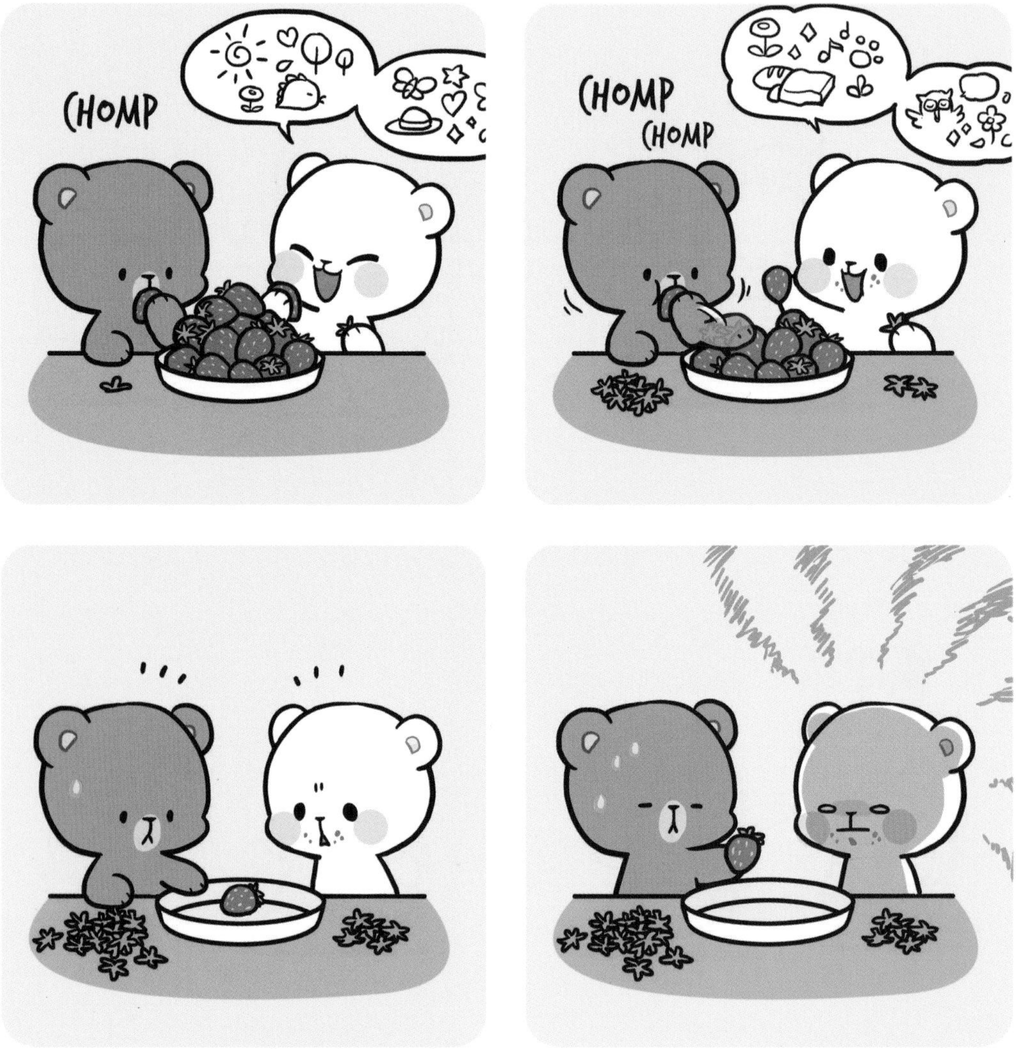
CHOMP
CHOMP
CHOMP

EPILOGUE

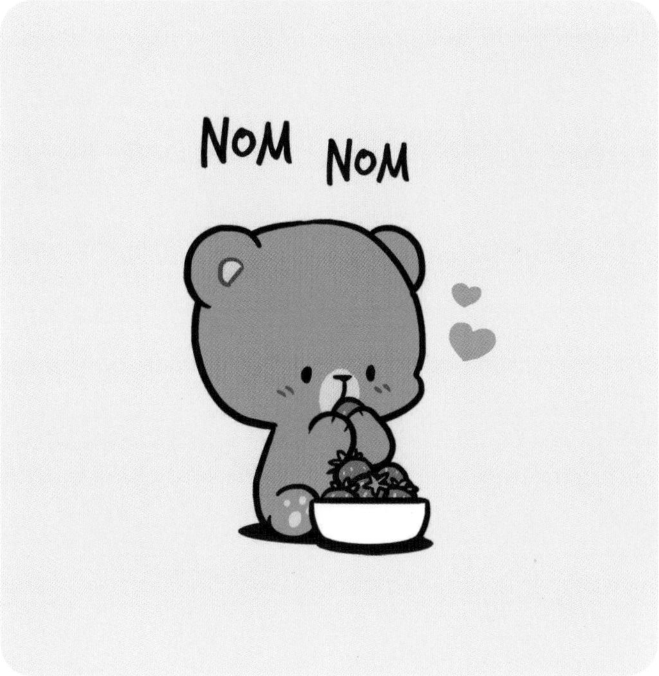
NOM NOM

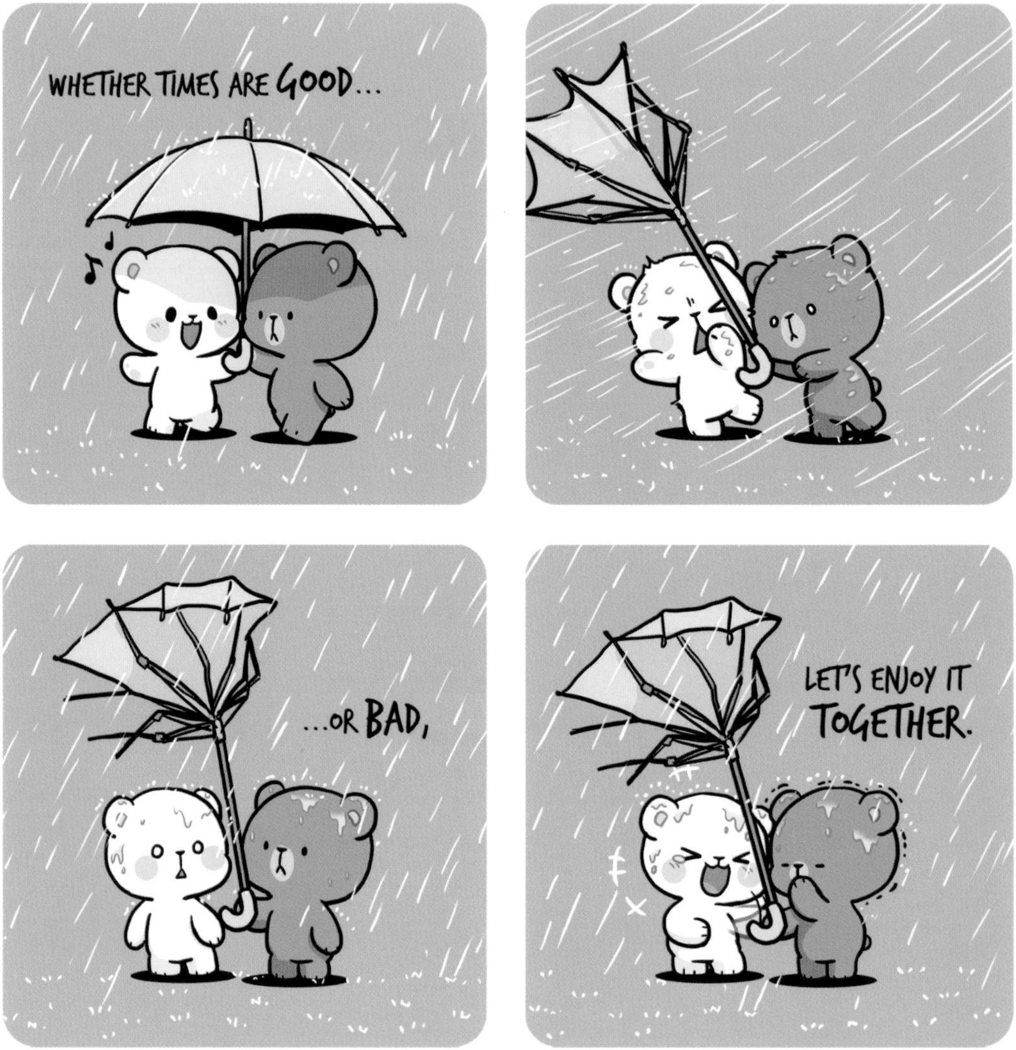
WHETHER TIMES ARE GOOD...
...OR BAD,
LET'S ENJOY IT TOGETHER.

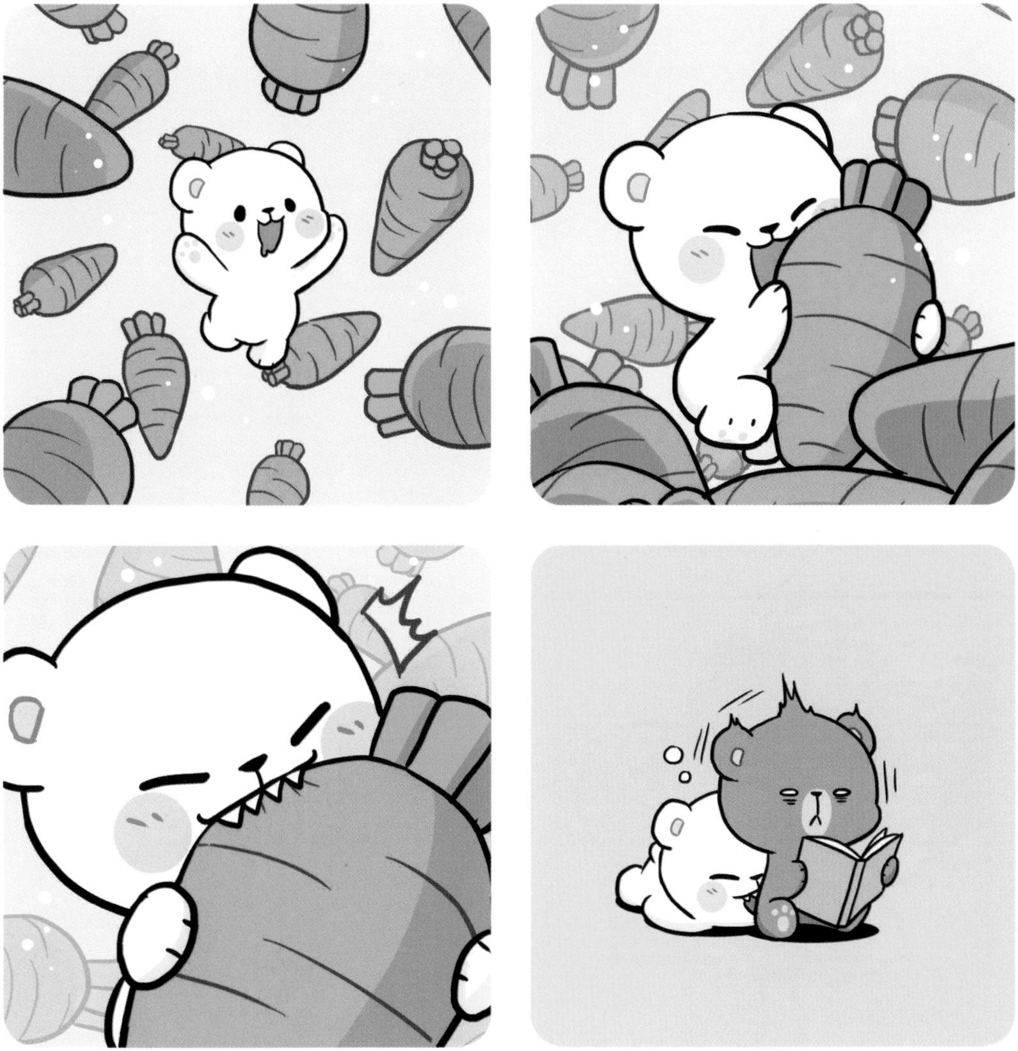

SOMETIMES I THINK...

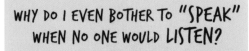

WHY DO I EVEN BOTHER TO "SPEAK" WHEN NO ONE WOULD LISTEN?

BUT THEN...

...THERE'S YOU.

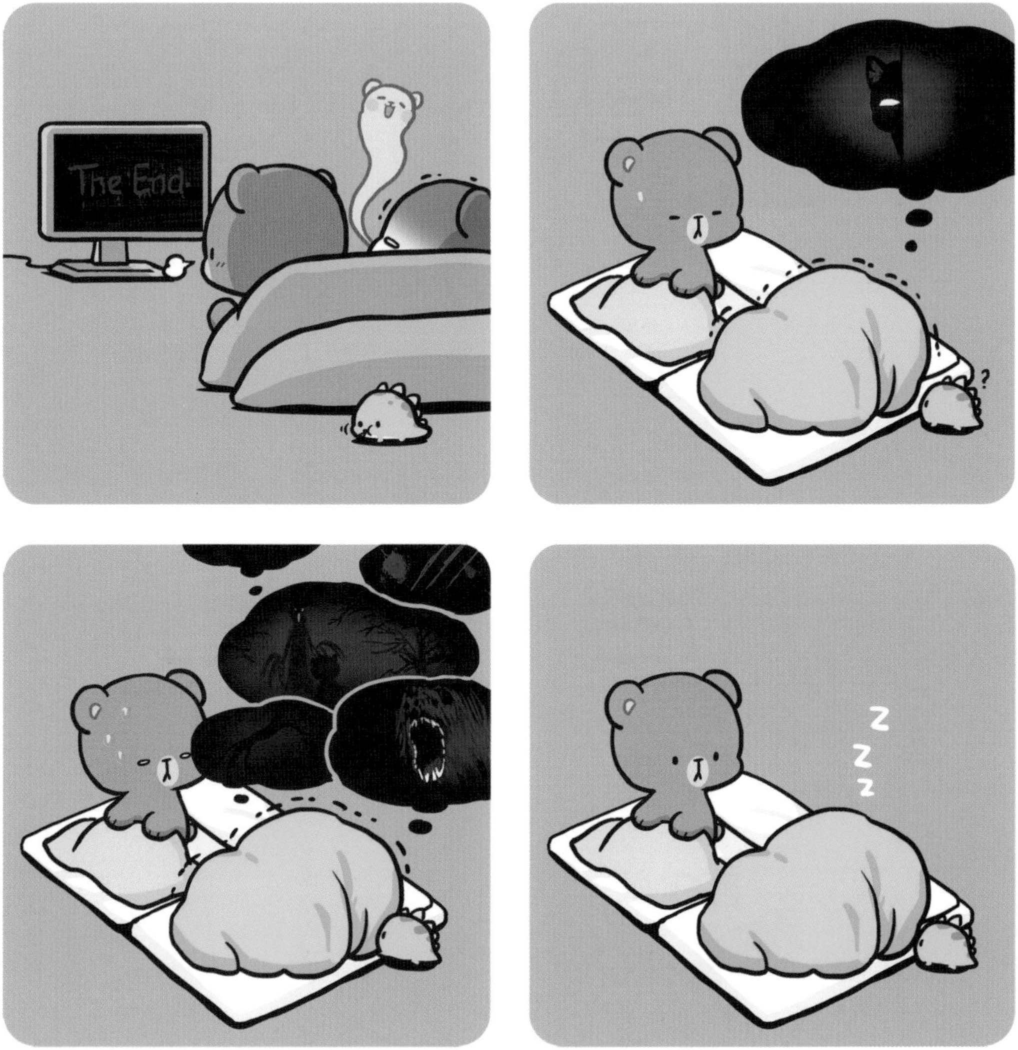
The End.
?
Z
Z
Z

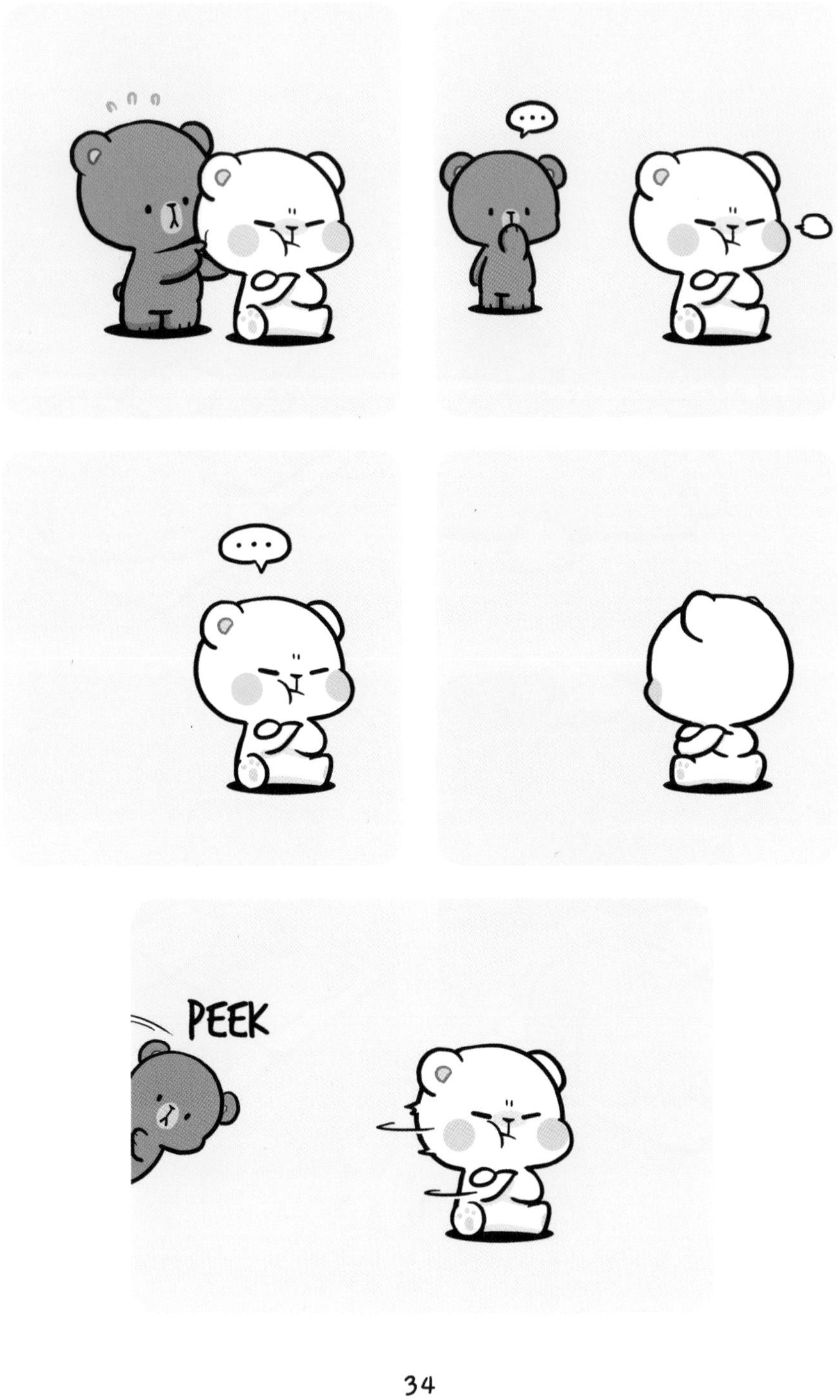
PEEK

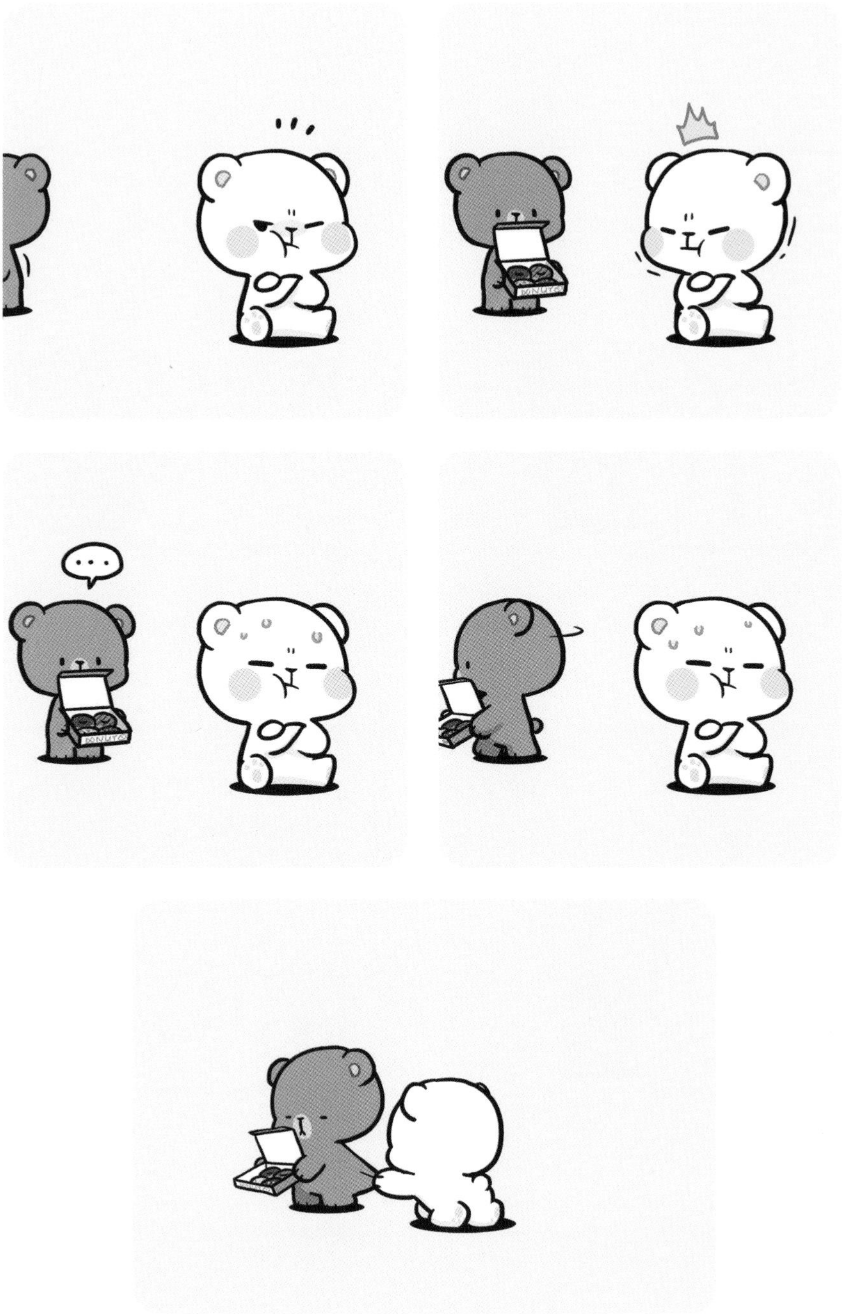

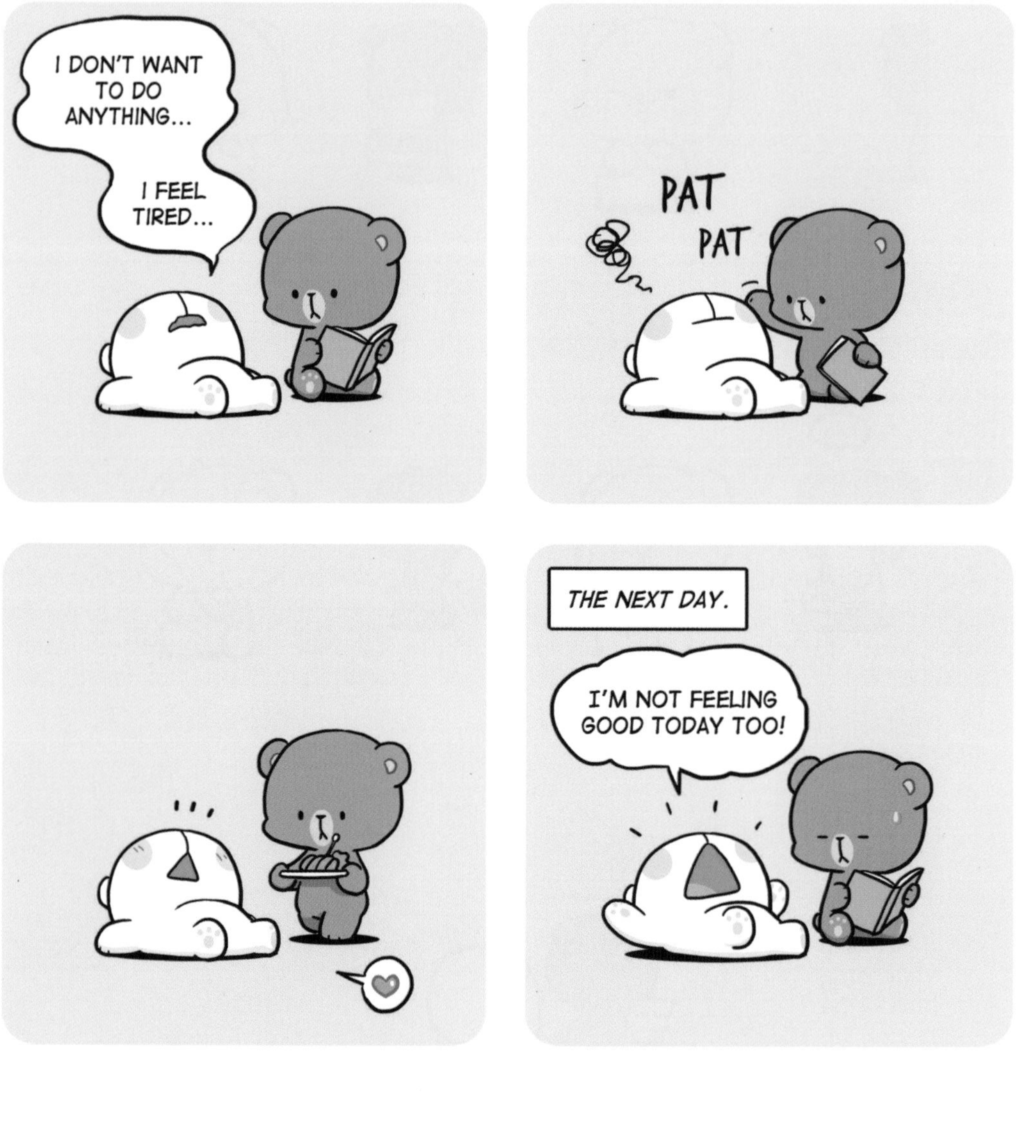
I DON'T WANT TO DO ANYTHING...
I FEEL TIRED...
PAT
PAT
THE NEXT DAY.
I'M NOT FEELING GOOD TODAY TOO!

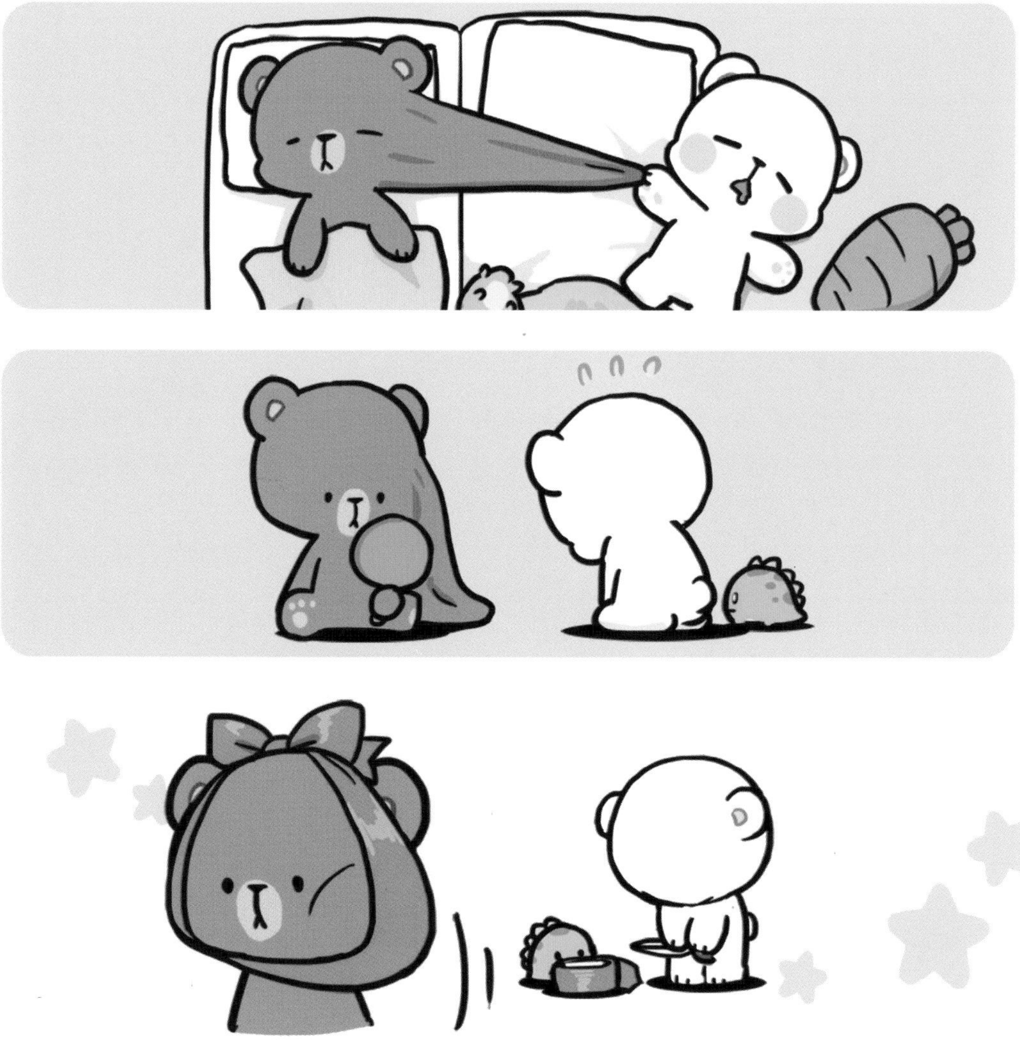

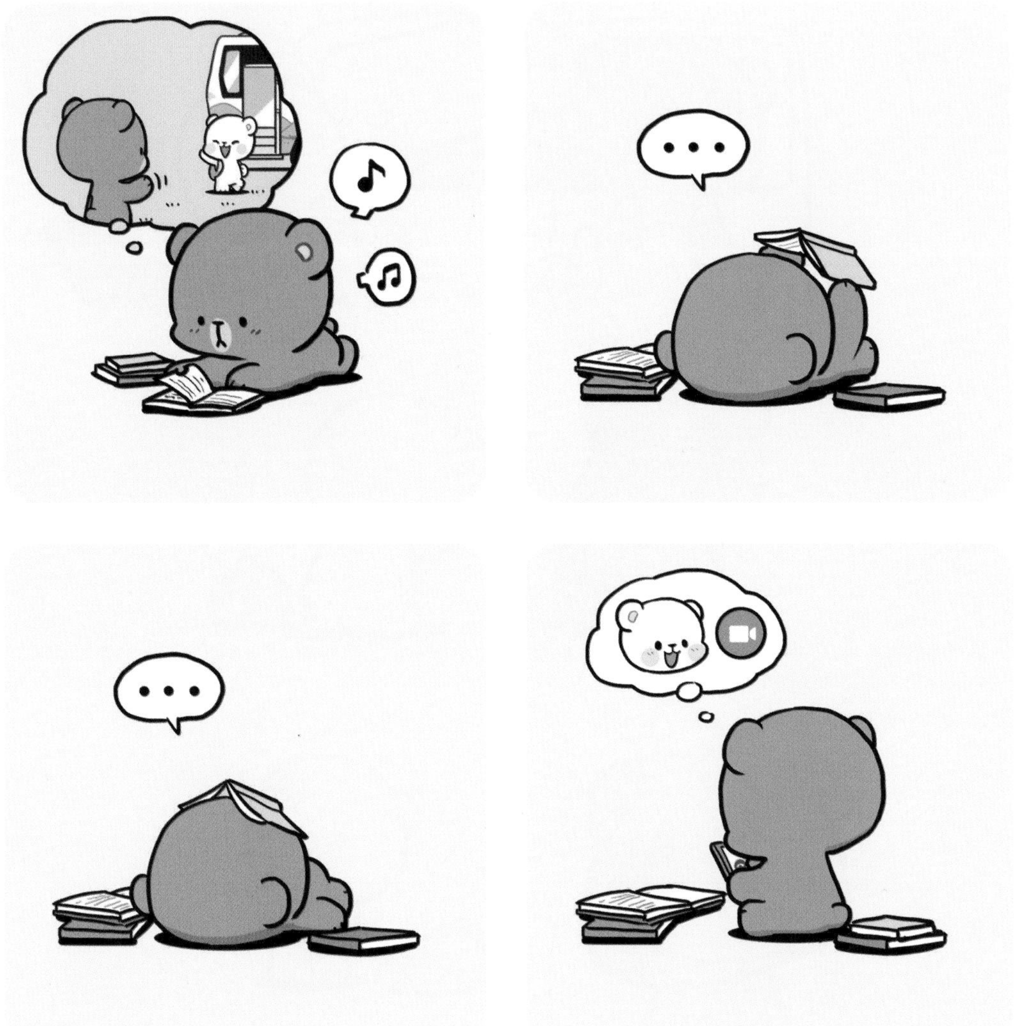
...
...

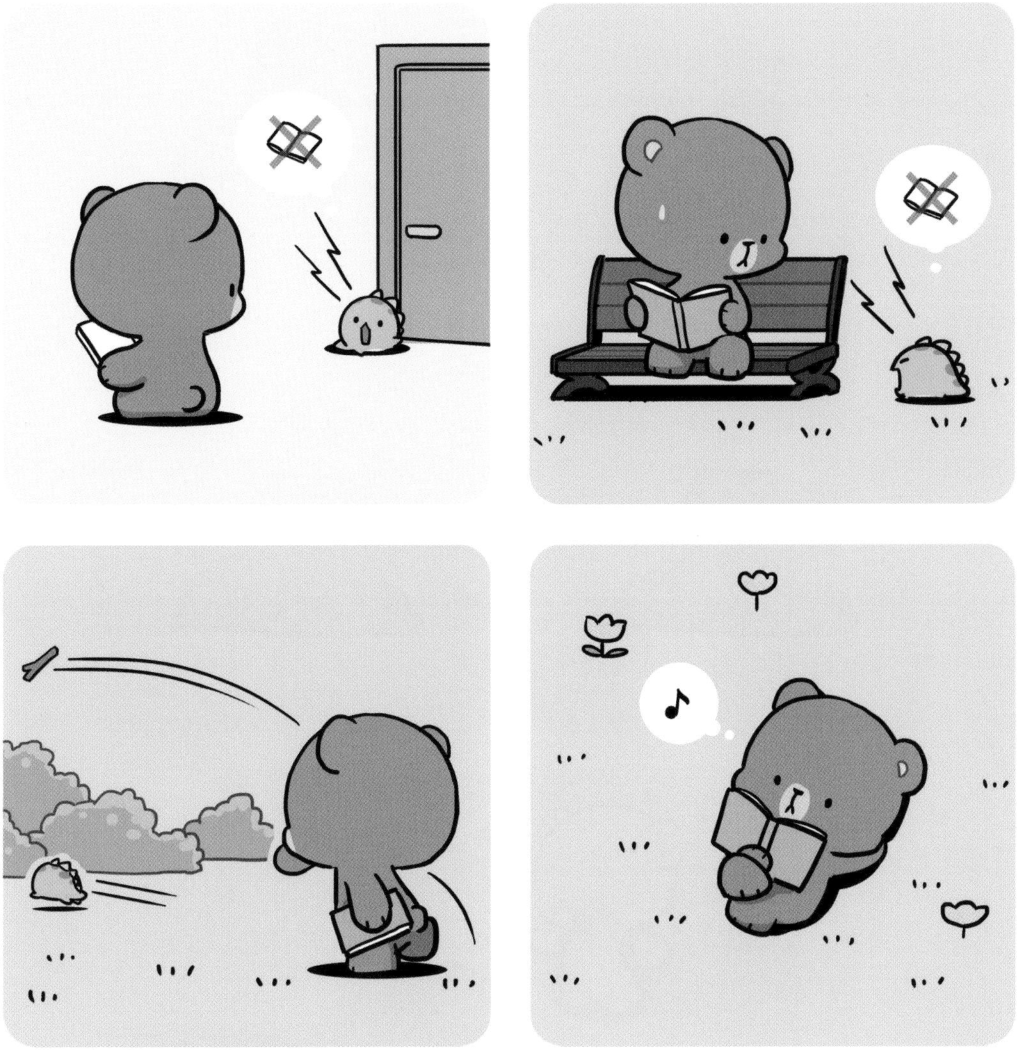

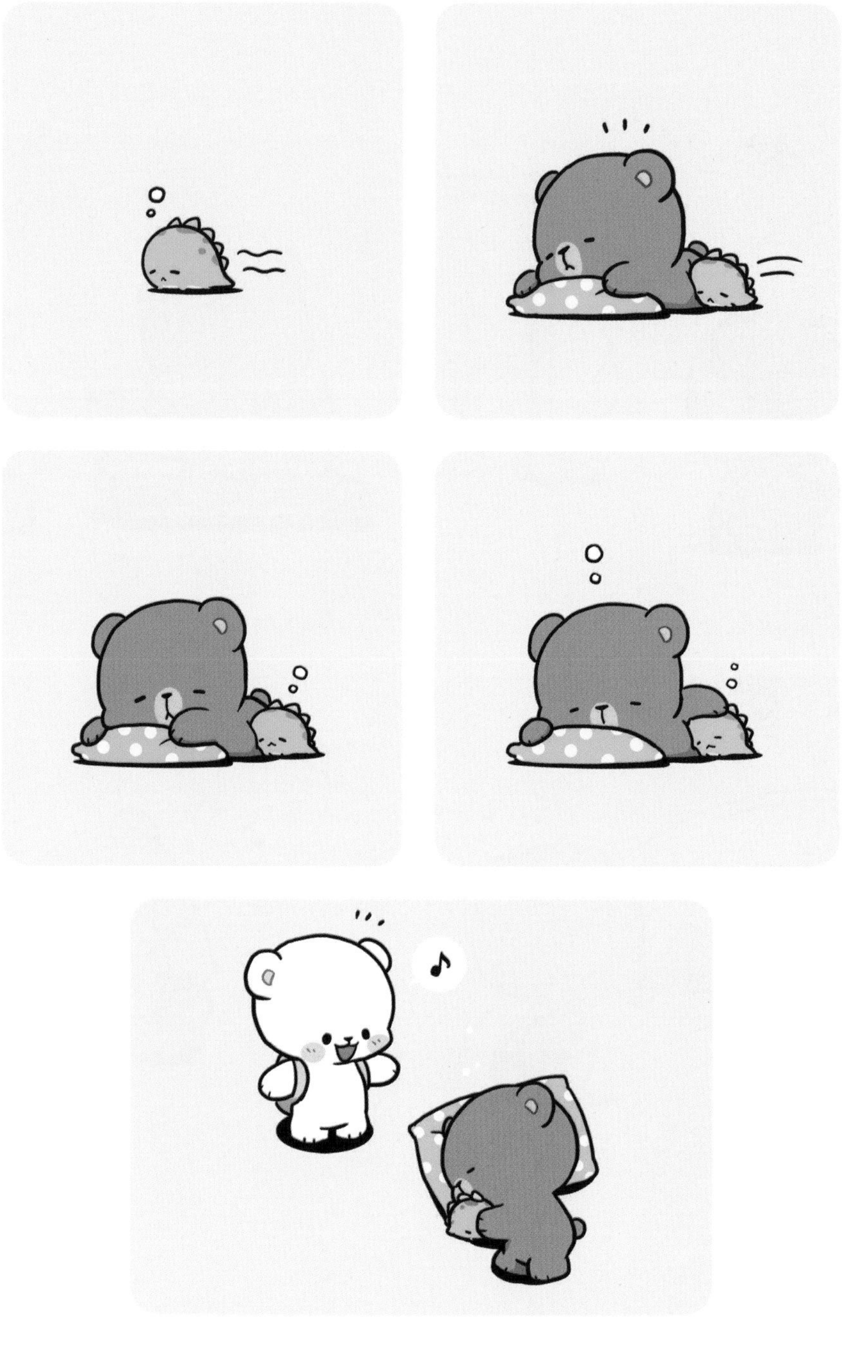

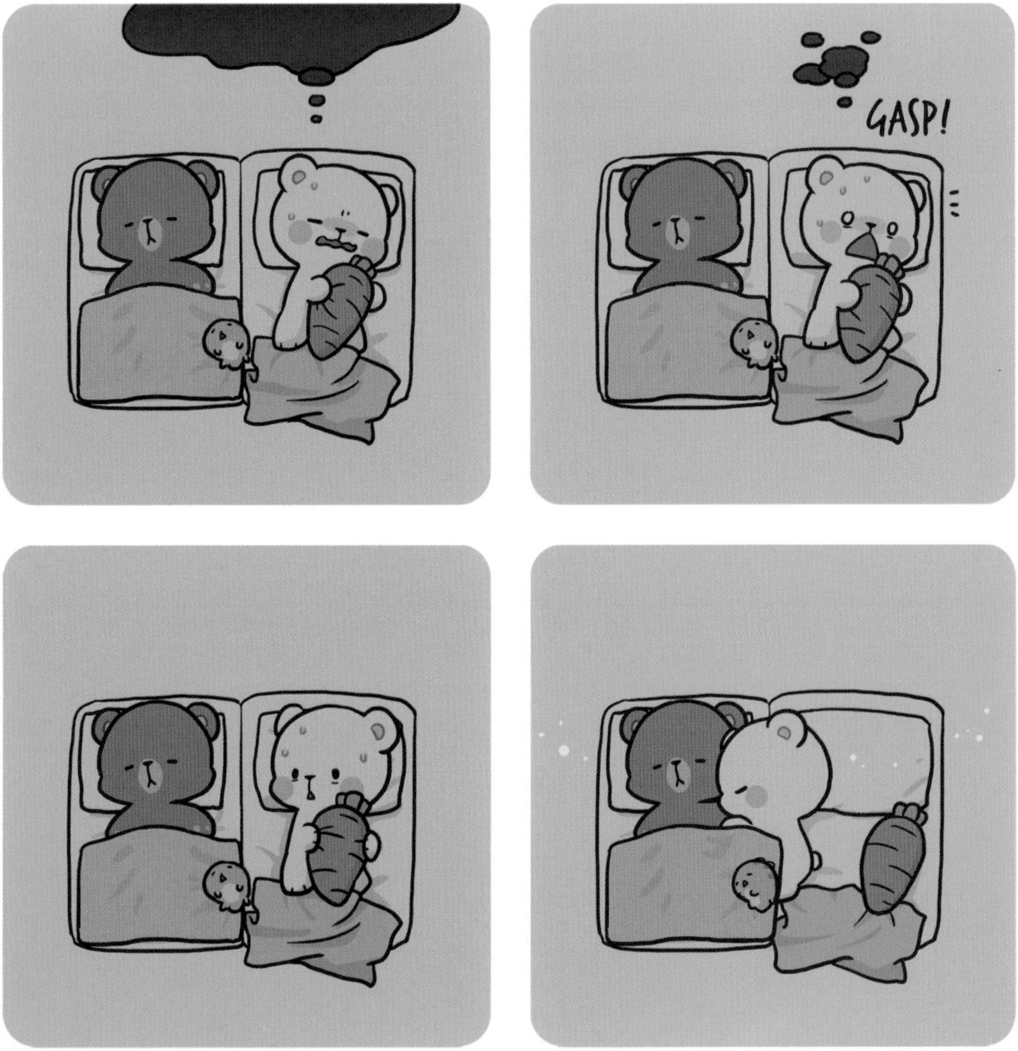
GASP!

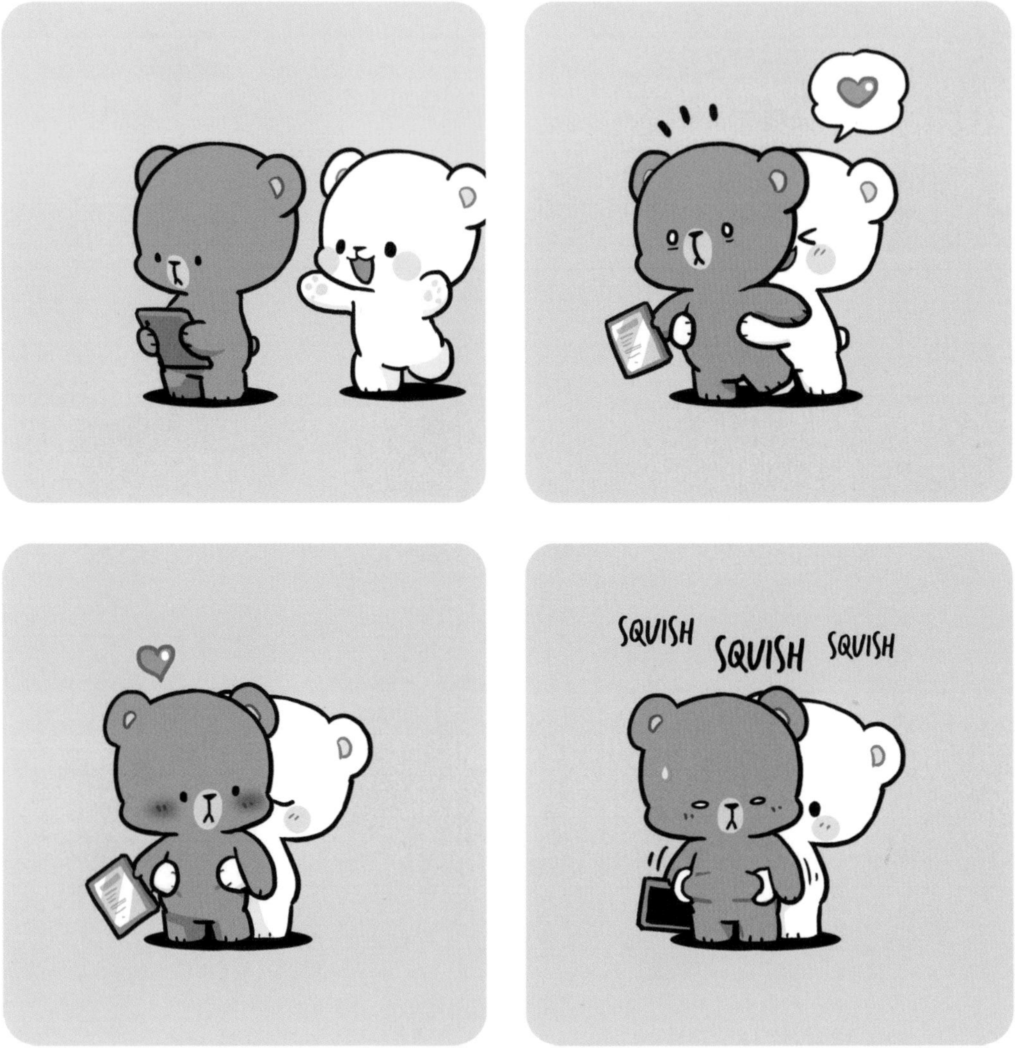
SQUISH
SQUISH
SQUISH

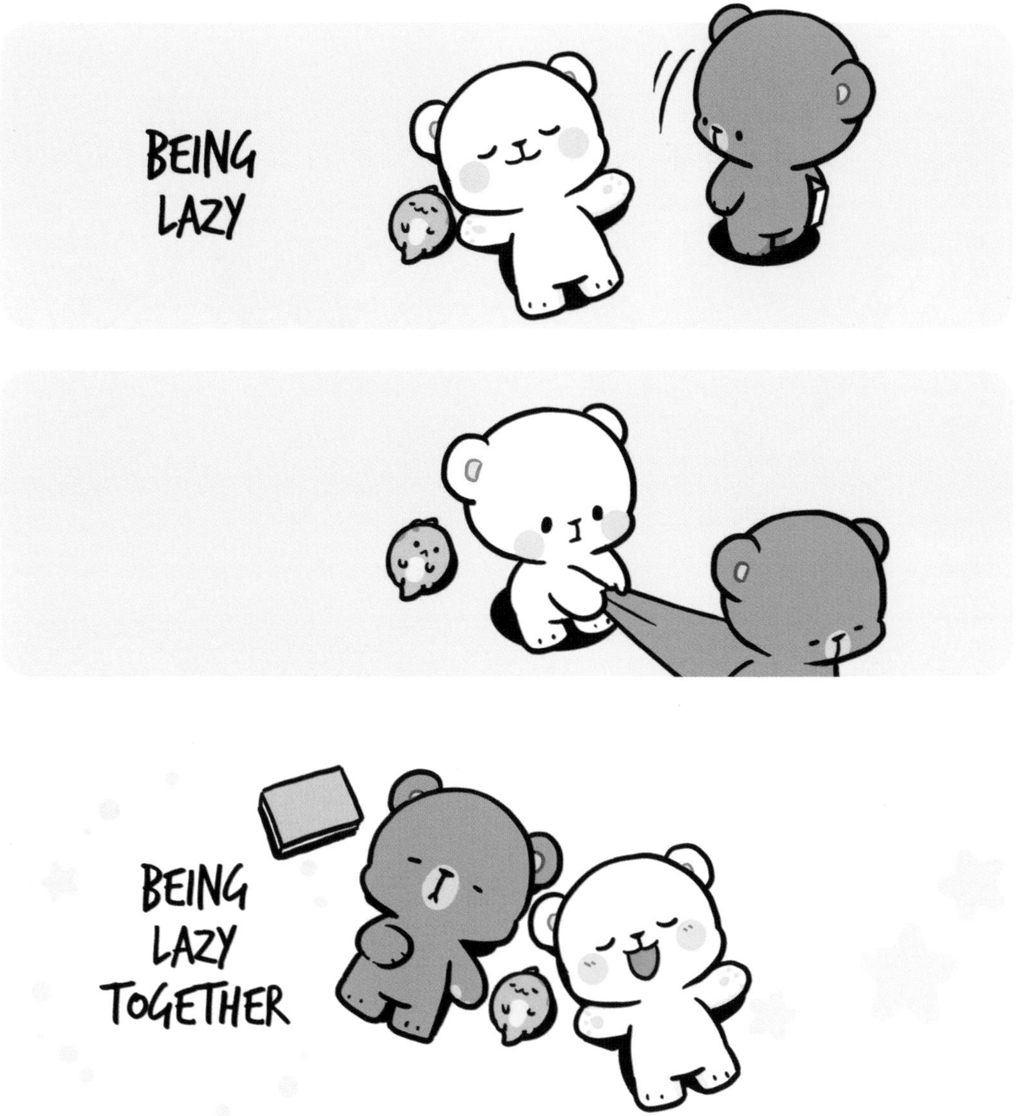
BEING LAZY
BEING LAZY TOGETHER

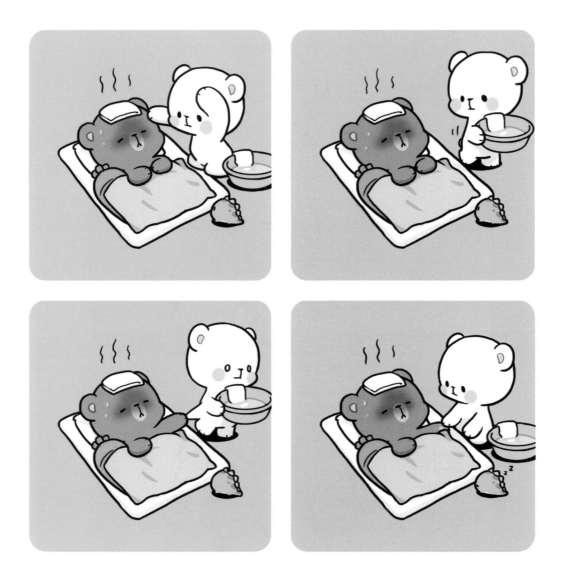

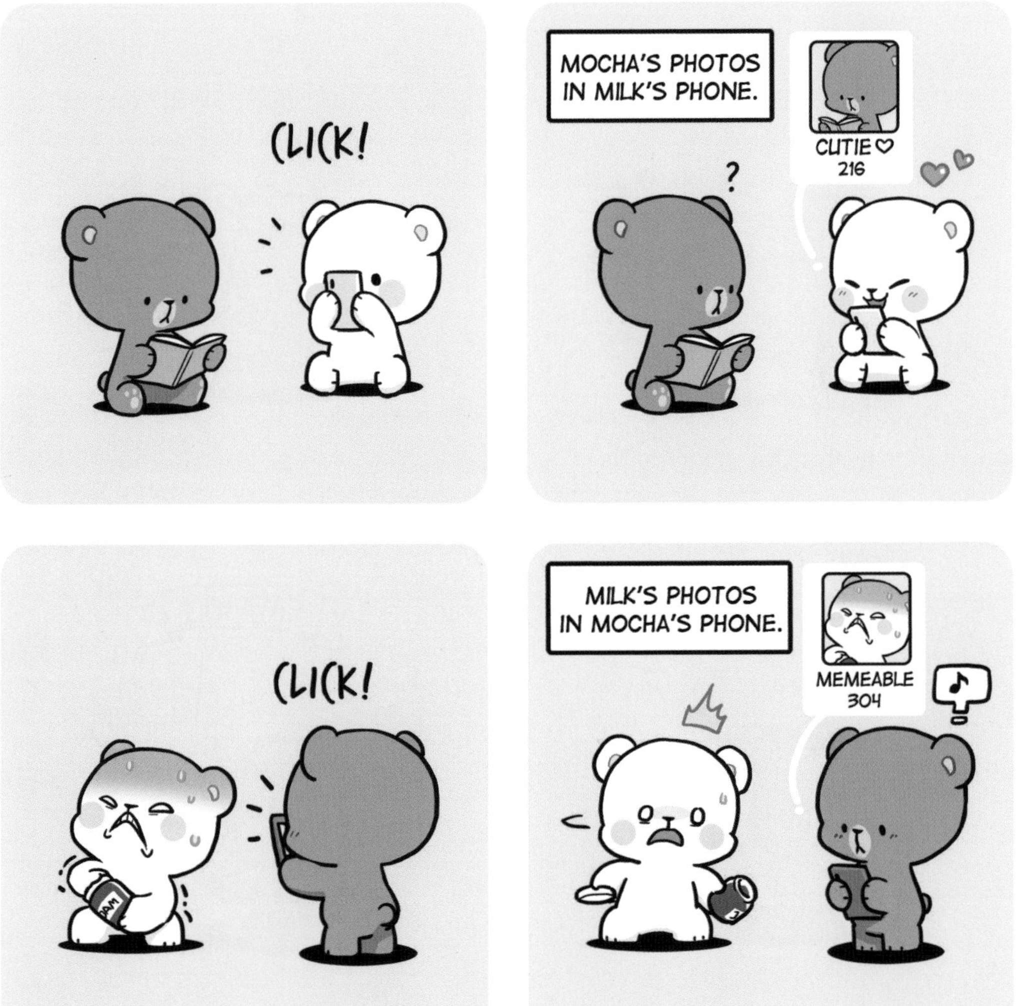
CLICK!
MOCHA'S PHOTOS IN MILK'S PHONE.
?
CUTIE ♡
216
CLICK!
JAM
MILK'S PHOTOS IN MOCHA'S PHONE.
MEMEABLE
304

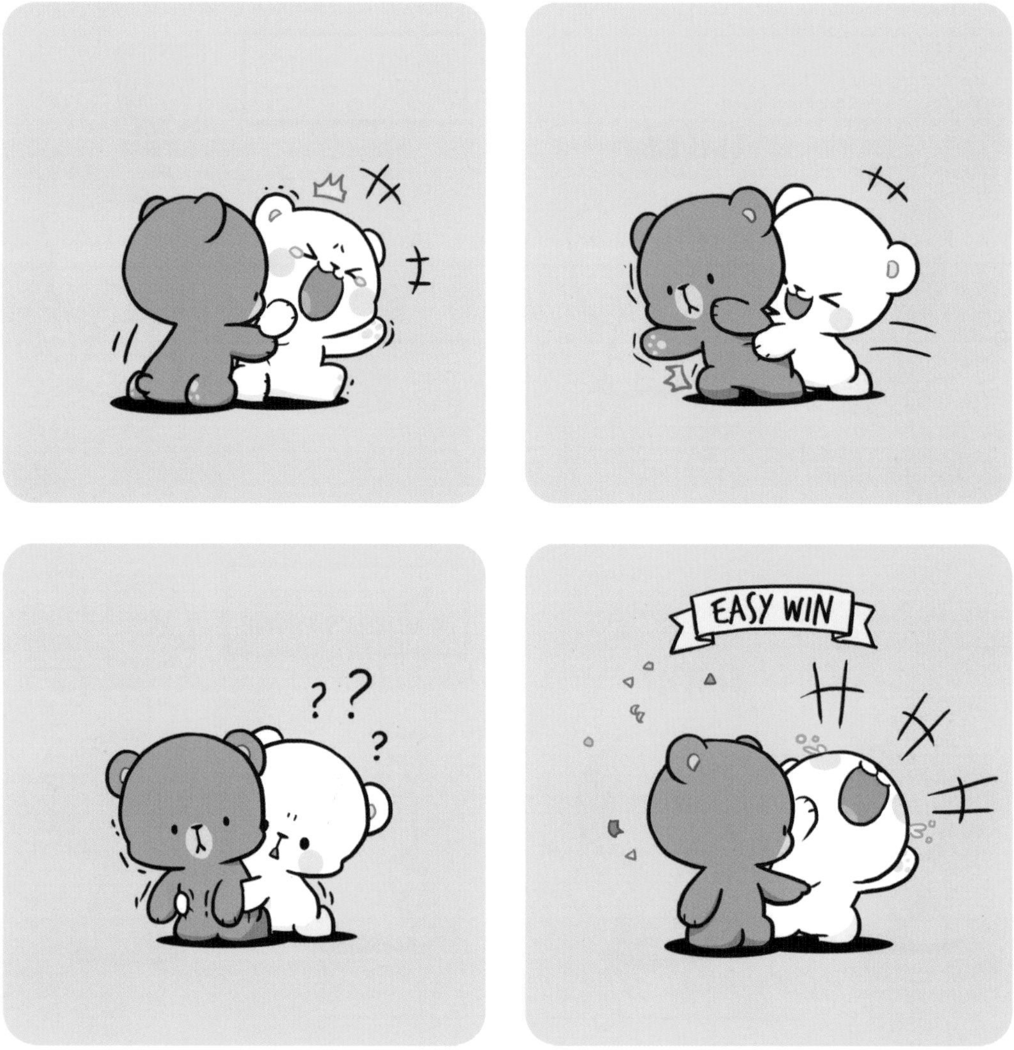
EASY WIN

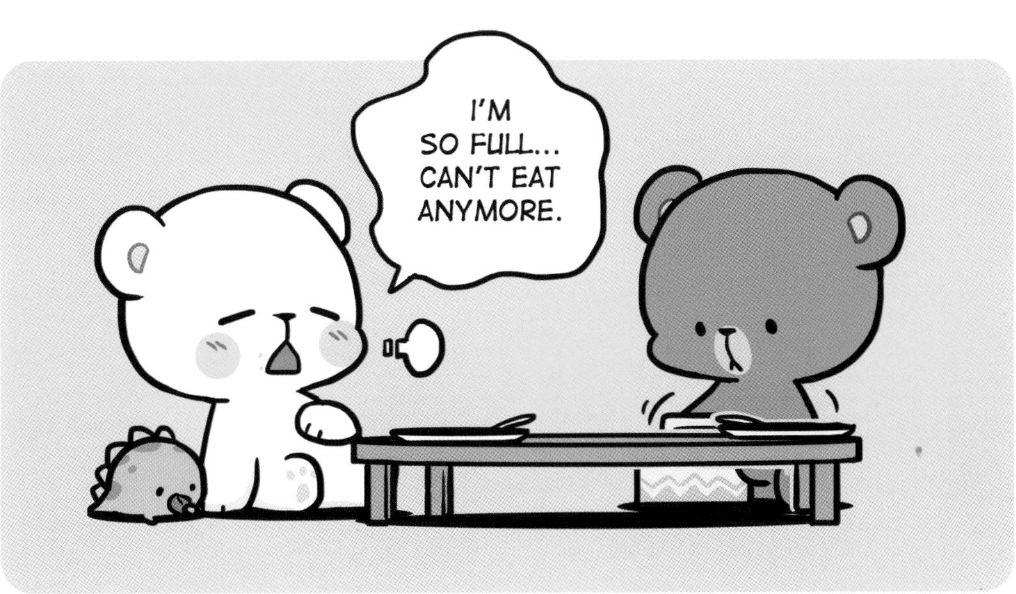
I'M
SO FULL...
CAN'T EAT
ANYMORE.

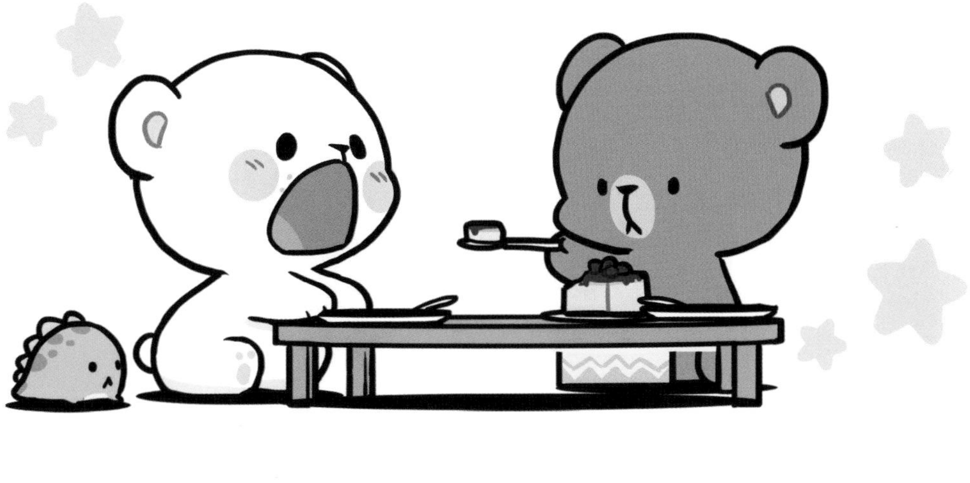

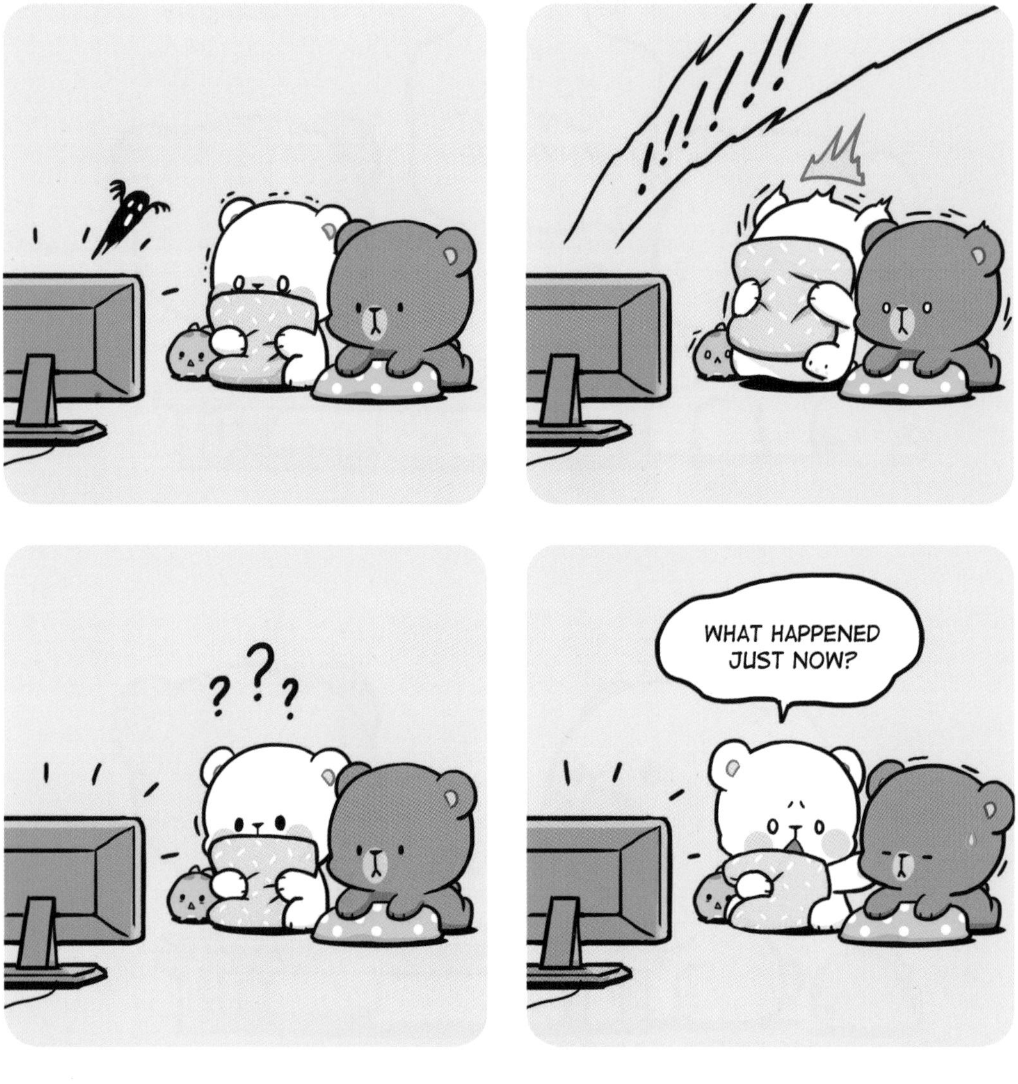
!!!!!!
???
WHAT HAPPENED JUST NOW?

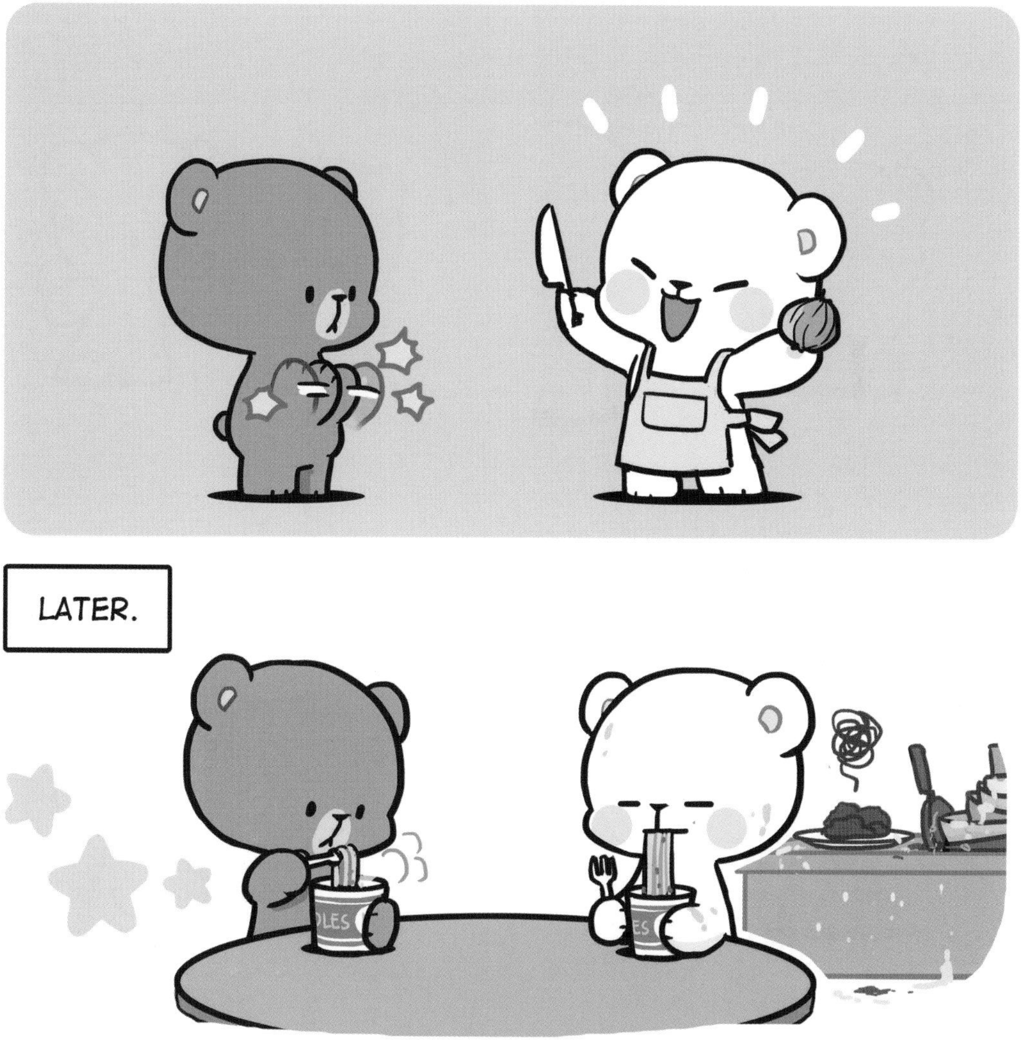
LATER.

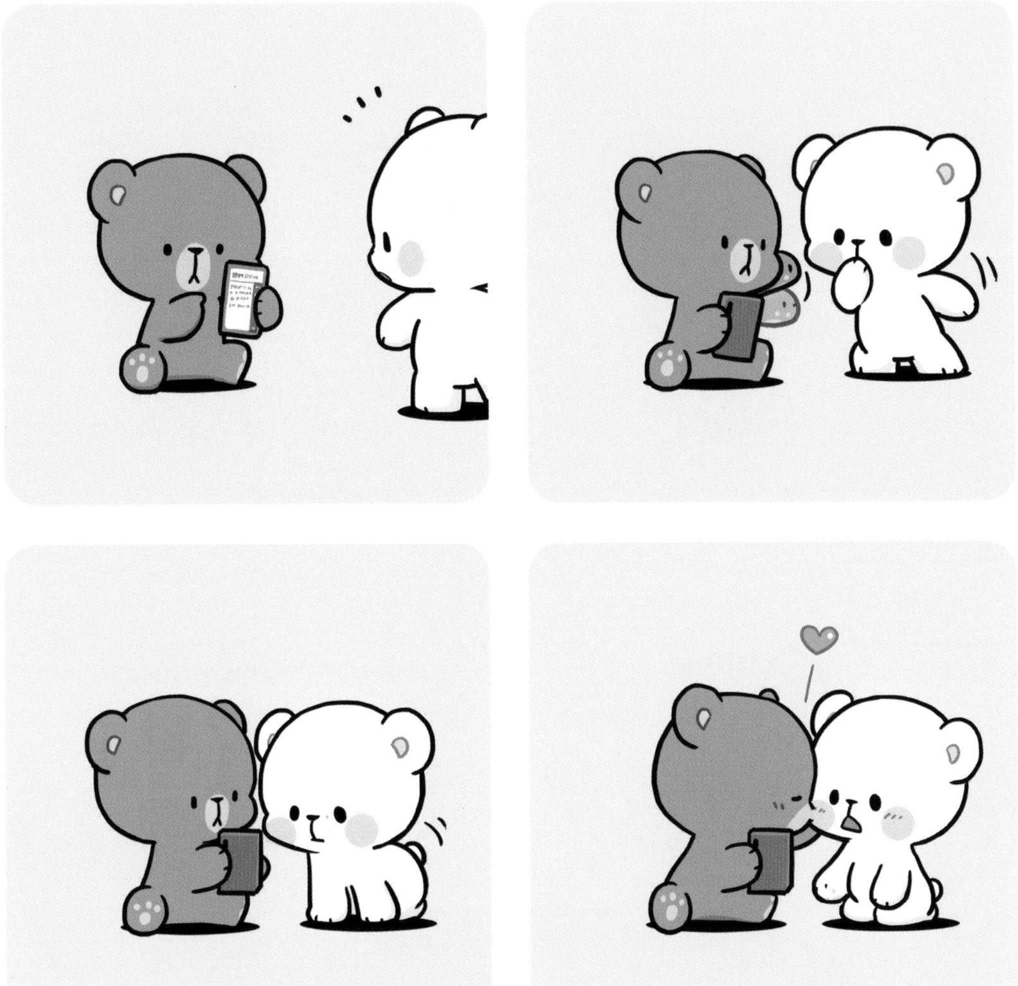

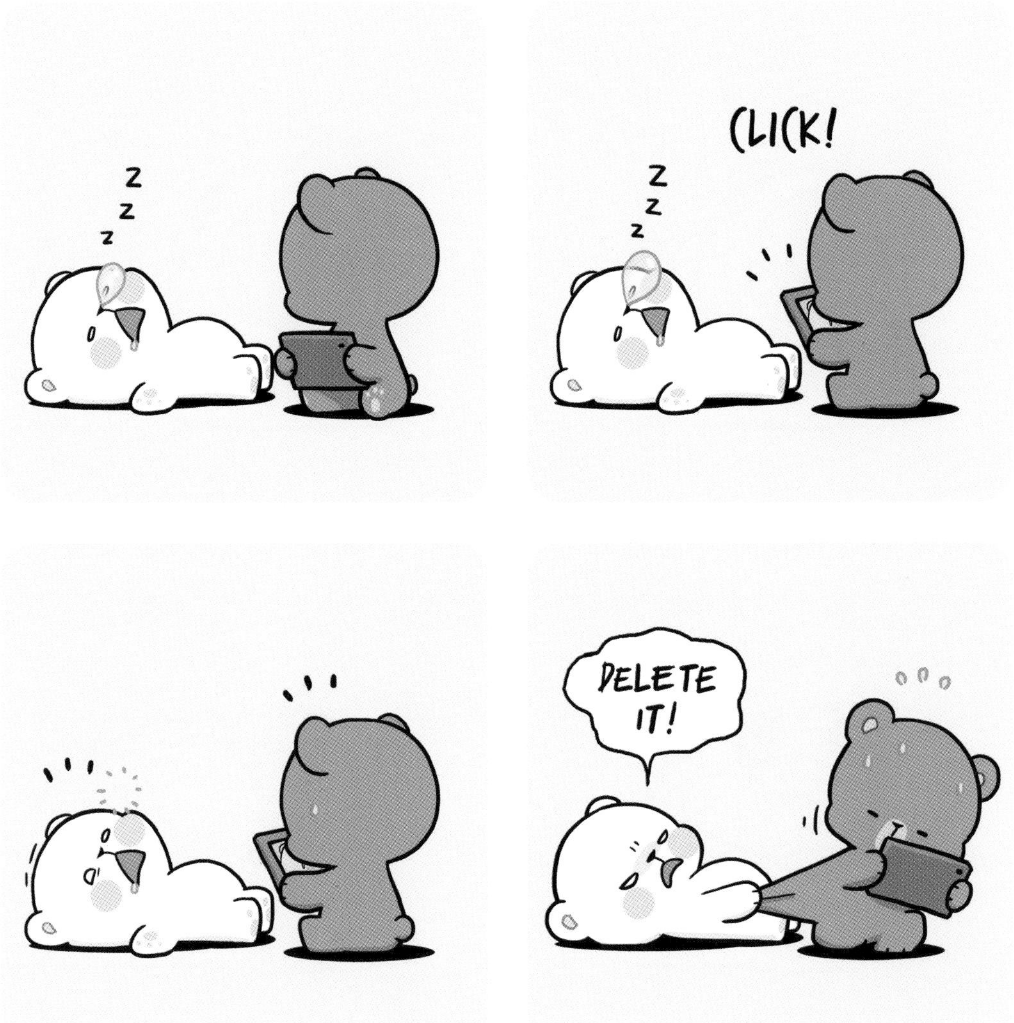
Z
Z
Z
Z
Z
Z
CLICK!
DELETE IT!

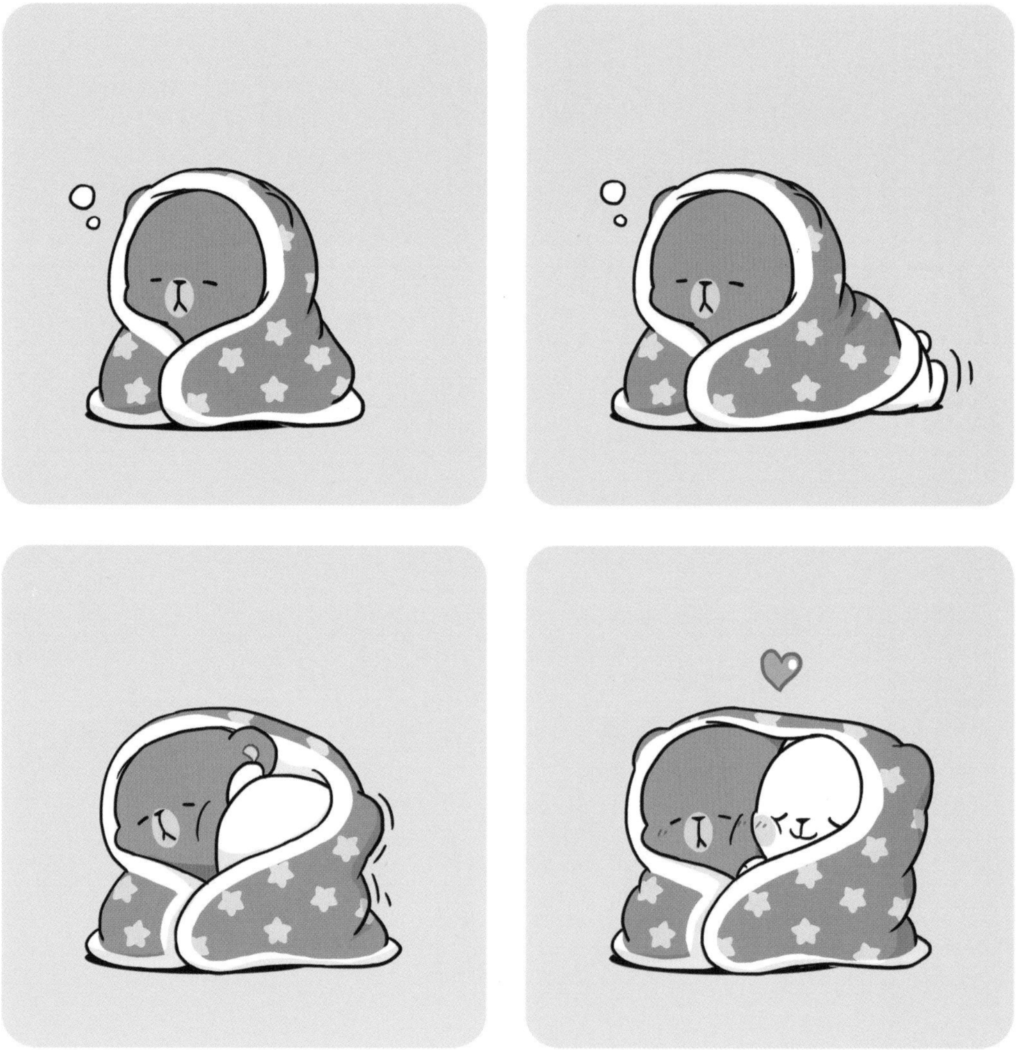

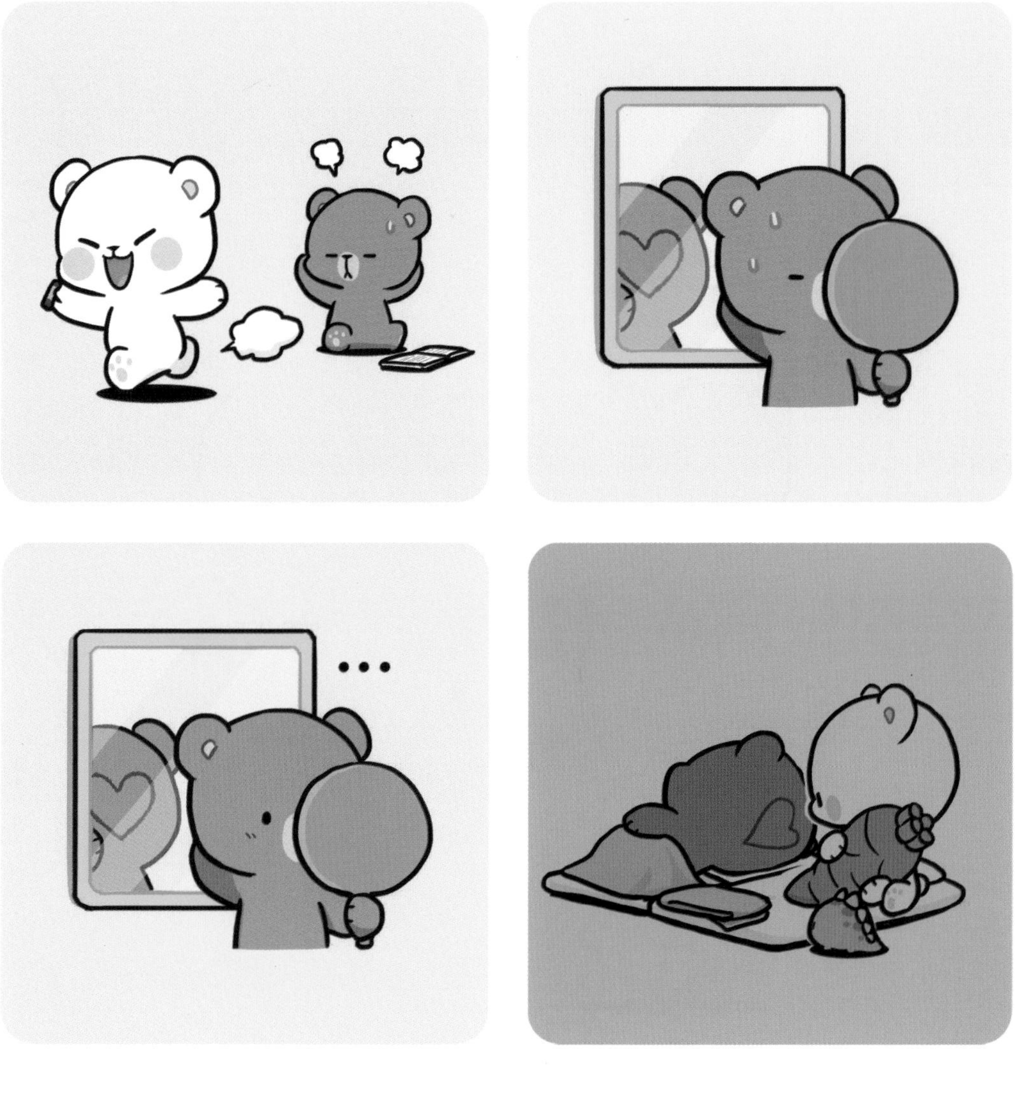

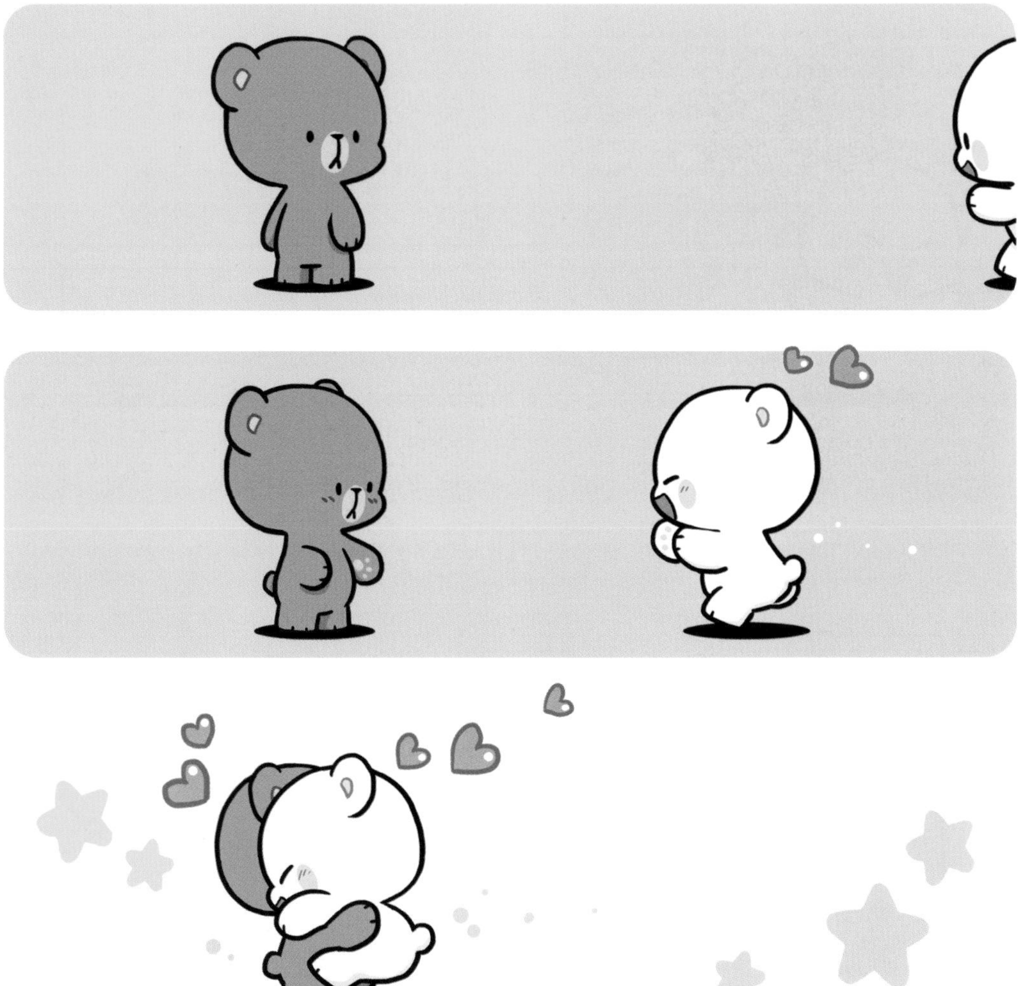

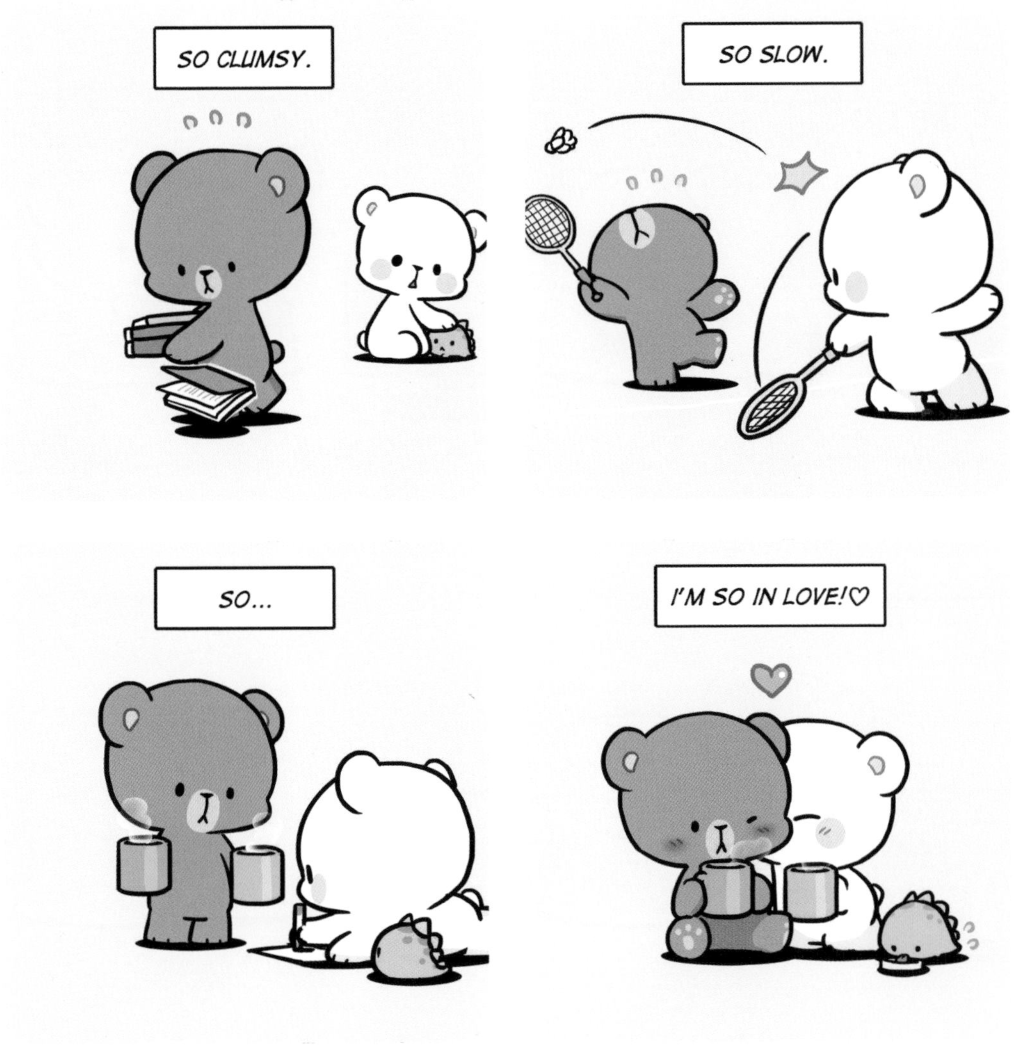
SO CLUMSY.
SO SLOW.
SO...
I'M SO IN LOVE!♡

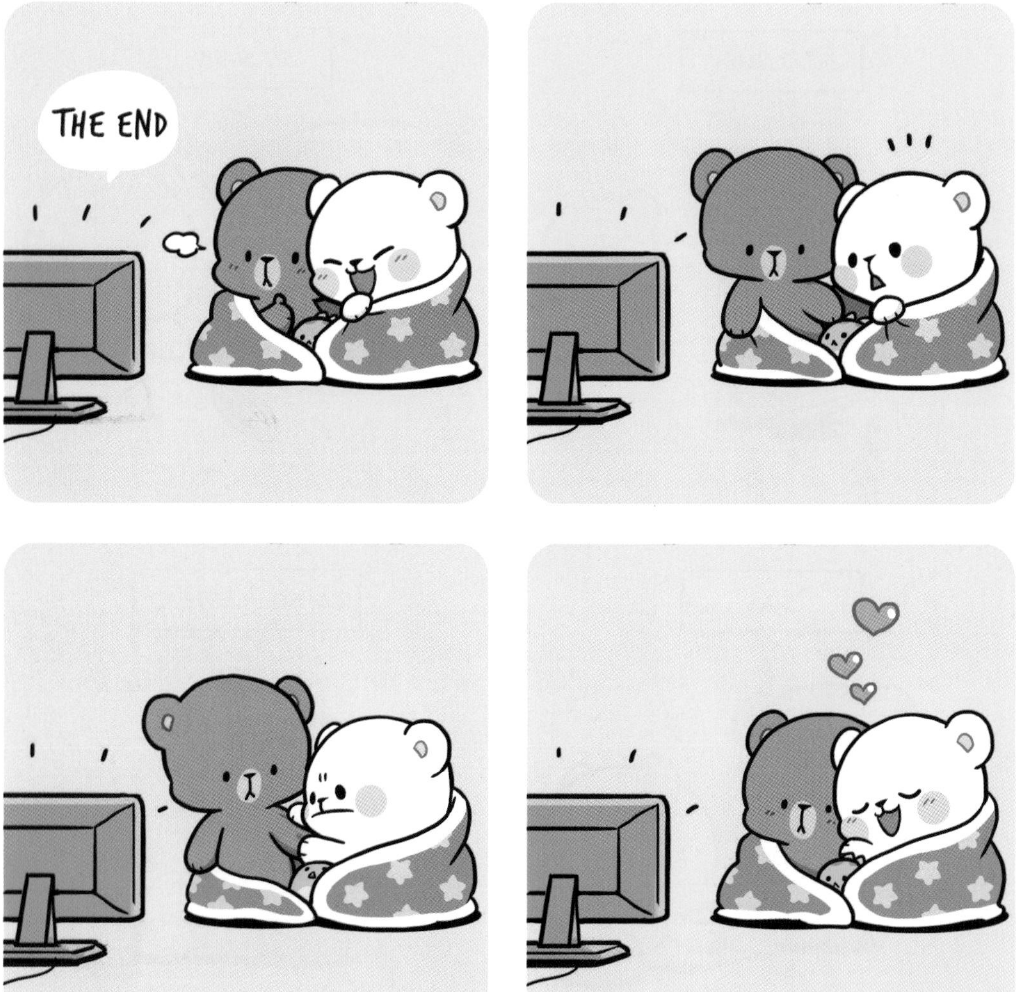
THE END

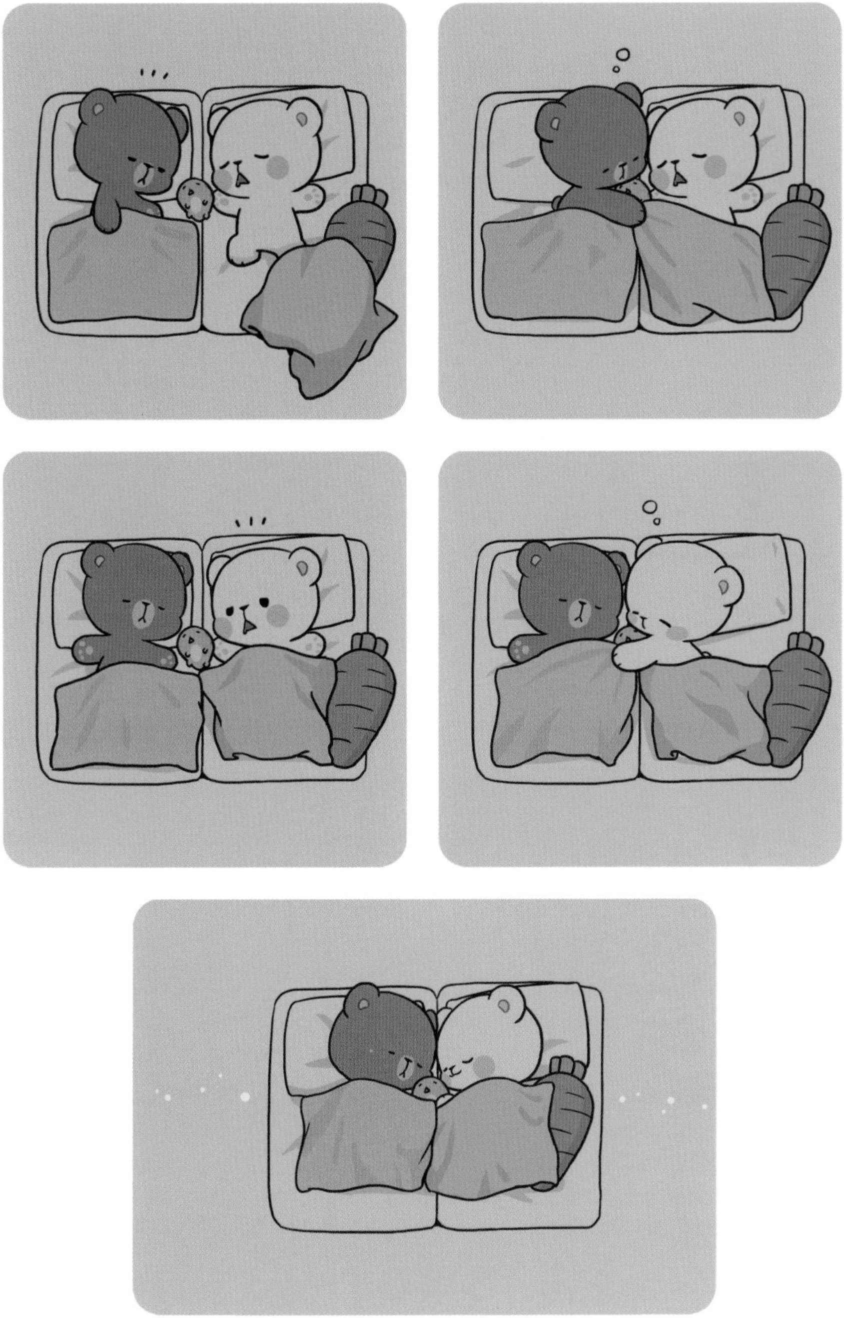

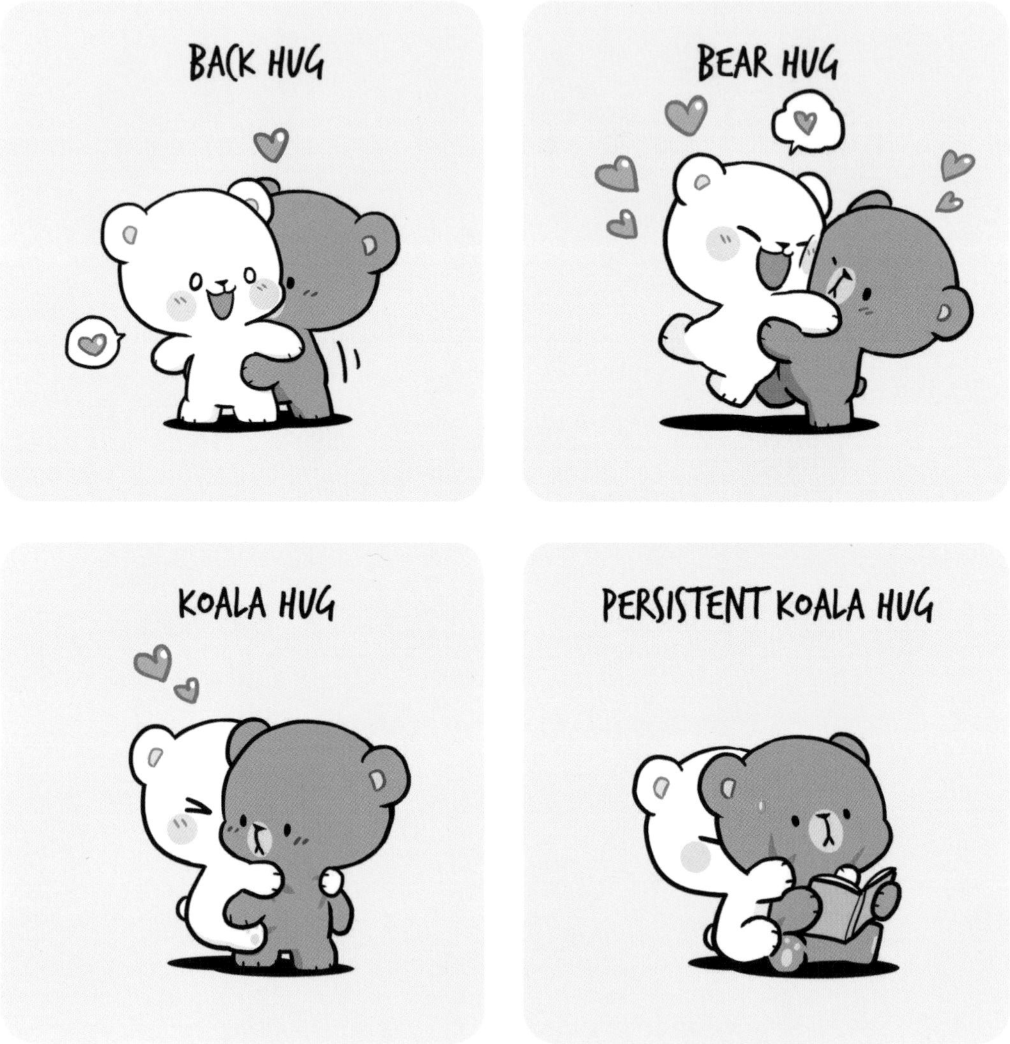
BACK HUG
BEAR HUG
KOALA HUG
PERSISTENT KOALA HUG

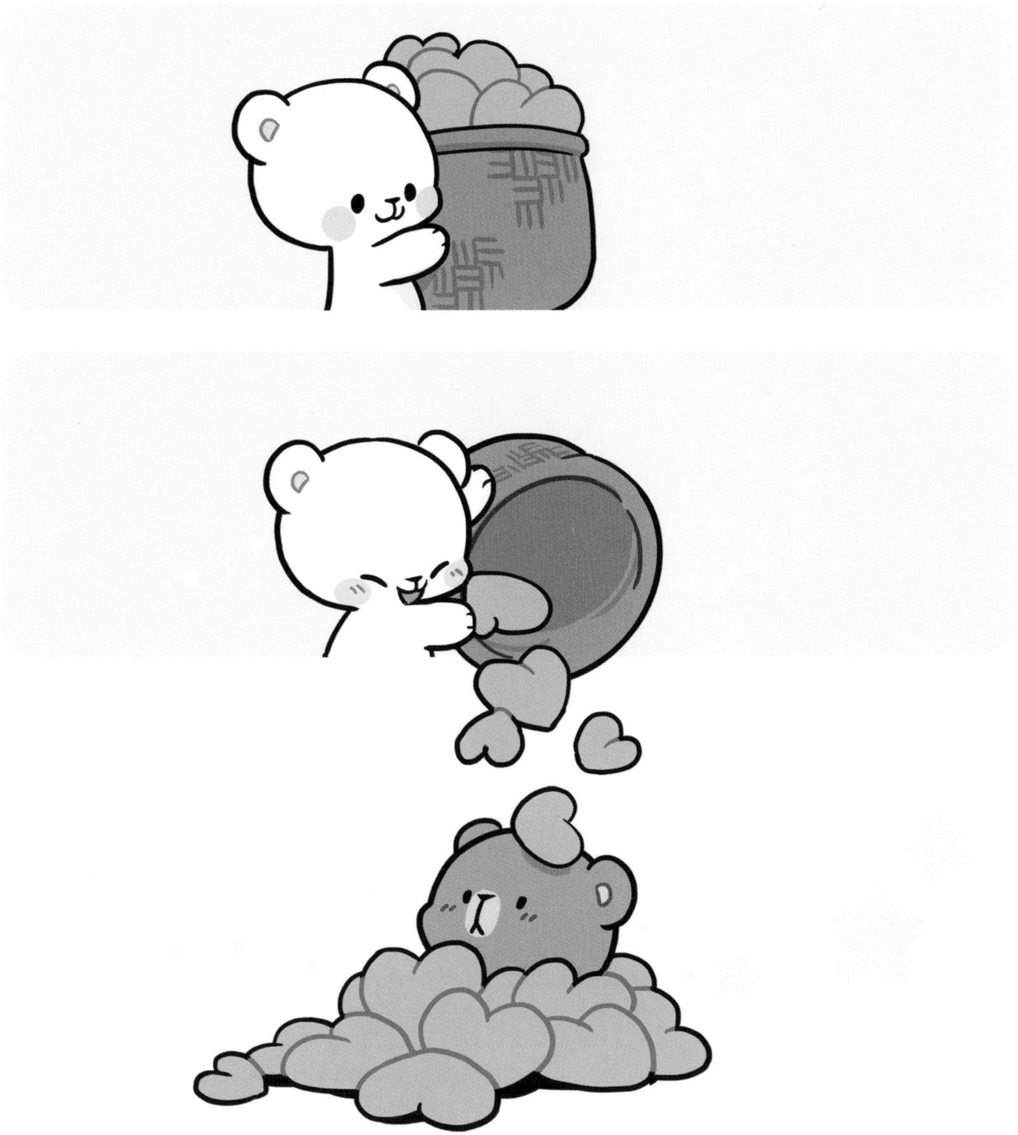

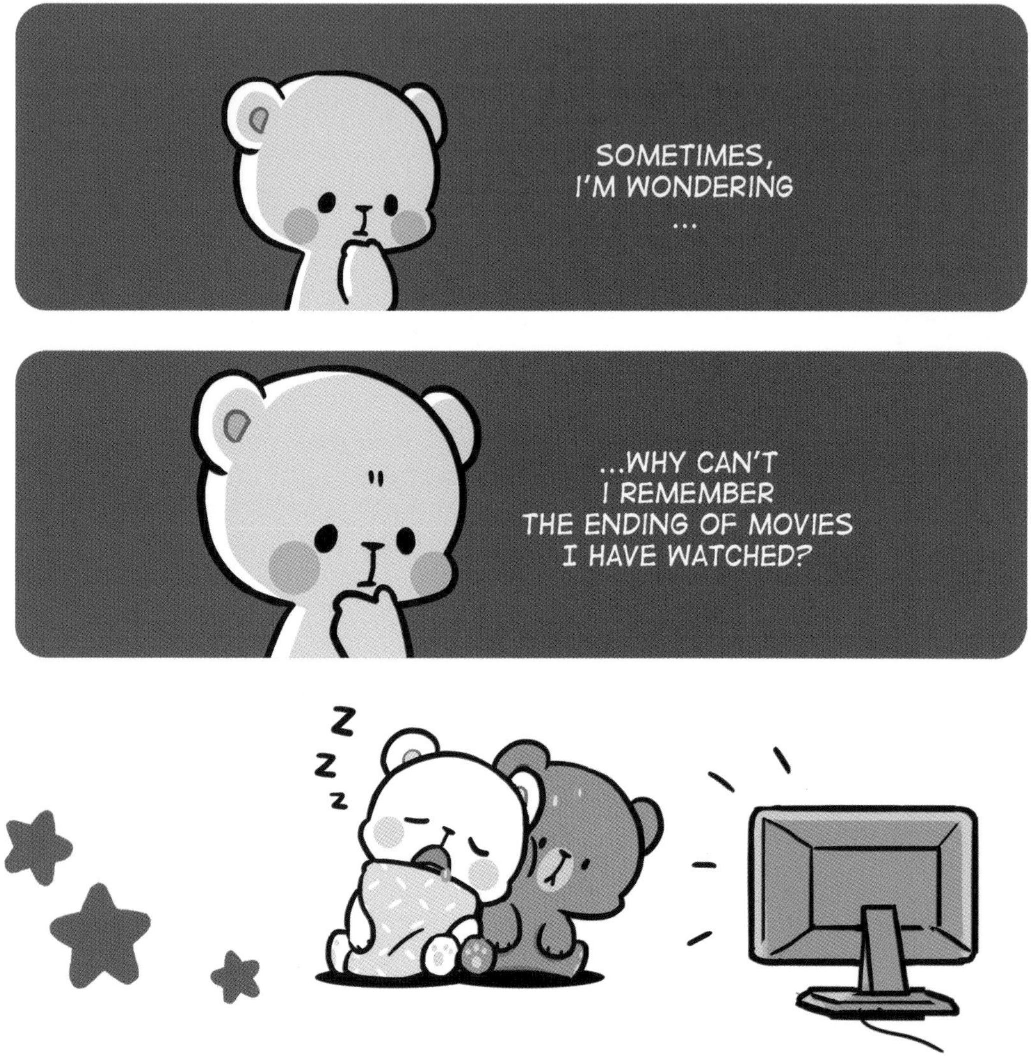
SOMETIMES,
I'M WONDERING
...
...WHY CAN'T
I REMEMBER
THE ENDING OF MOVIES
I HAVE WATCHED?
Z
Z
Z

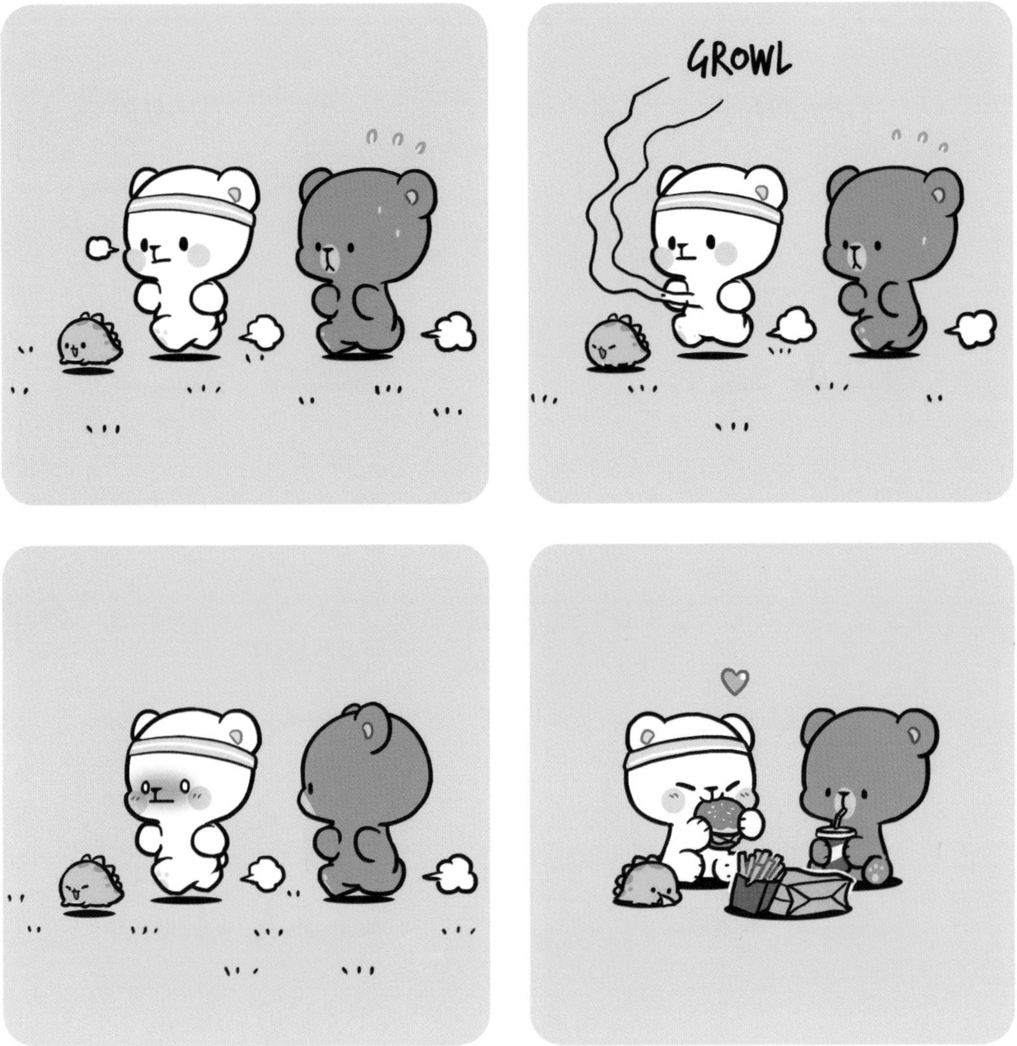
GROWL

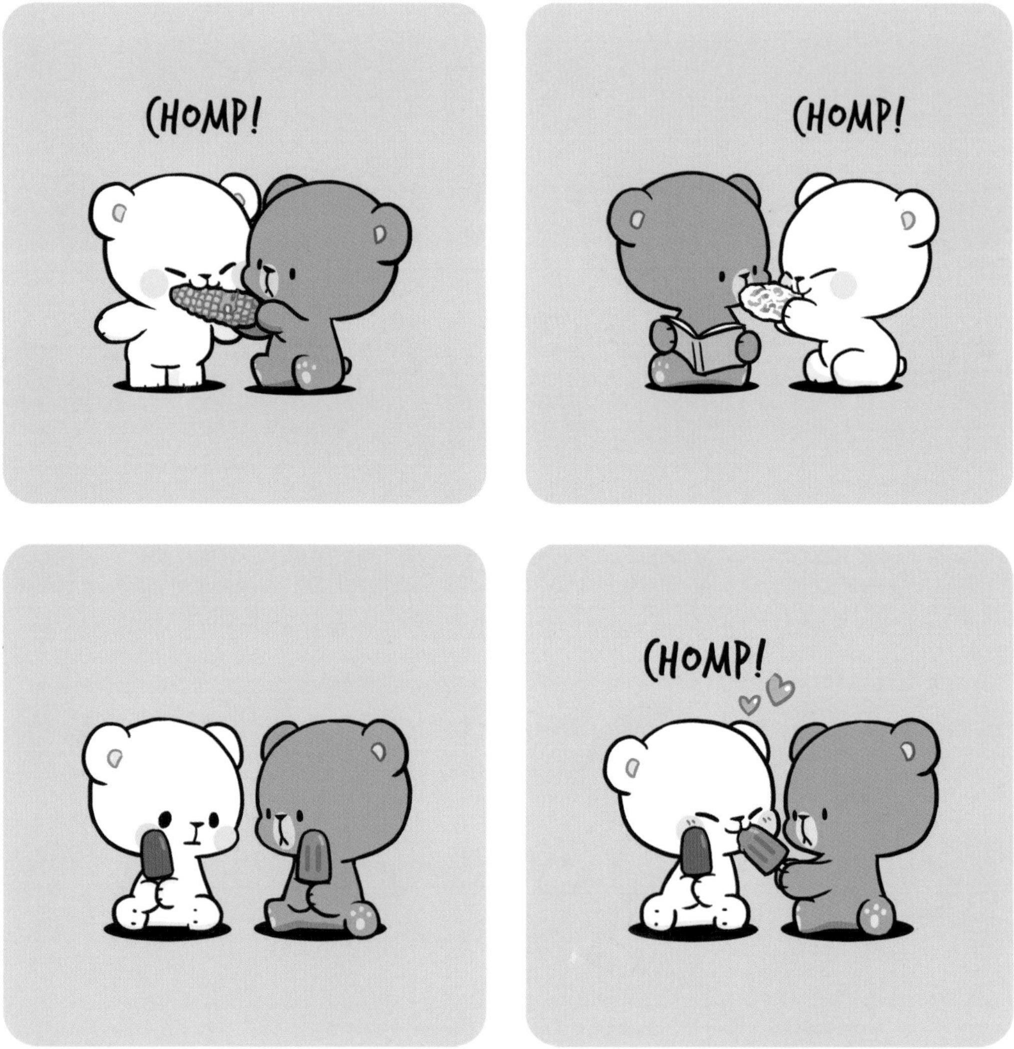
CHOMP!
CHOMP!
CHOMP!

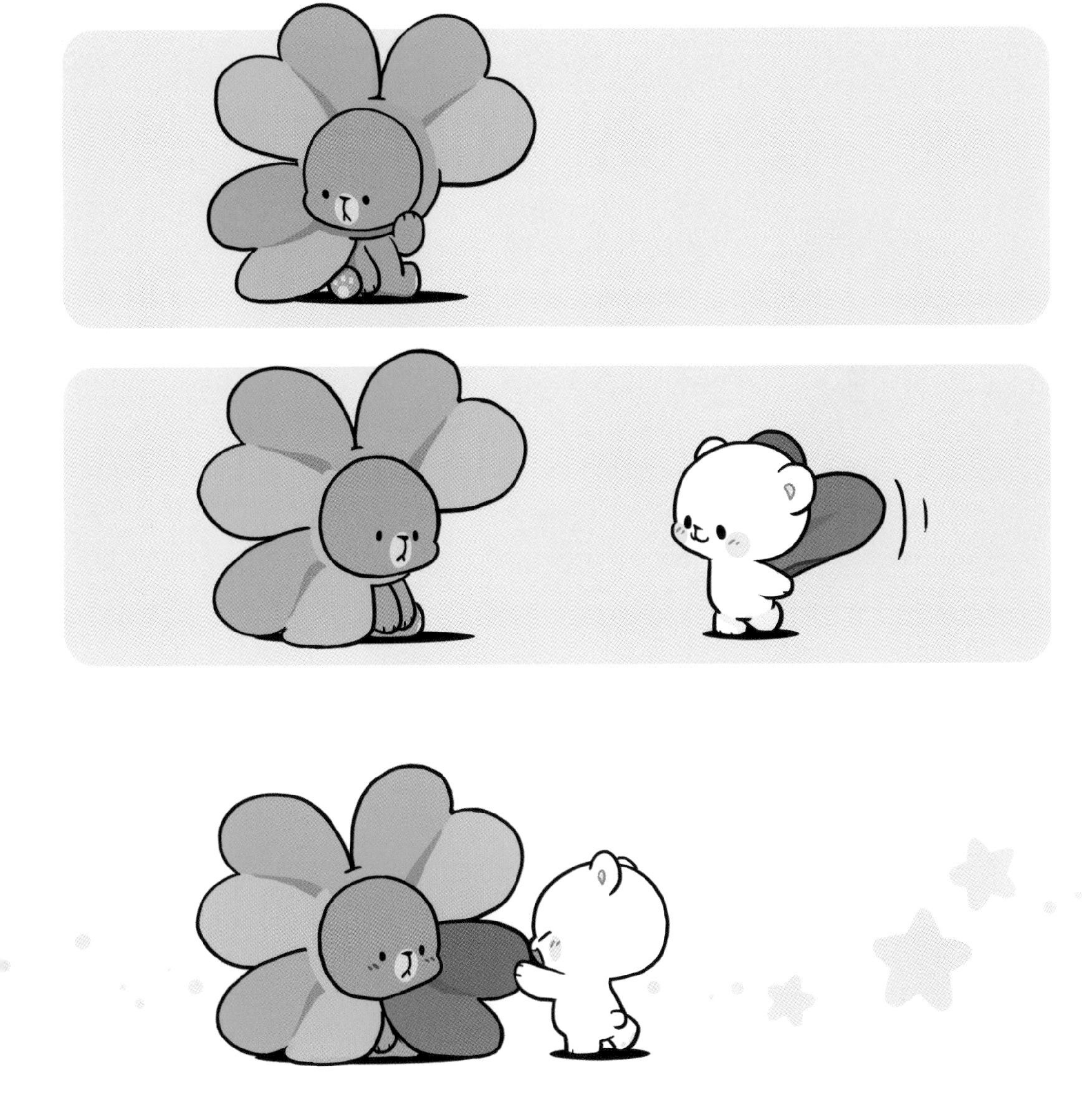

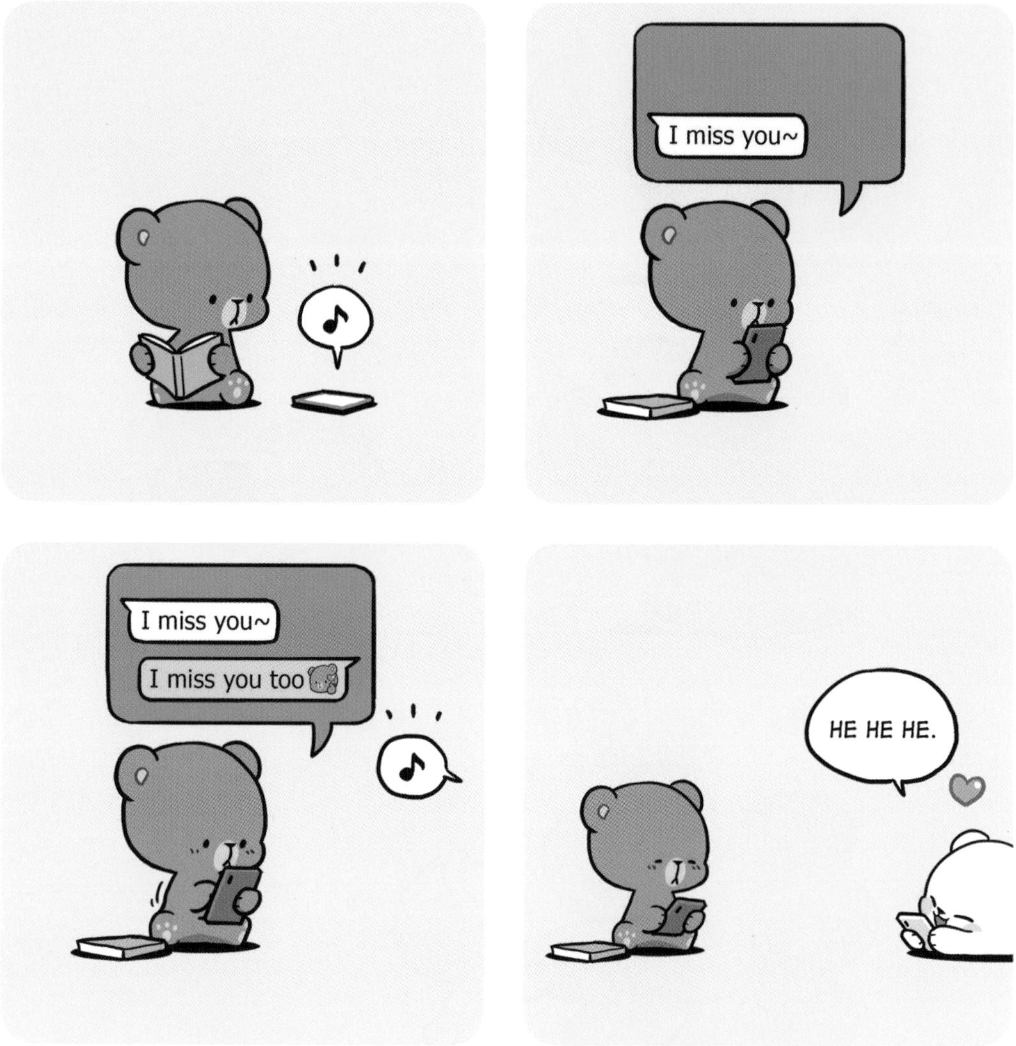
I miss you~
I miss you~
I miss you too
HE HE HE.

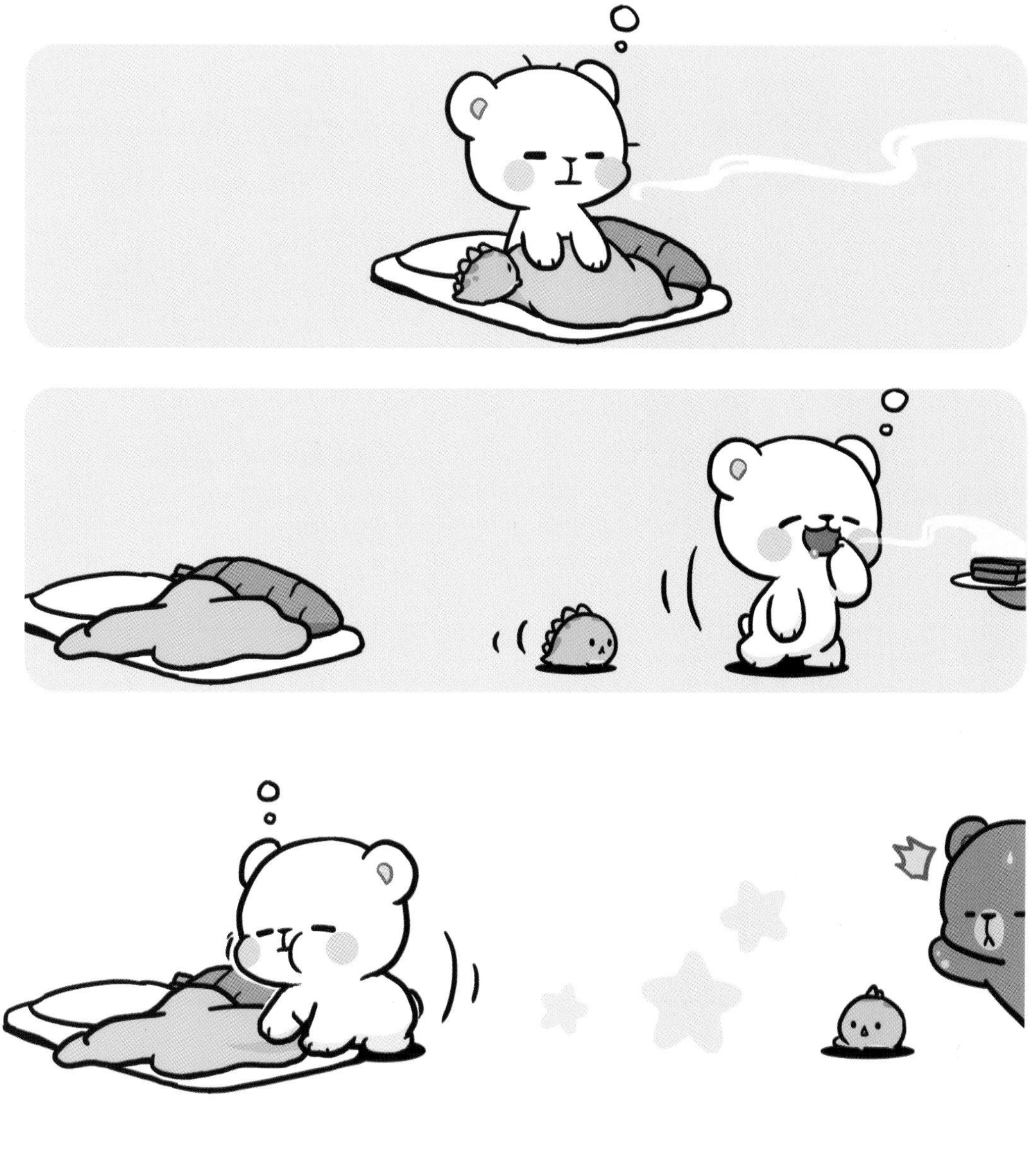

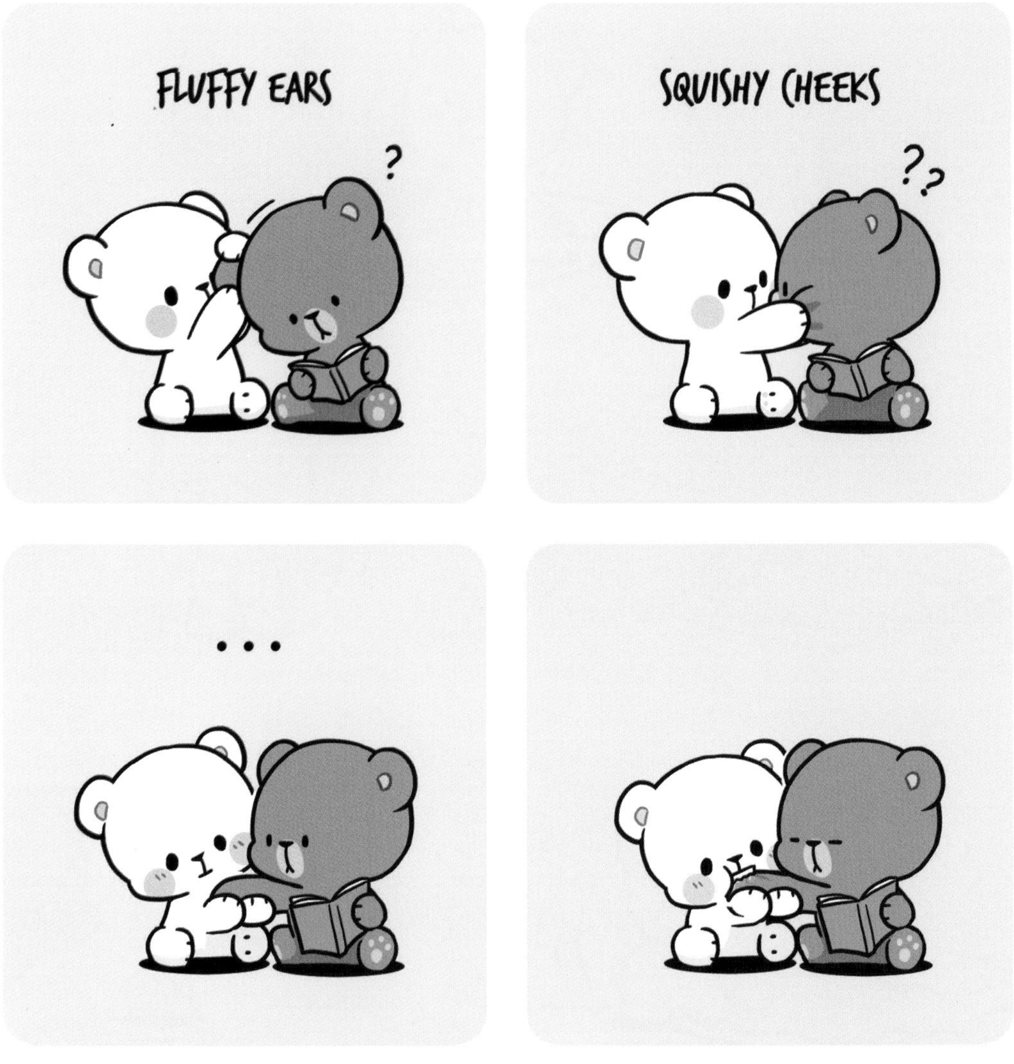
FLUFFY EARS
?
SQUISHY CHEEKS
??
. . .

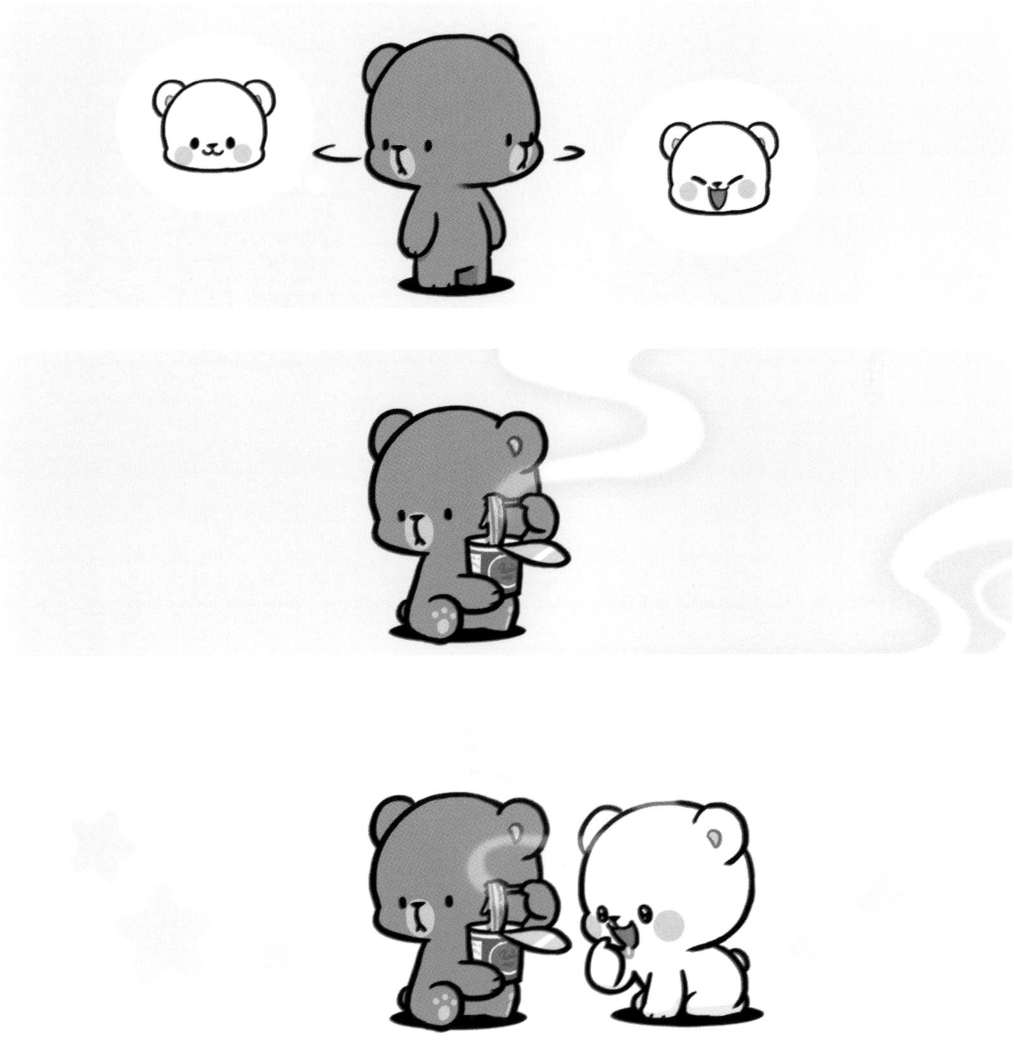

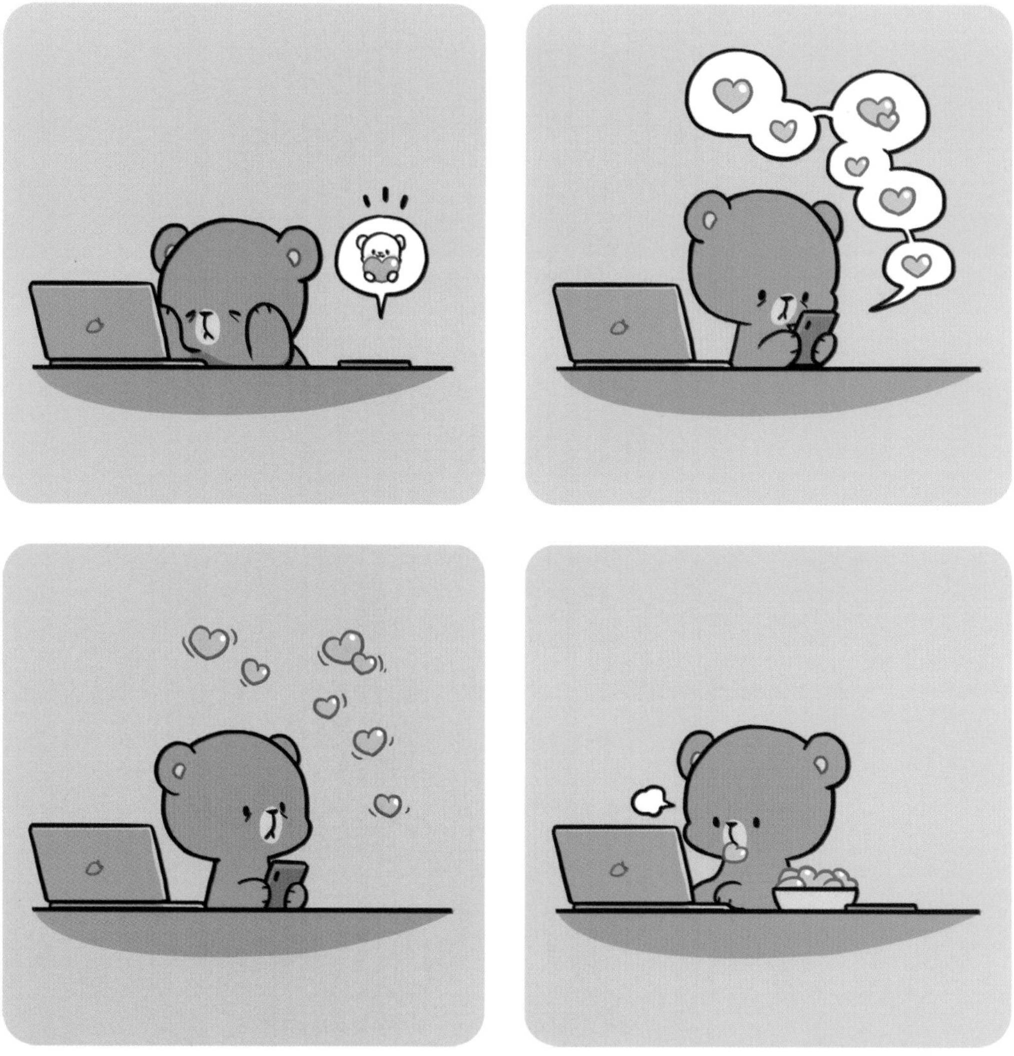

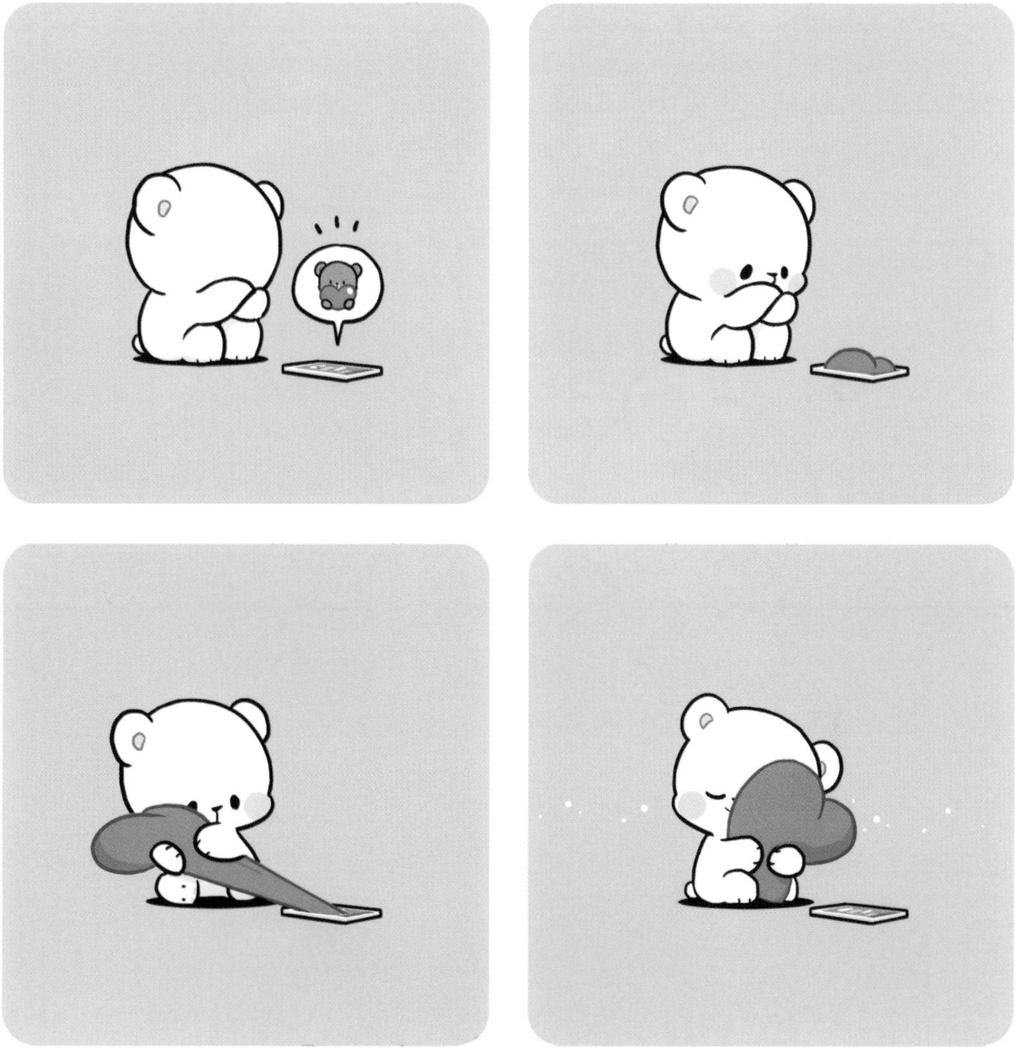

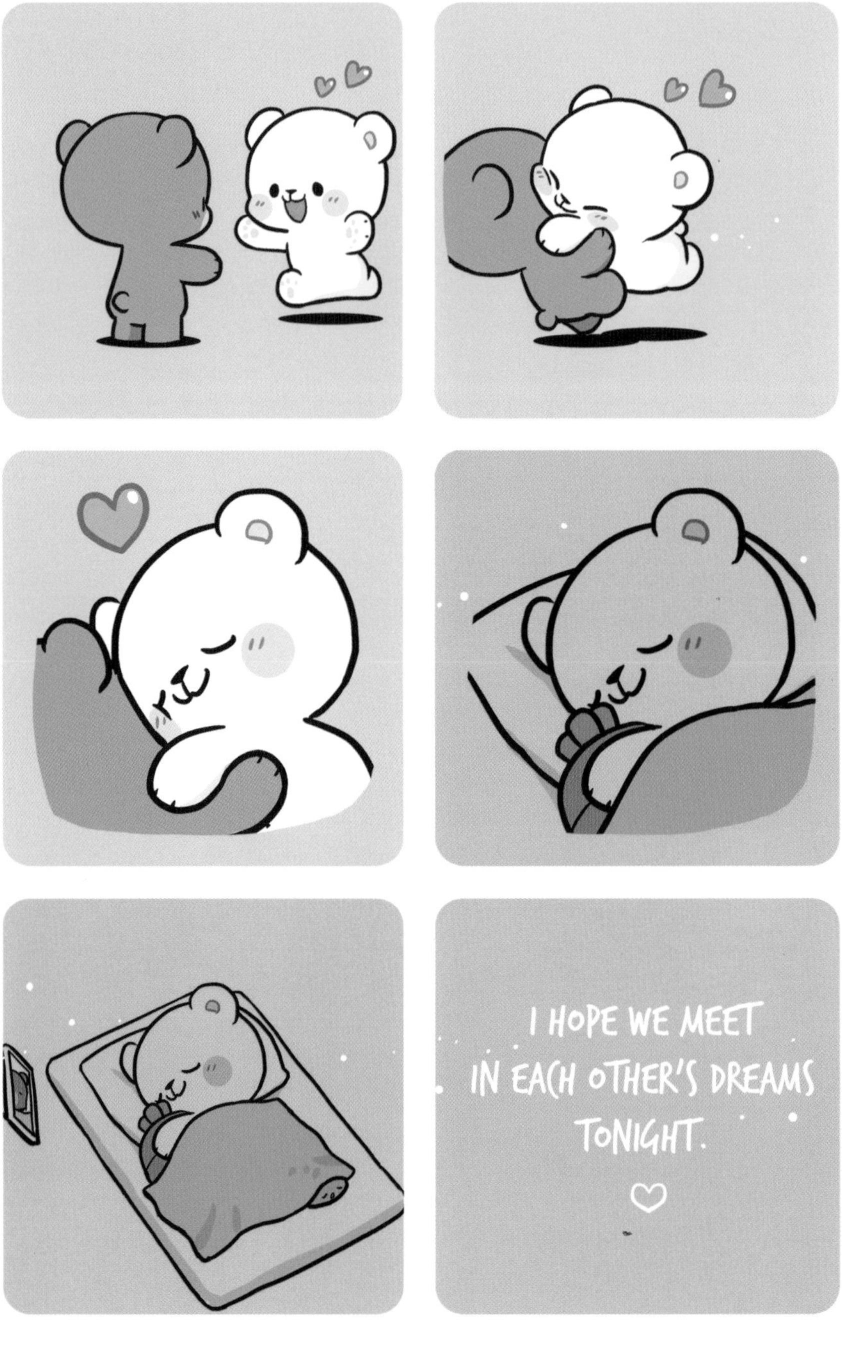
I HOPE WE MEET
IN EACH OTHER'S DREAMS
TONIGHT.

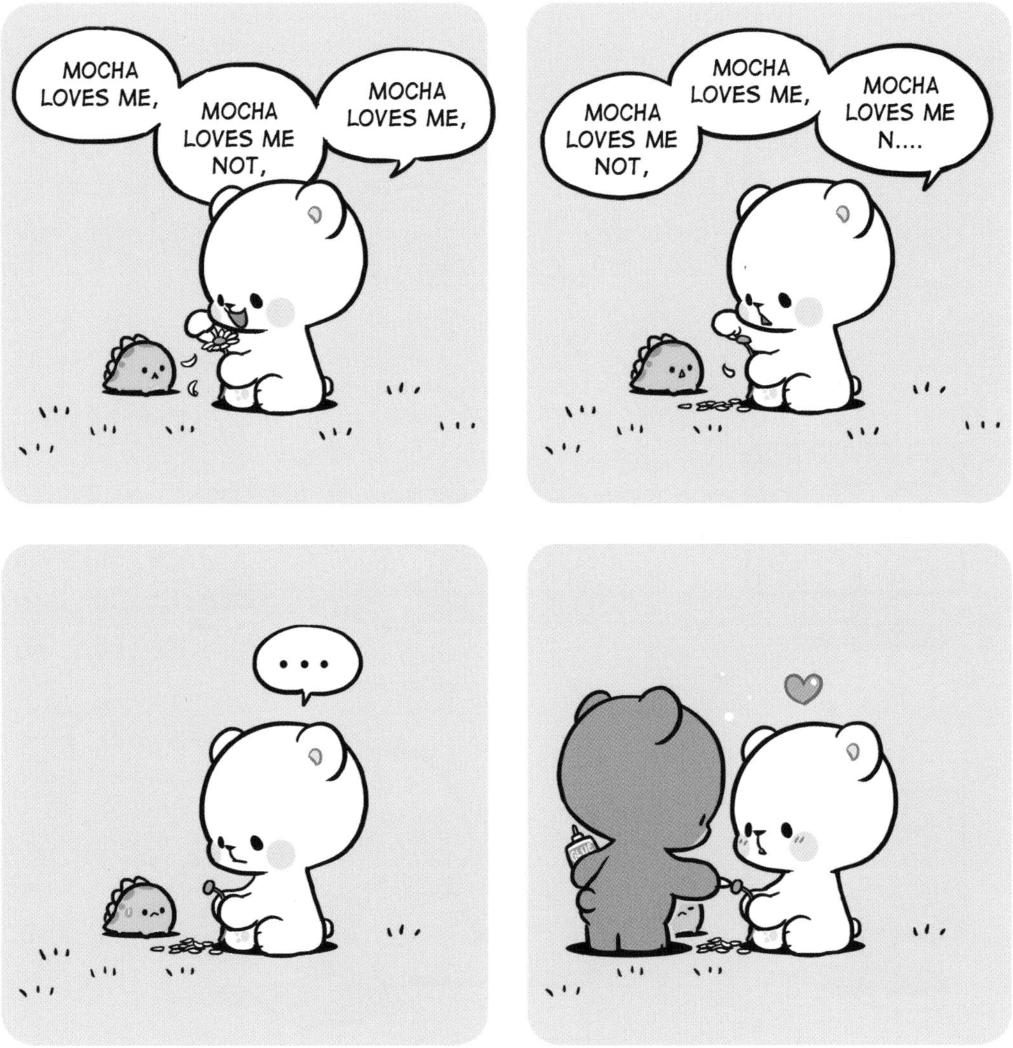
MOCHA LOVES ME,
MOCHA LOVES ME NOT,
MOCHA LOVES ME,
MOCHA LOVES ME NOT,
MOCHA LOVES ME,
MOCHA LOVES ME N....
...
GLUE

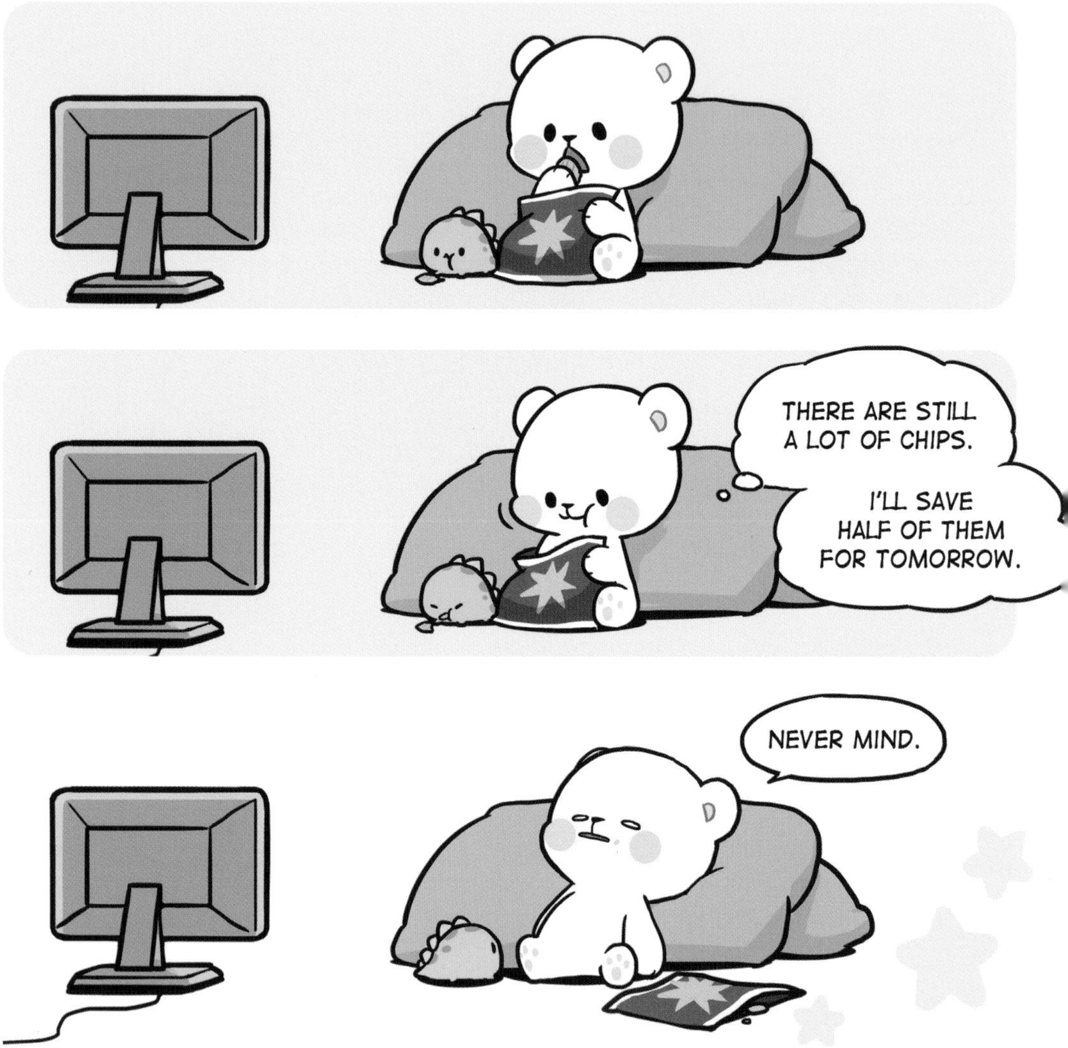
THERE ARE STILL A LOT OF CHIPS.
I'LL SAVE HALF OF THEM FOR TOMORROW.
NEVER MIND.

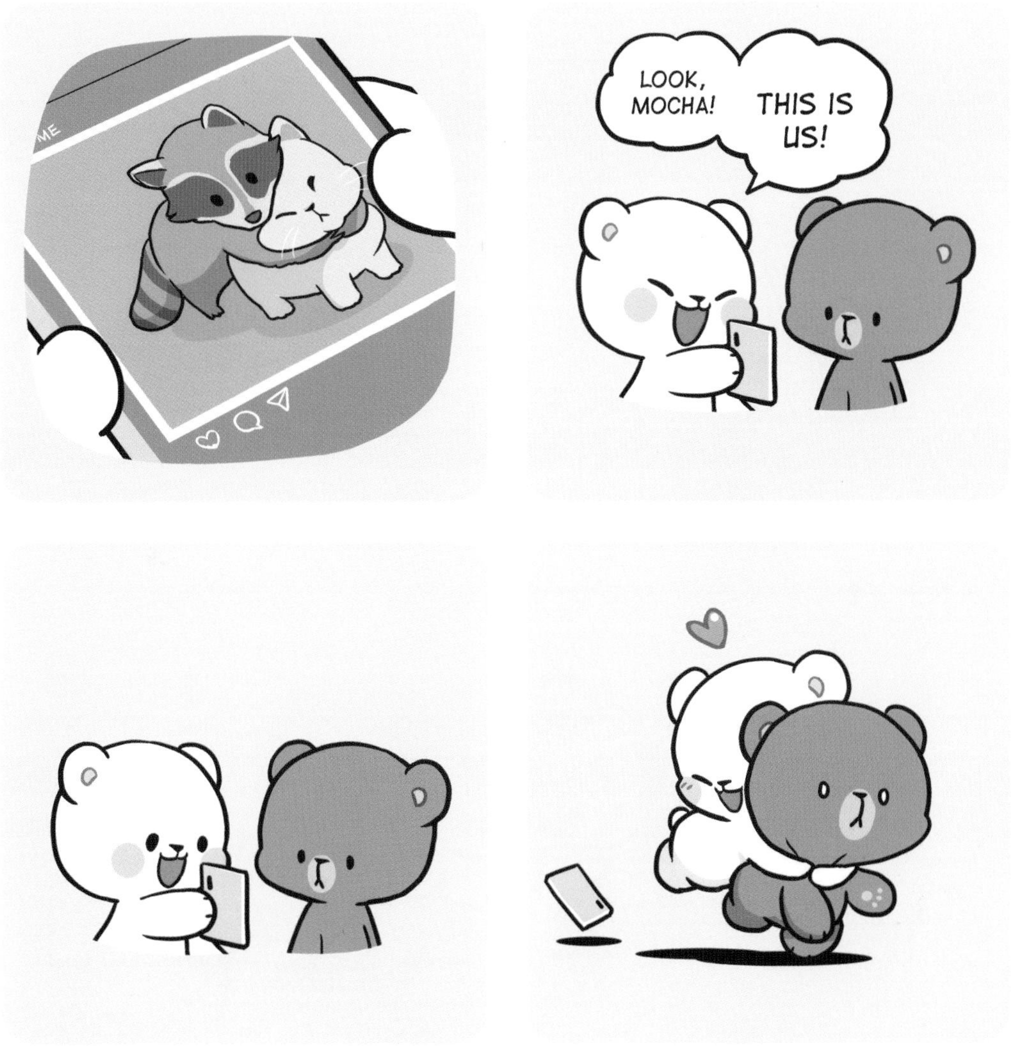
LOOK, MOCHA!
THIS IS US!

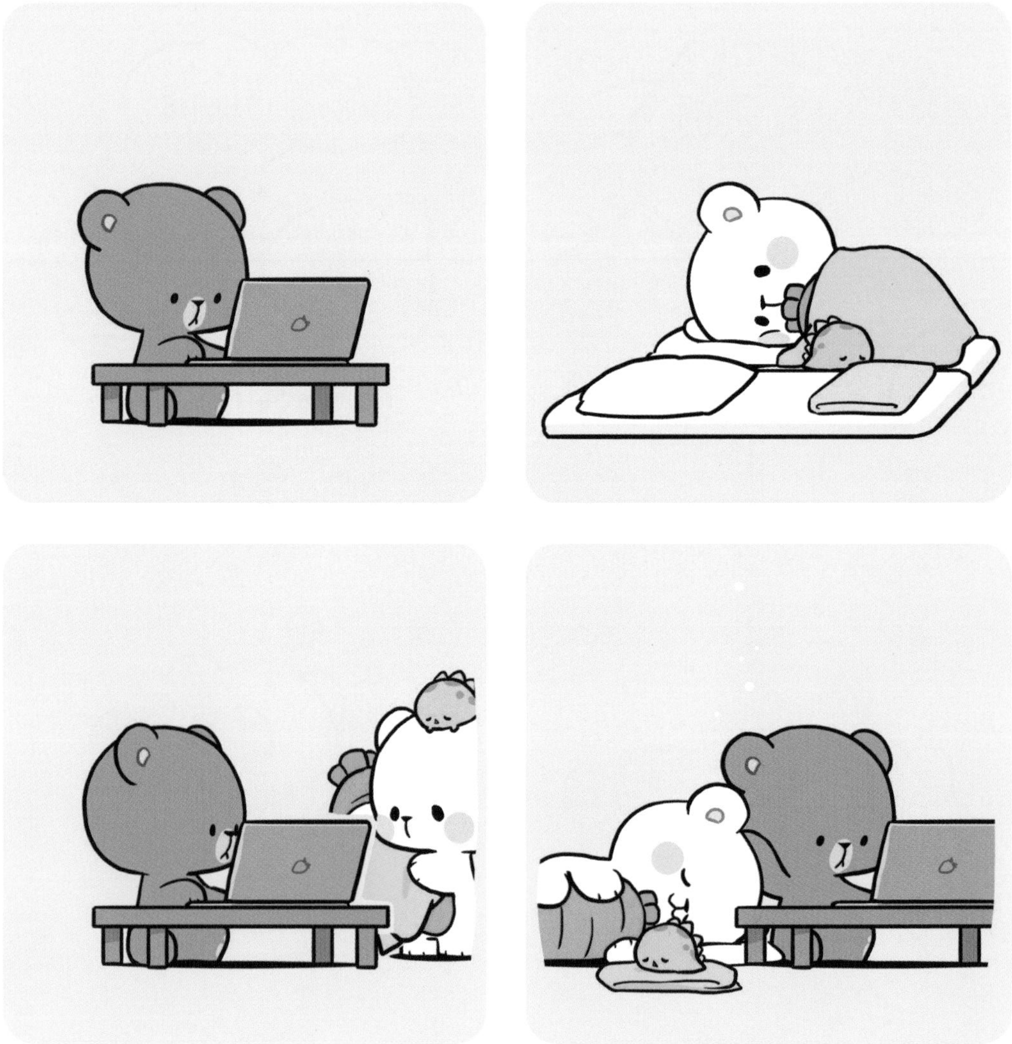

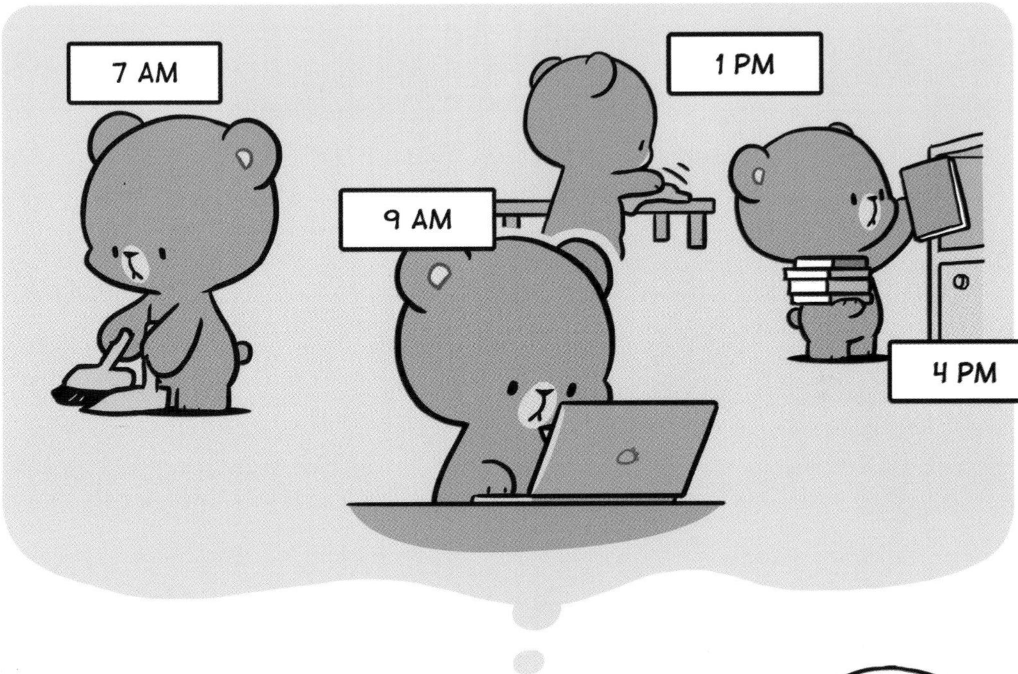
7 AM
9 AM
1 PM
4 PM

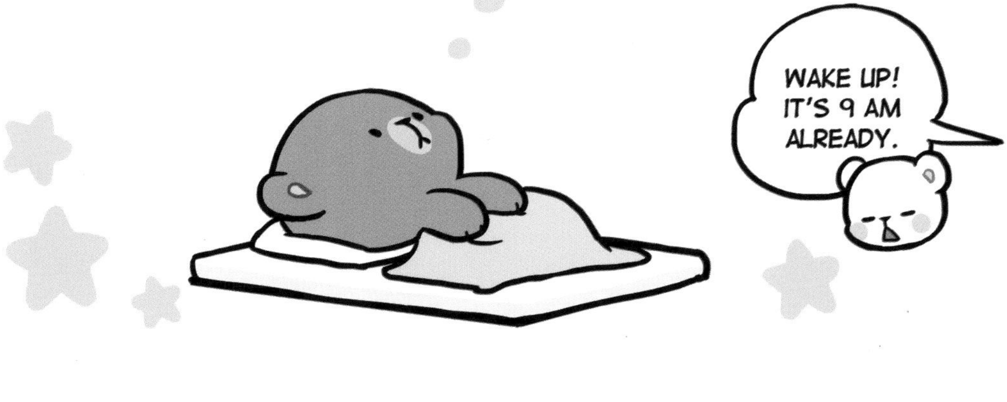
WAKE UP! IT'S 9 AM ALREADY.

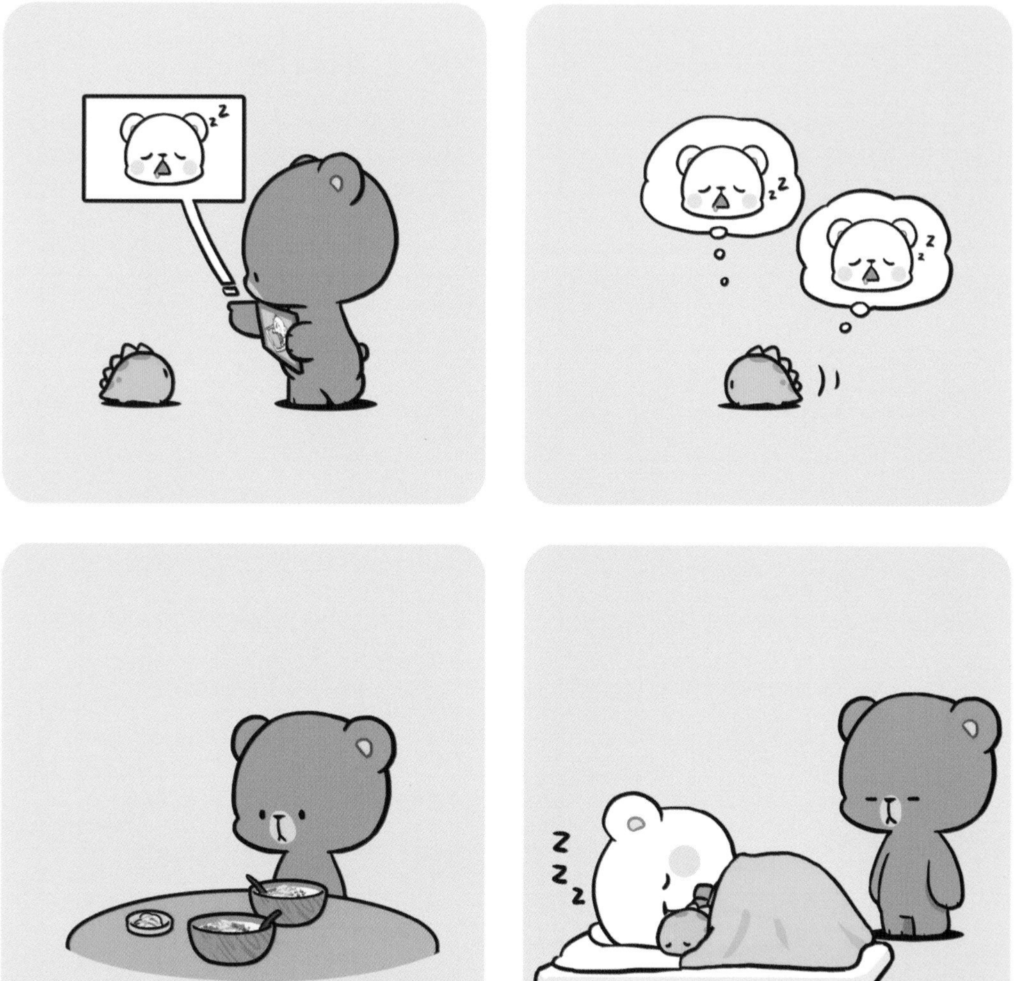

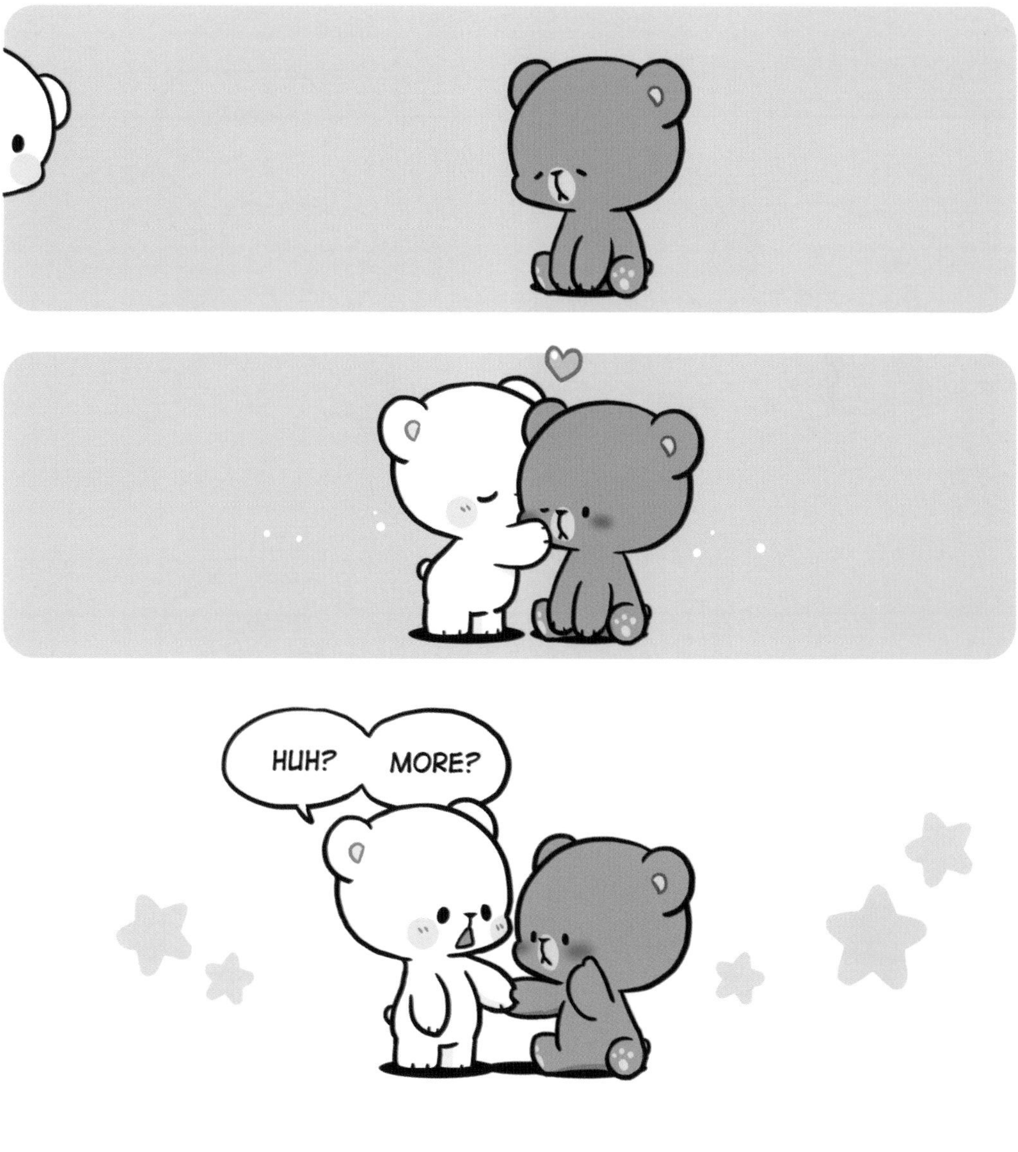
HUH?
MORE?

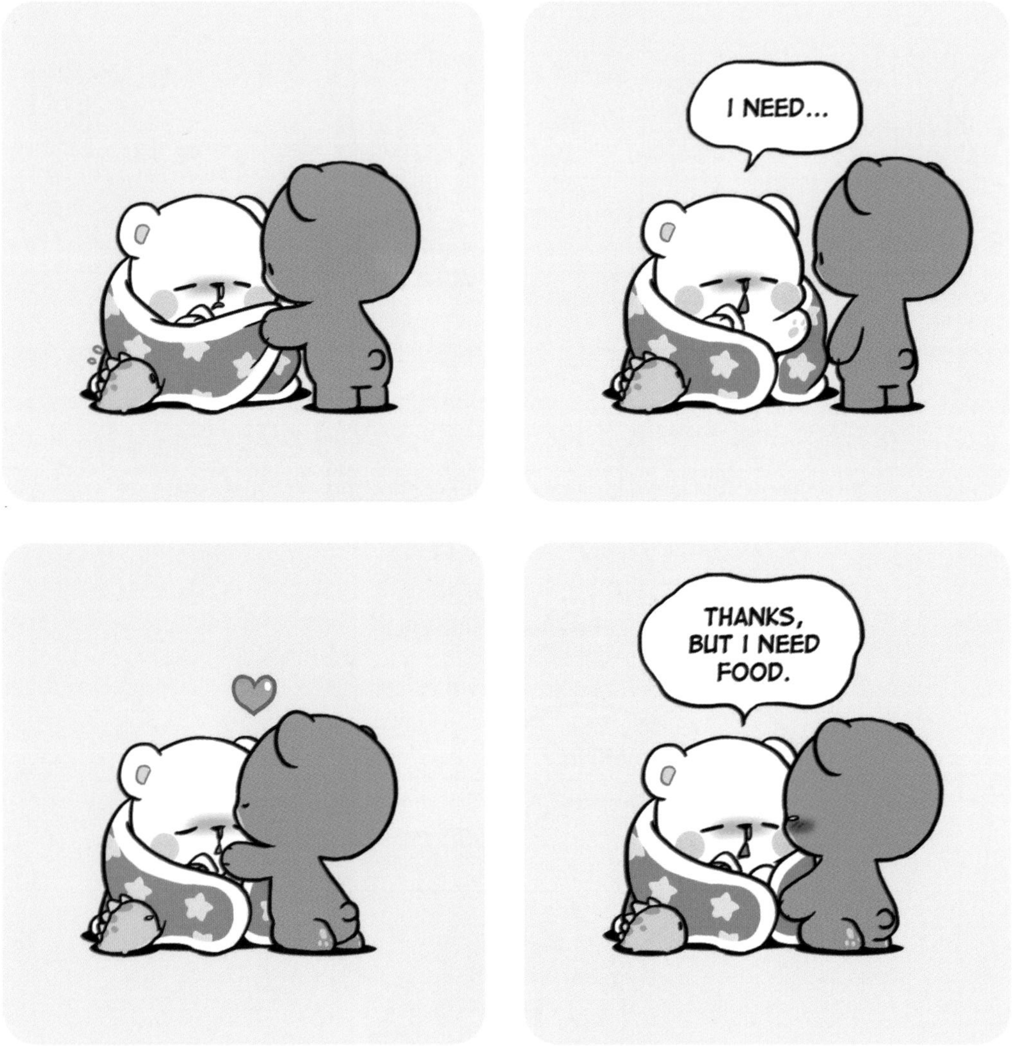
I NEED...
THANKS, BUT I NEED FOOD.

EPILOGUE

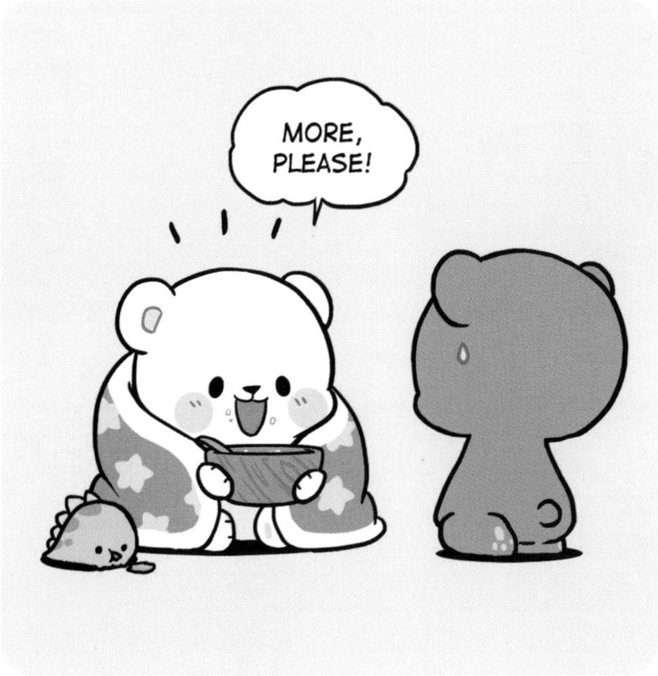
MORE, PLEASE!

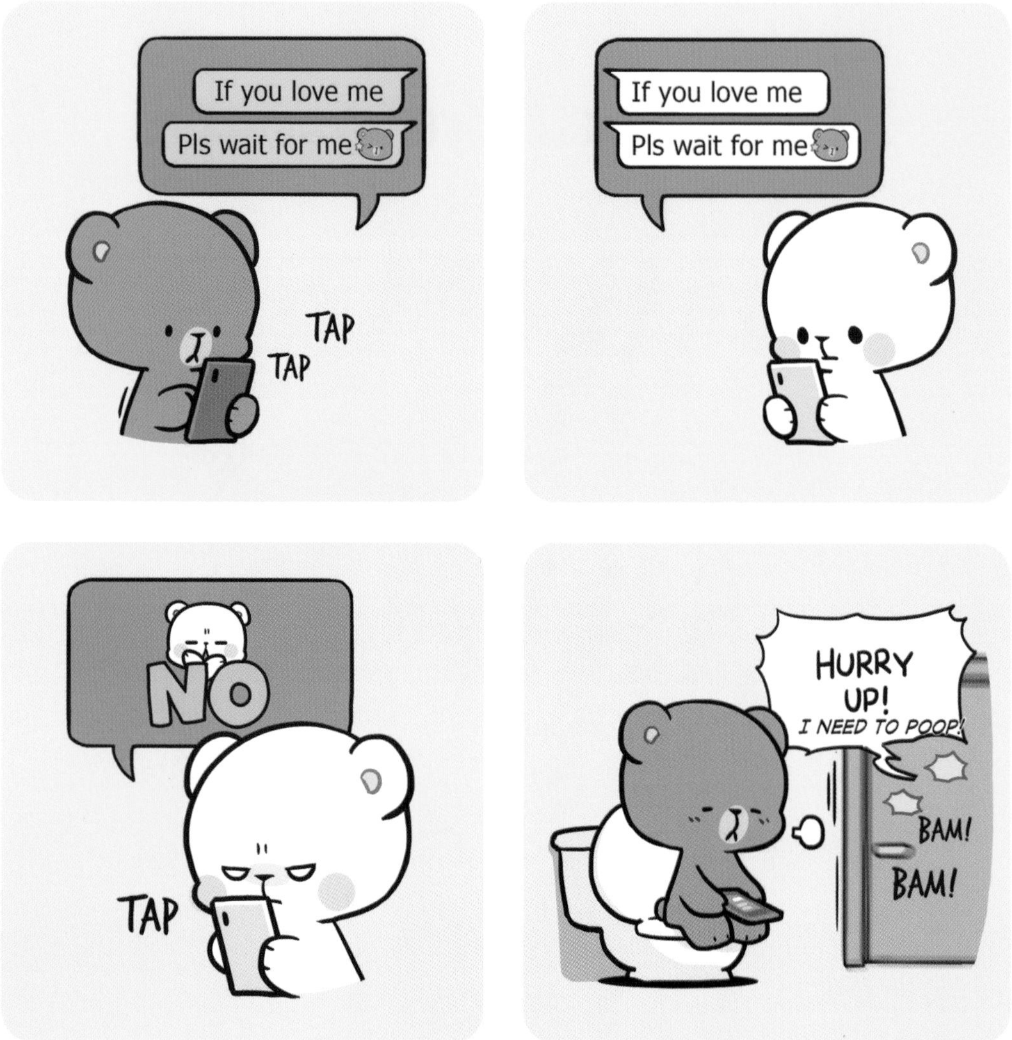
If you love me
Pls wait for me
TAP
TAP
If you love me
Pls wait for me
NO
TAP
HURRY UP!
I NEED TO POOP!
BAM!
BAM!

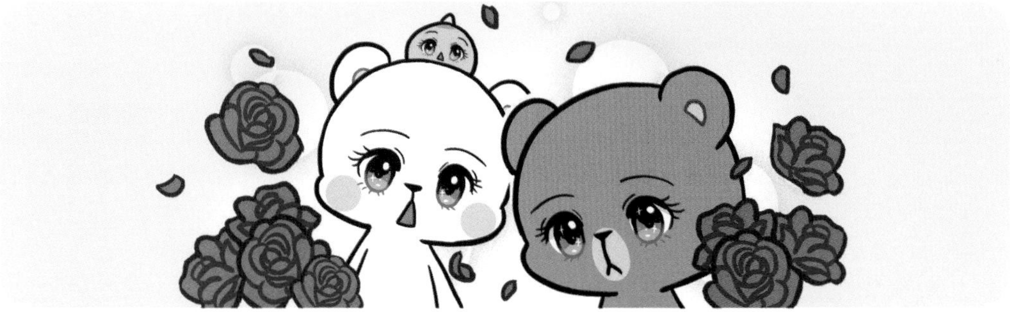

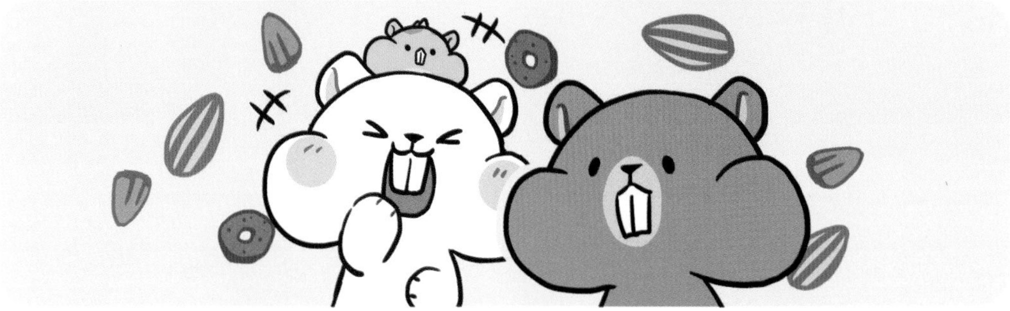

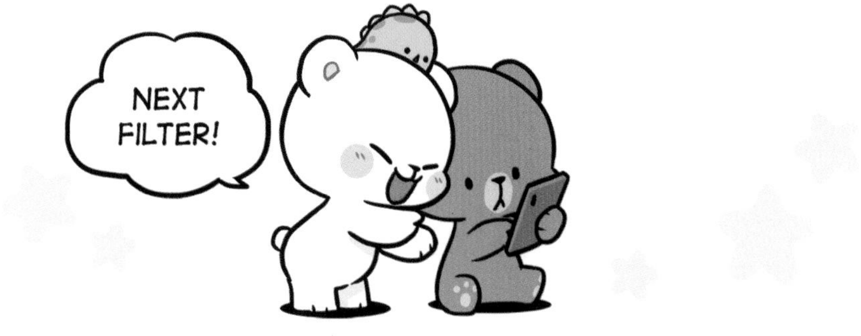
NEXT FILTER!

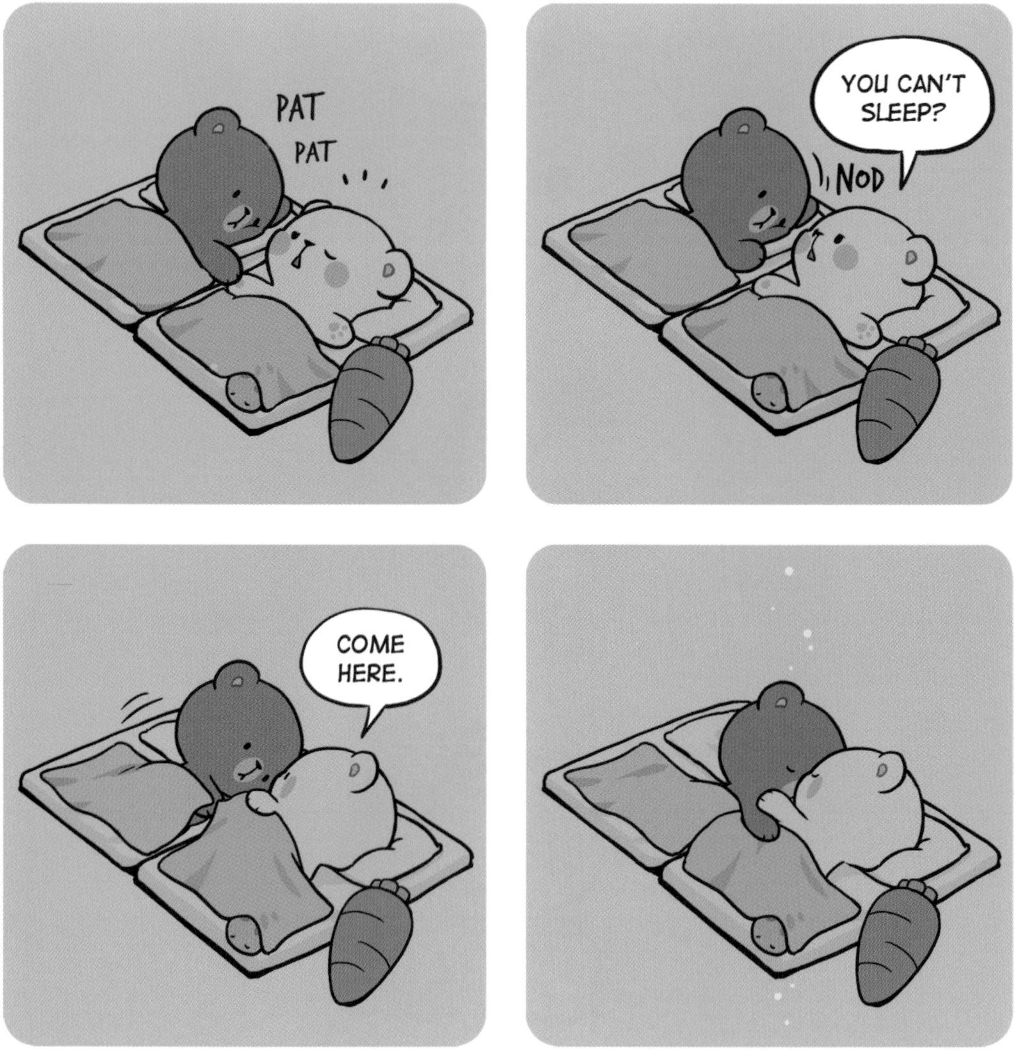
PAT
PAT
YOU CAN'T SLEEP?
NOD
COME HERE.

EPILOGUE

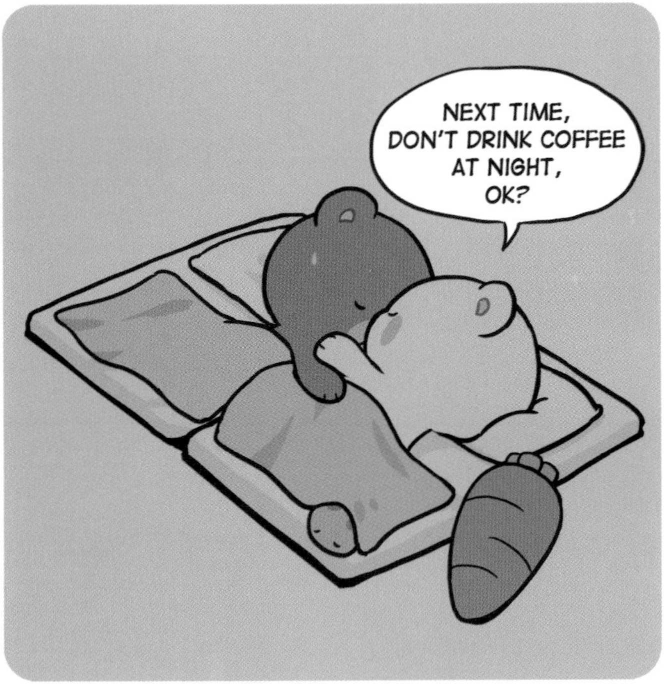
NEXT TIME, DON'T DRINK COFFEE AT NIGHT, OK?

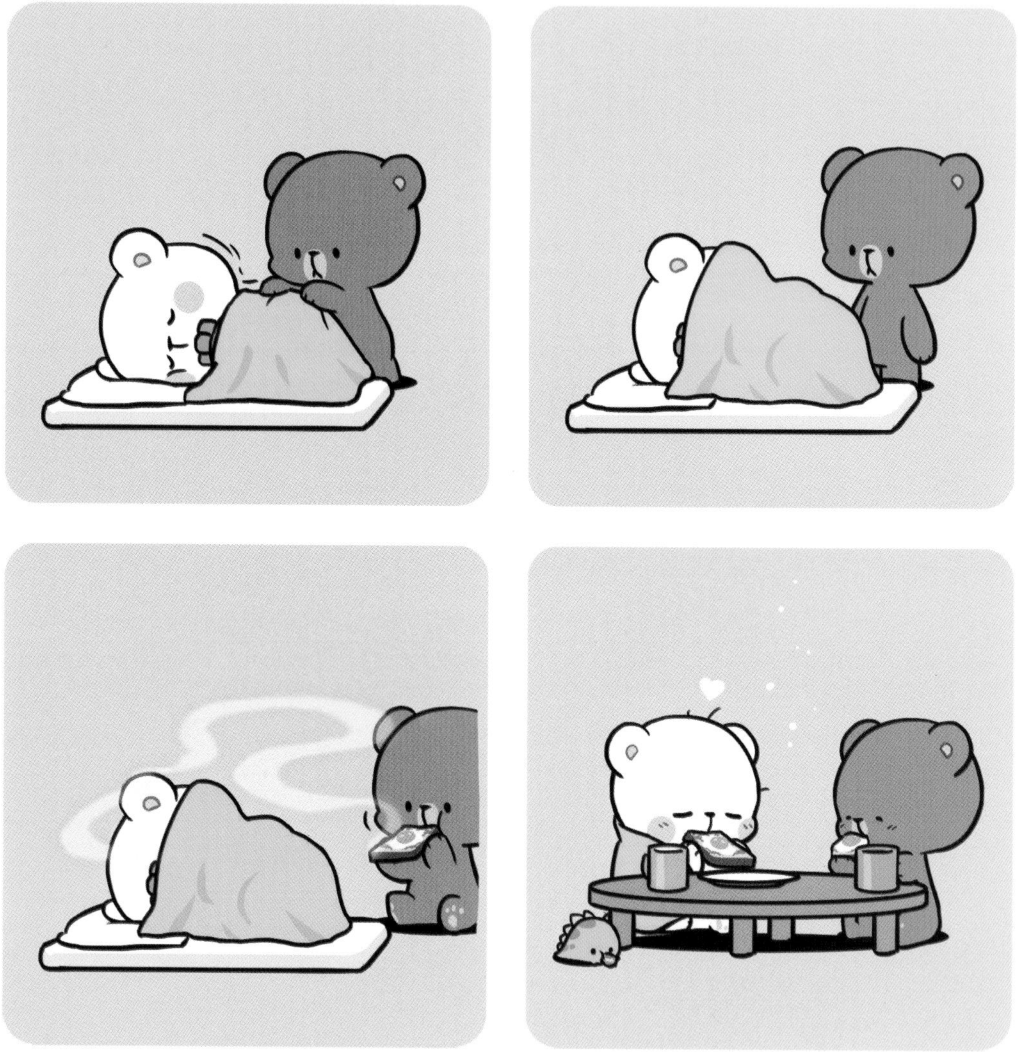

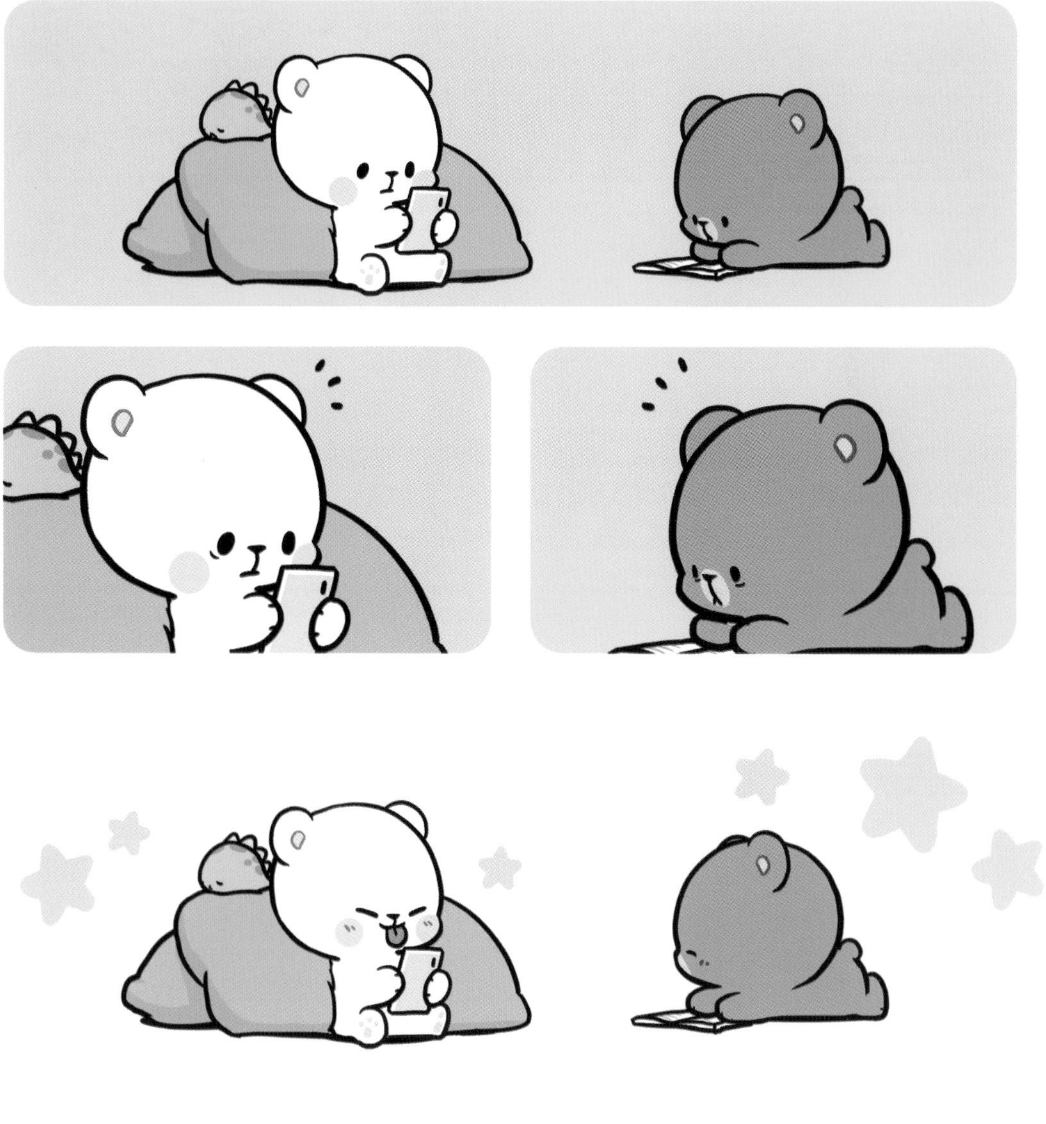

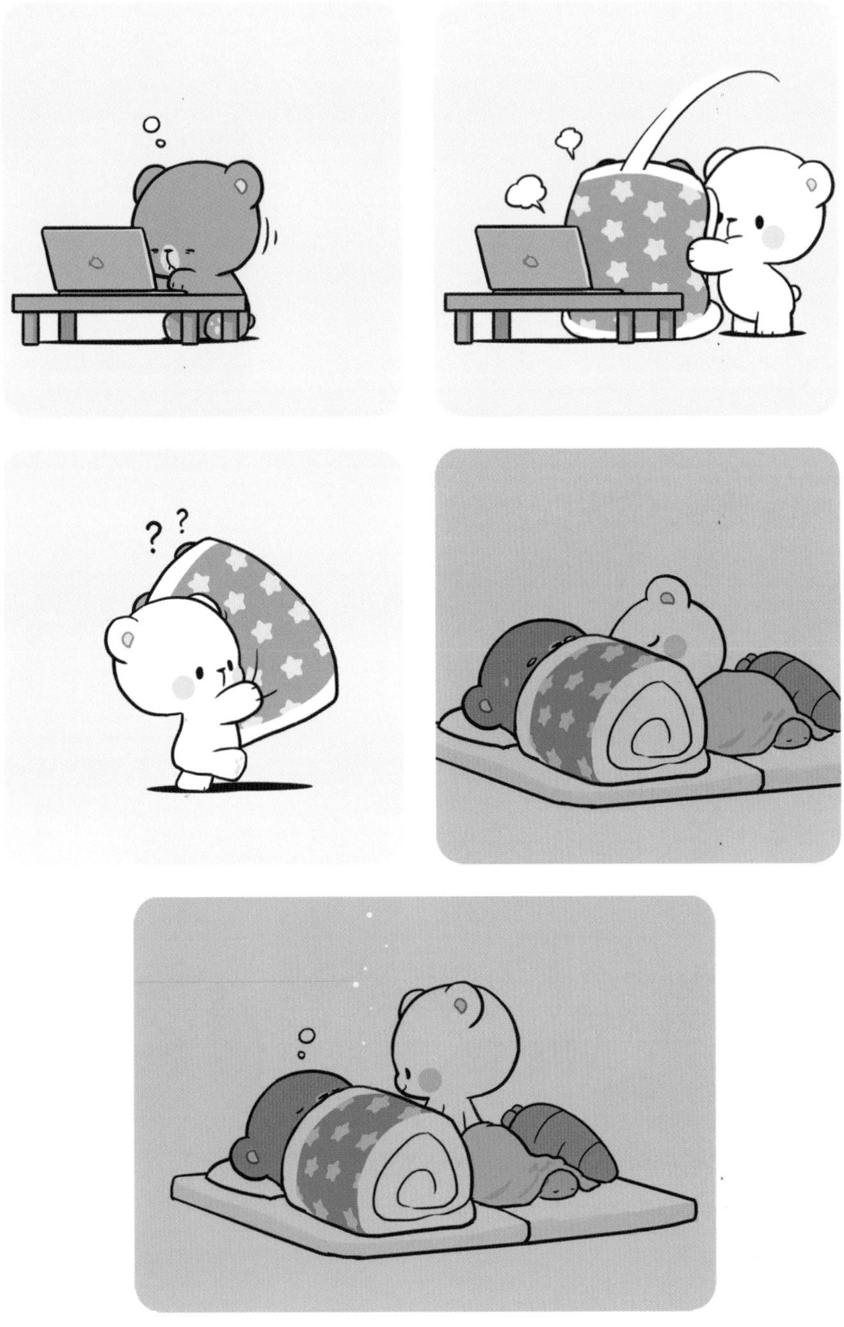

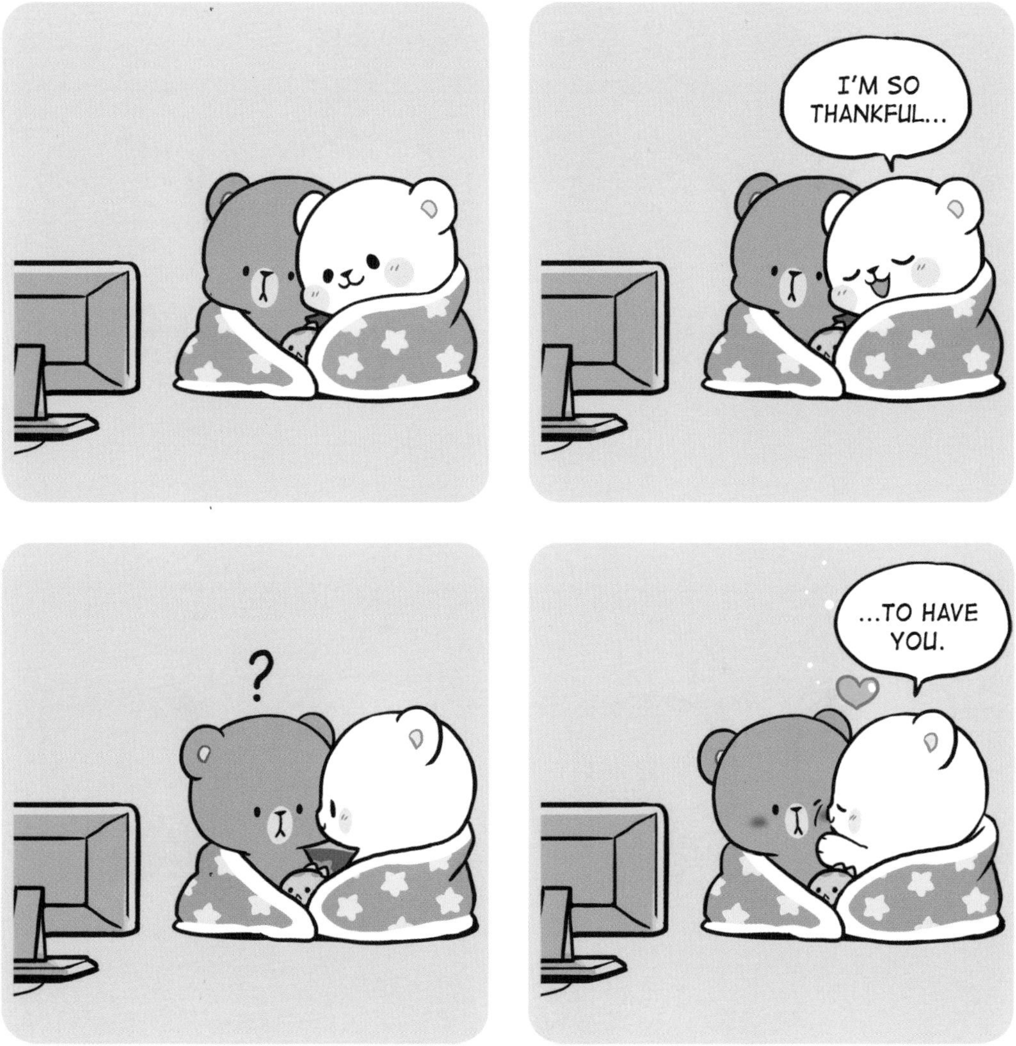
I'M SO THANKFUL...
?
...TO HAVE YOU.

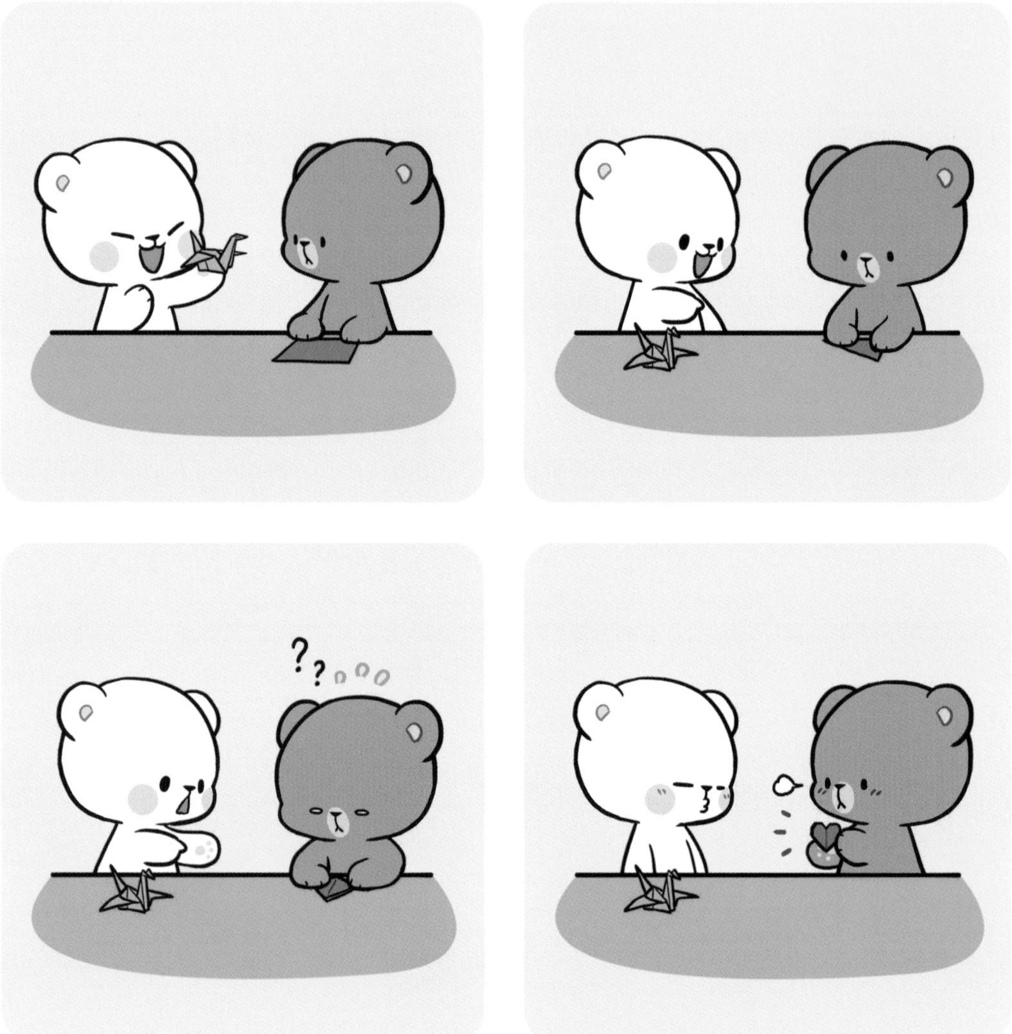

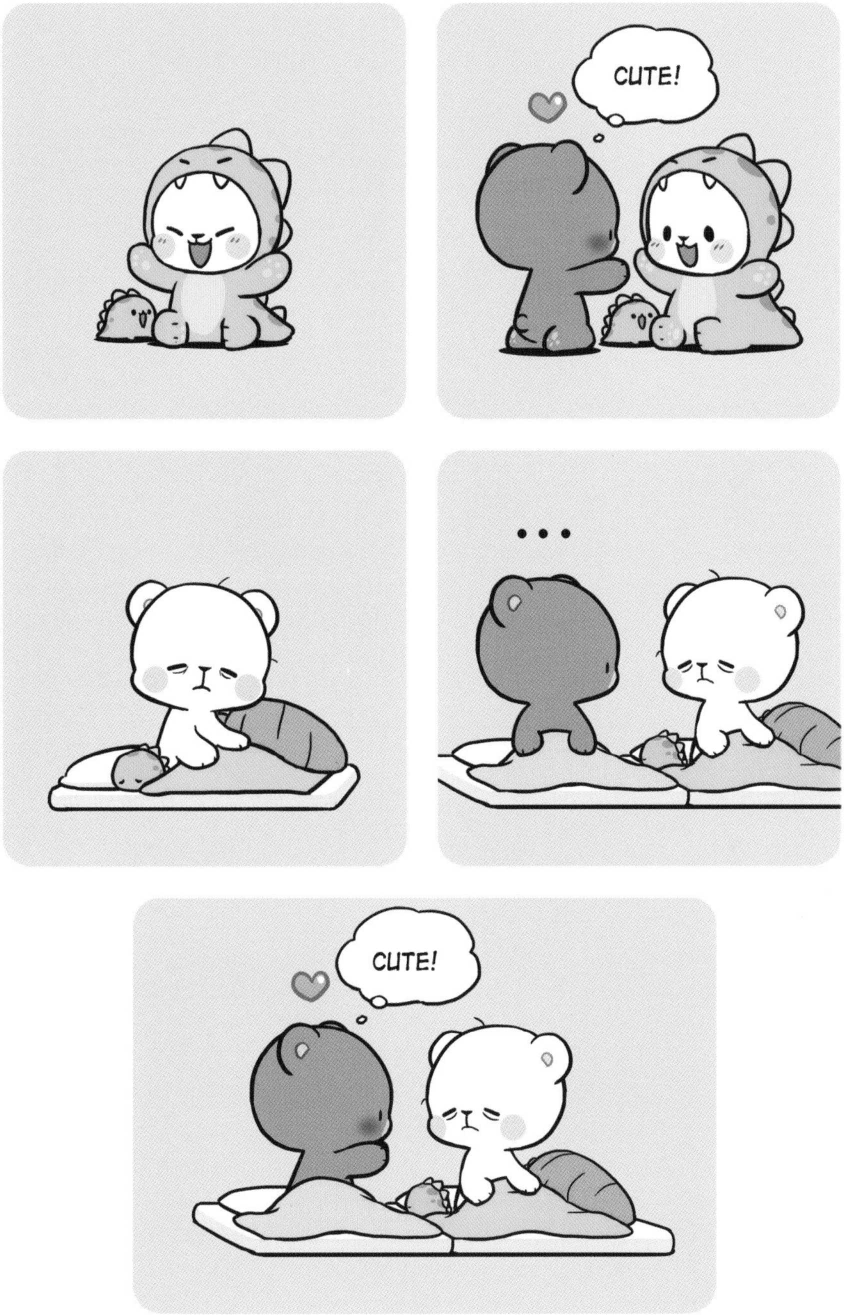
CUTE!
...
CUTE!

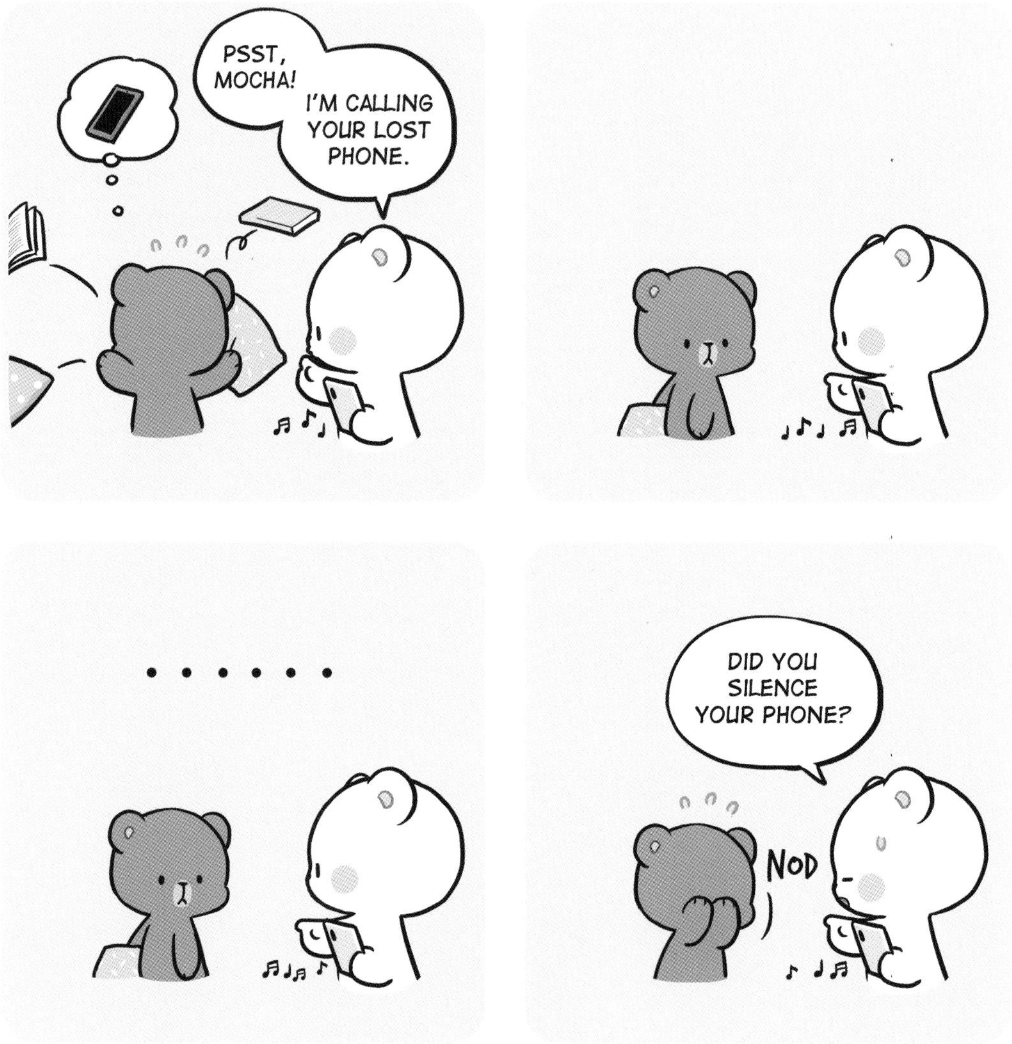
PSST, MOCHA!
I'M CALLING YOUR LOST PHONE.
• • • • • •
DID YOU SILENCE YOUR PHONE?
NOD

EPILOGUE

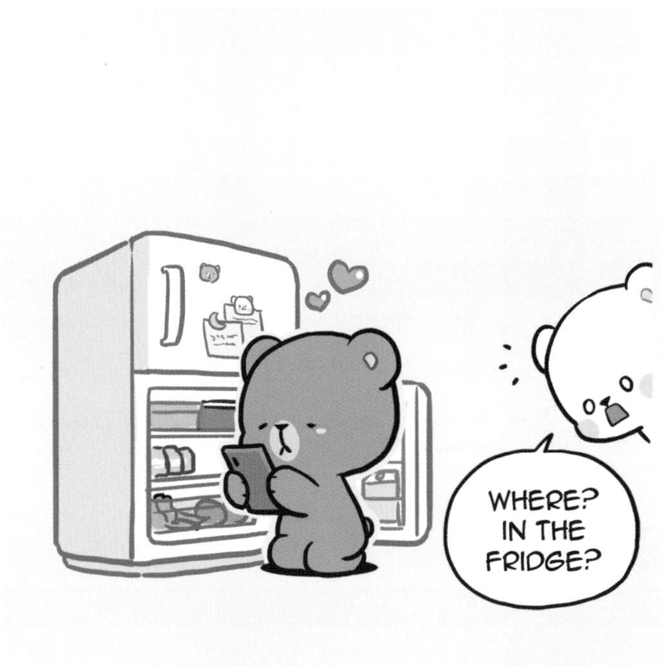
WHERE? IN THE FRIDGE?

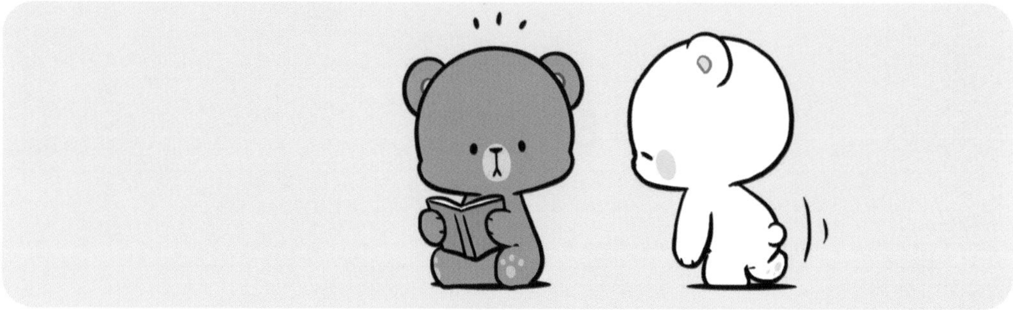
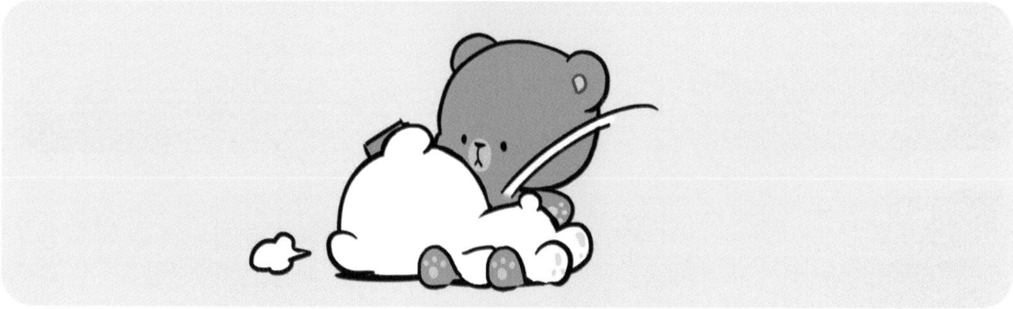
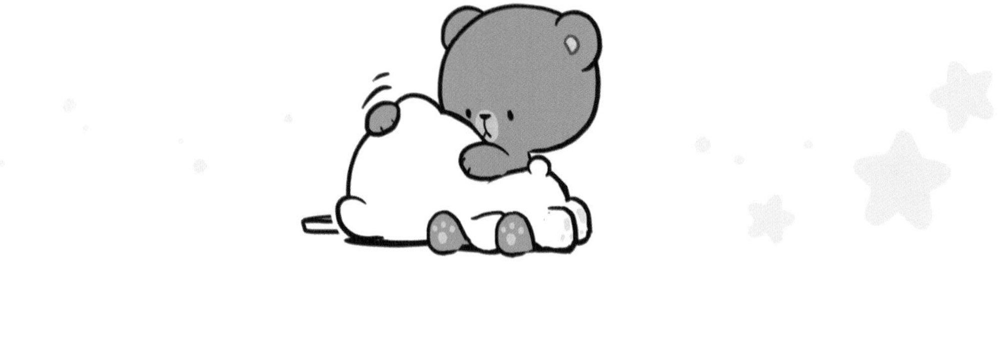

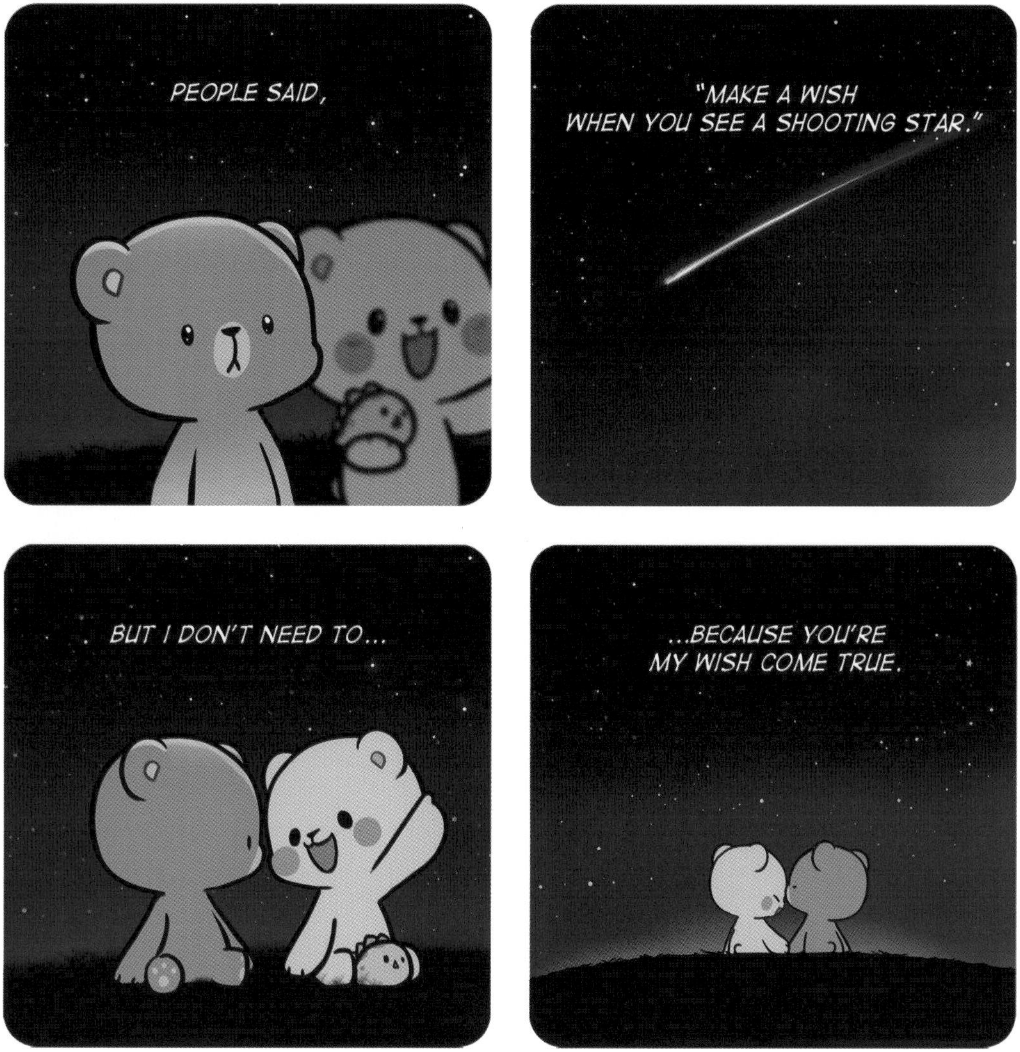
PEOPLE SAID,
"MAKE A WISH
WHEN YOU SEE A SHOOTING STAR."
BUT I DON'T NEED TO...
...BECAUSE YOU'RE
MY WISH COME TRUE.

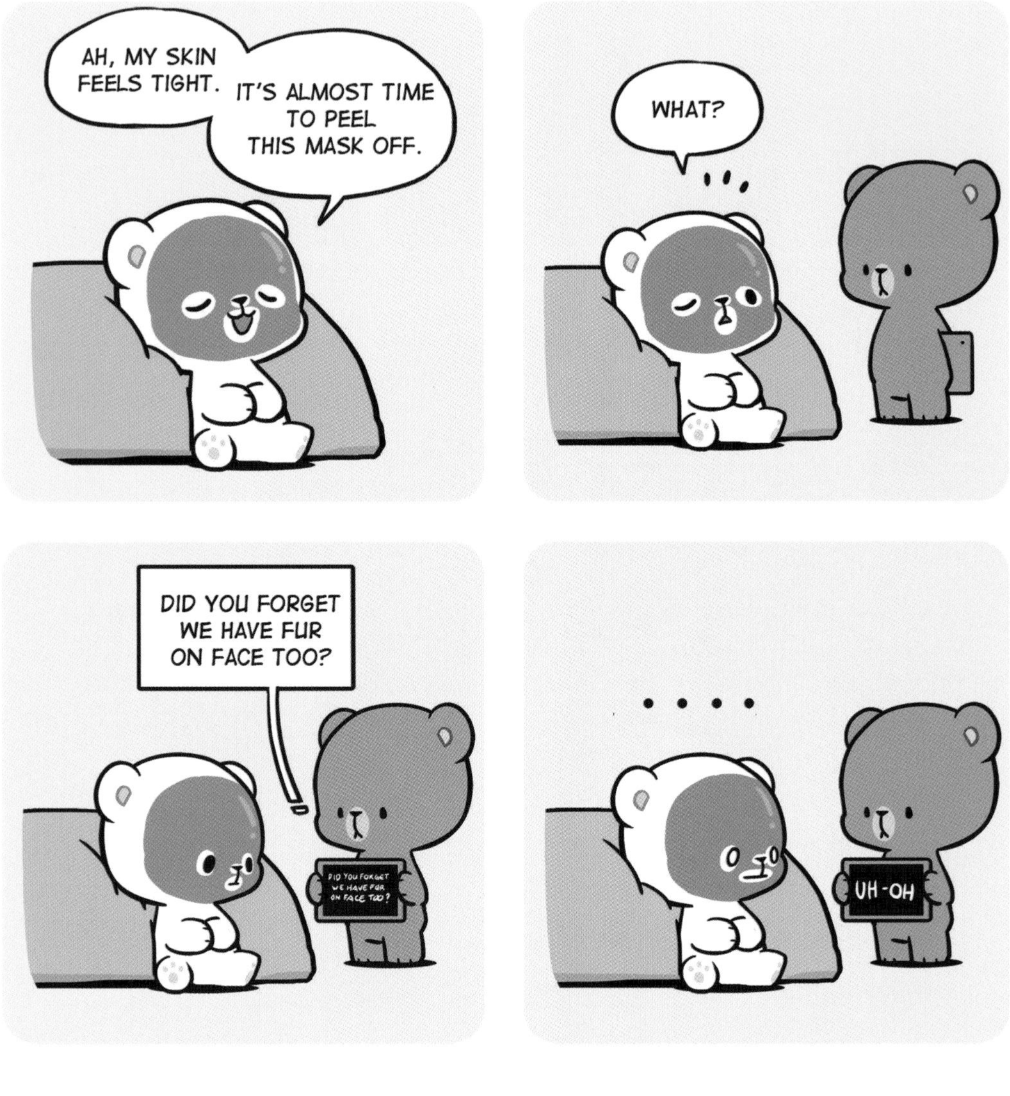
AH, MY SKIN FEELS TIGHT.
IT'S ALMOST TIME TO PEEL THIS MASK OFF.
WHAT?
DID YOU FORGET WE HAVE FUR ON FACE TOO?
DID YOU FORGET WE HAVE FUR ON FACE TOO?
....
UH-OH

EPILOGUE

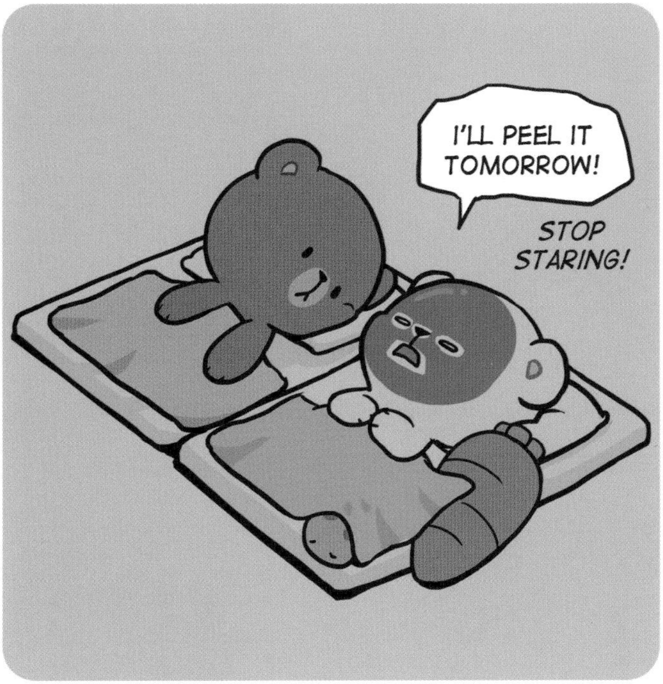

I'LL PEEL IT TOMORROW!
STOP STARING!

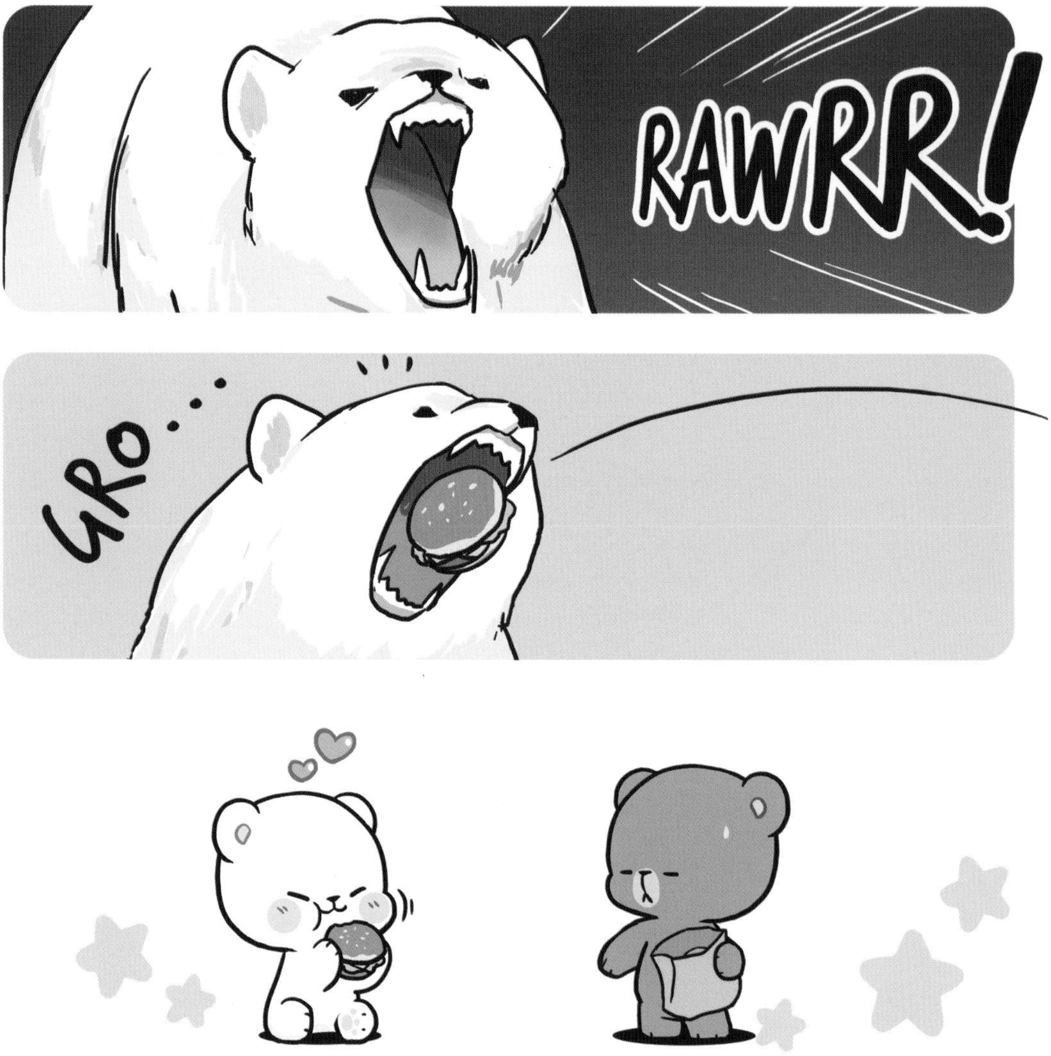
RAWRR!
GRO...

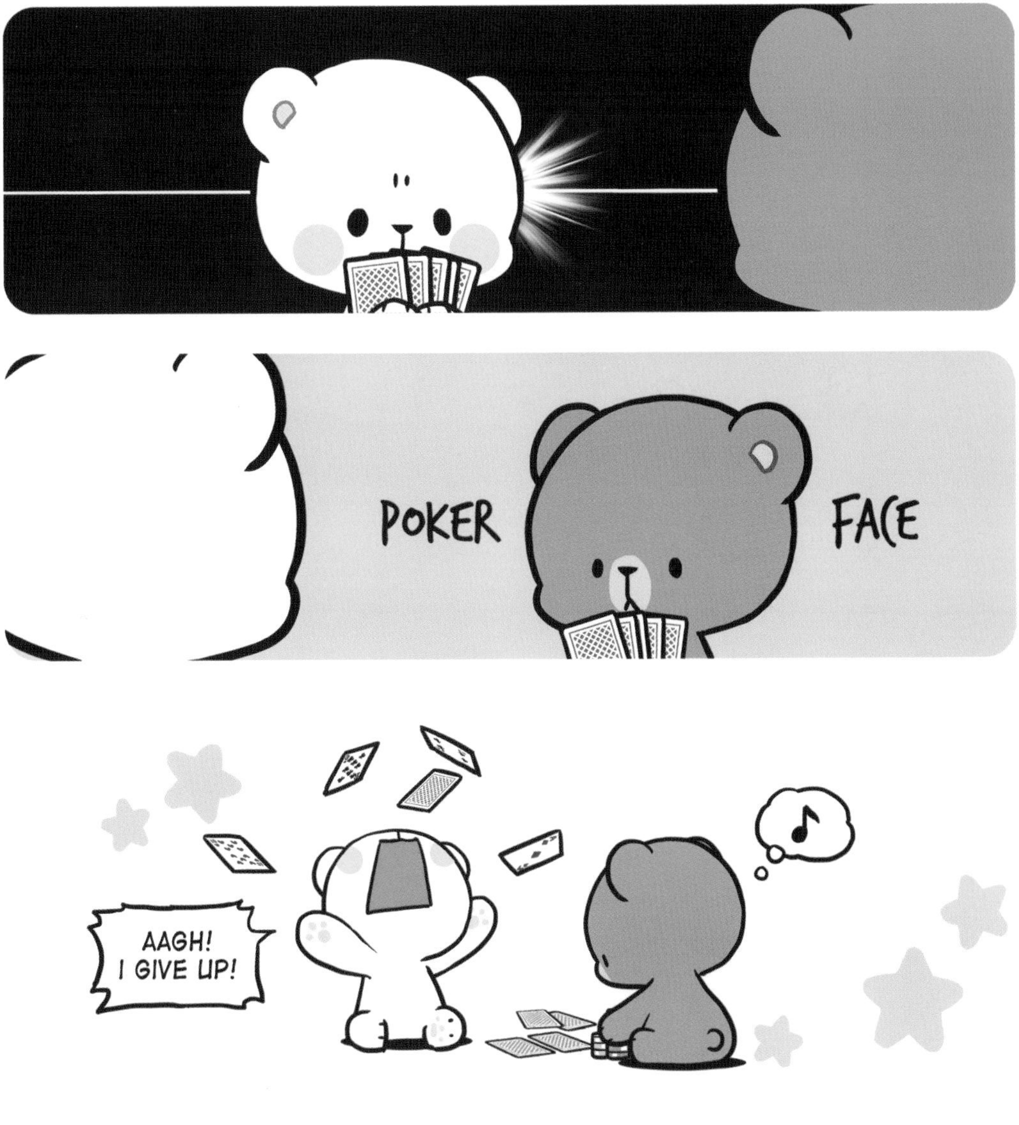
POKER
FACE
AAGH! I GIVE UP!

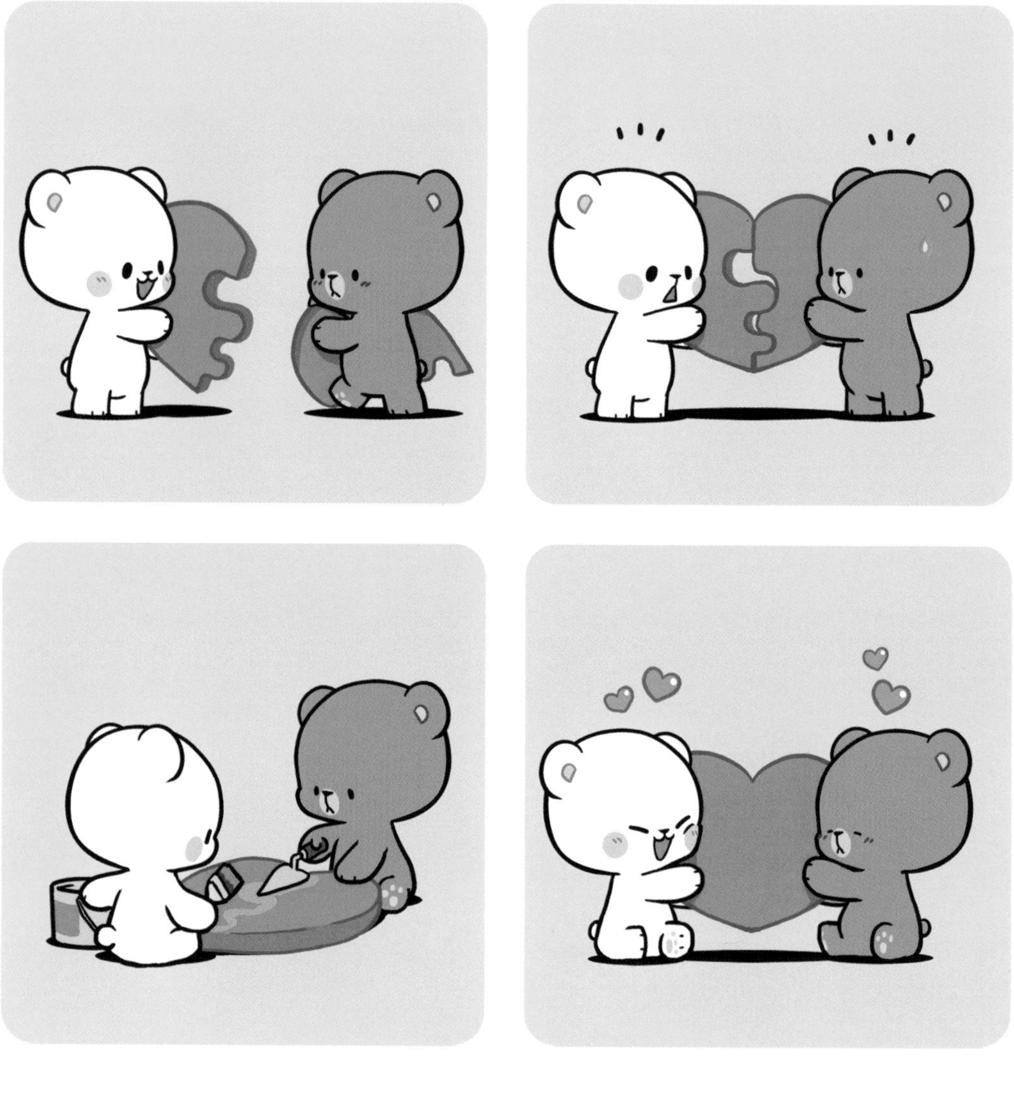

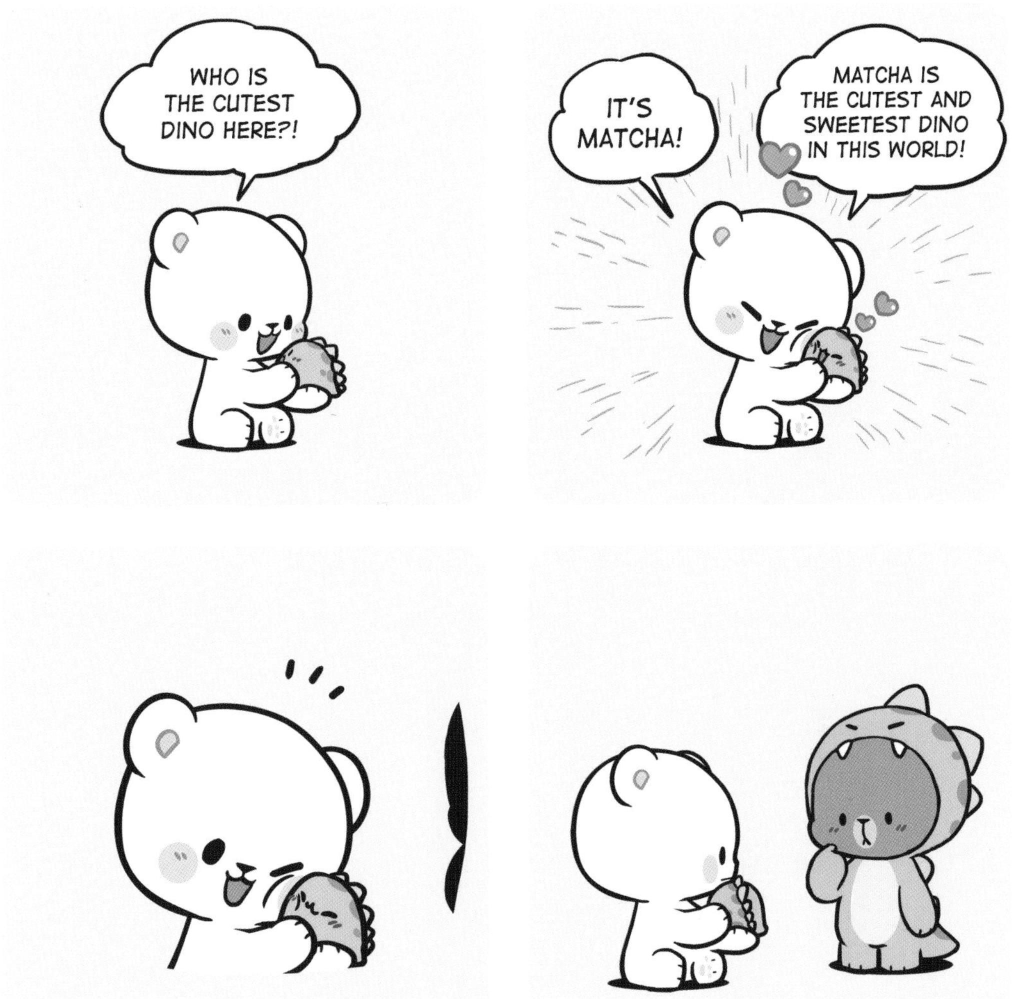
WHO IS THE CUTEST DINO HERE?!
IT'S MATCHA!
MATCHA IS THE CUTEST AND SWEETEST DINO IN THIS WORLD!

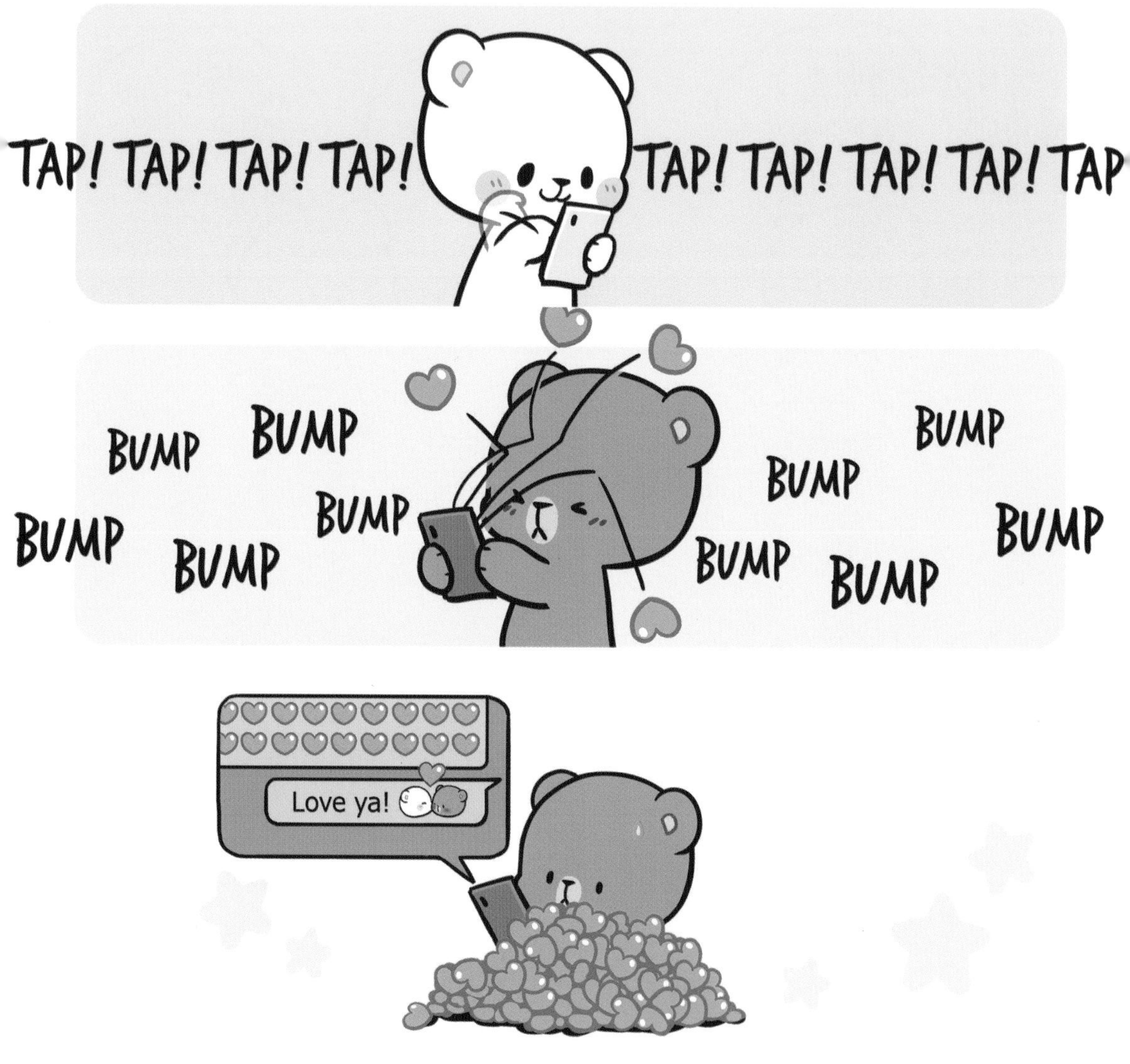

TAP! TAP! TAP! TAP!
TAP! TAP! TAP! TAP! TAP
BUMP
BUMP
BUMP
BUMP
BUMP
BUMP
BUMP
BUMP
BUMP
BUMP
Love ya!

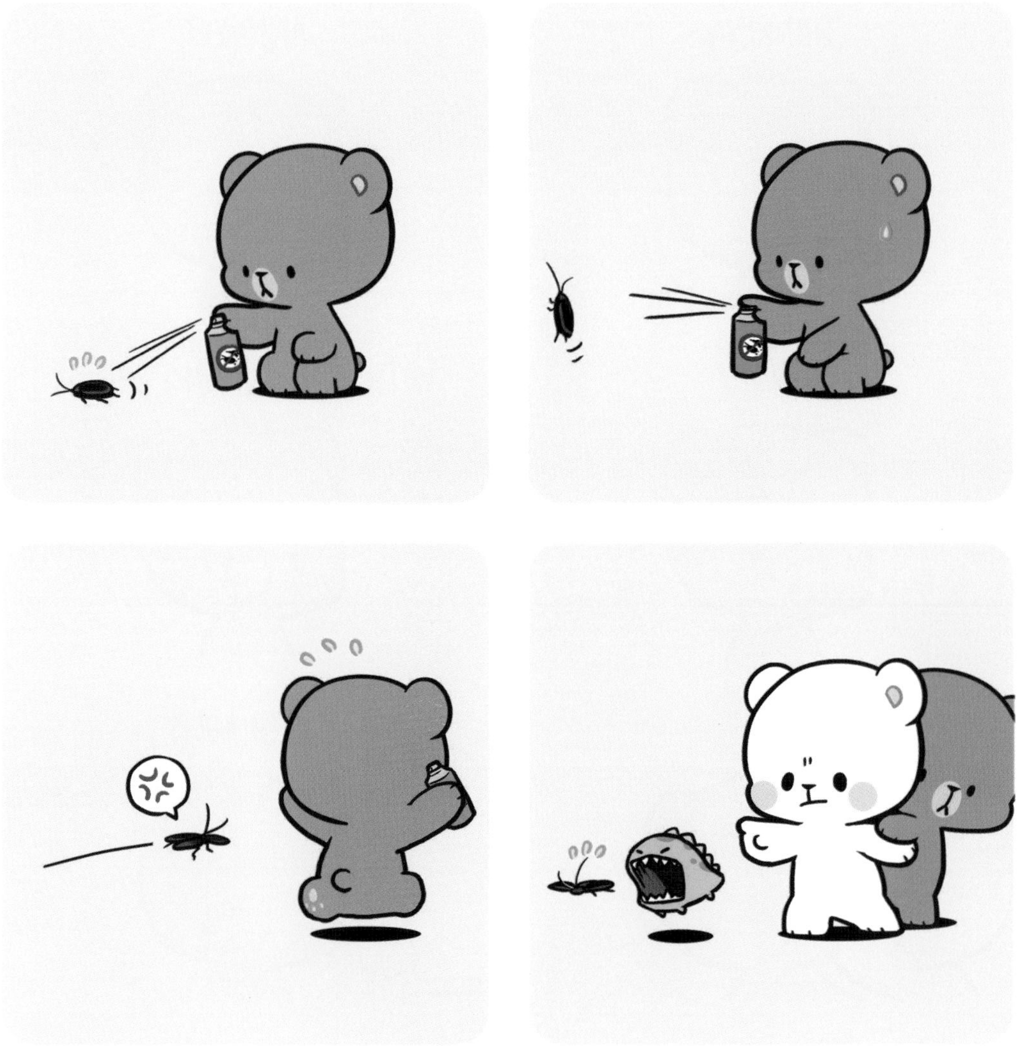

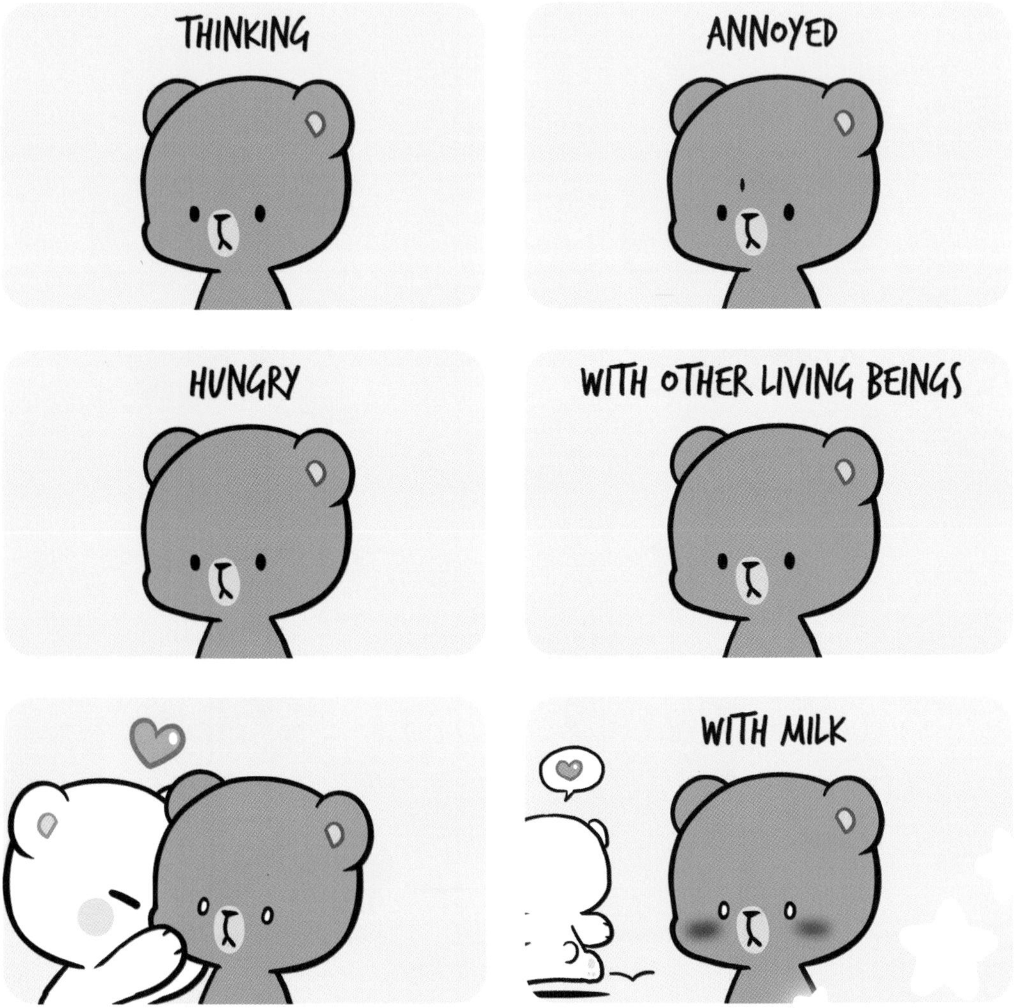

THINKING
ANNOYED
HUNGRY
WITH OTHER LIVING BEINGS
WITH MILK

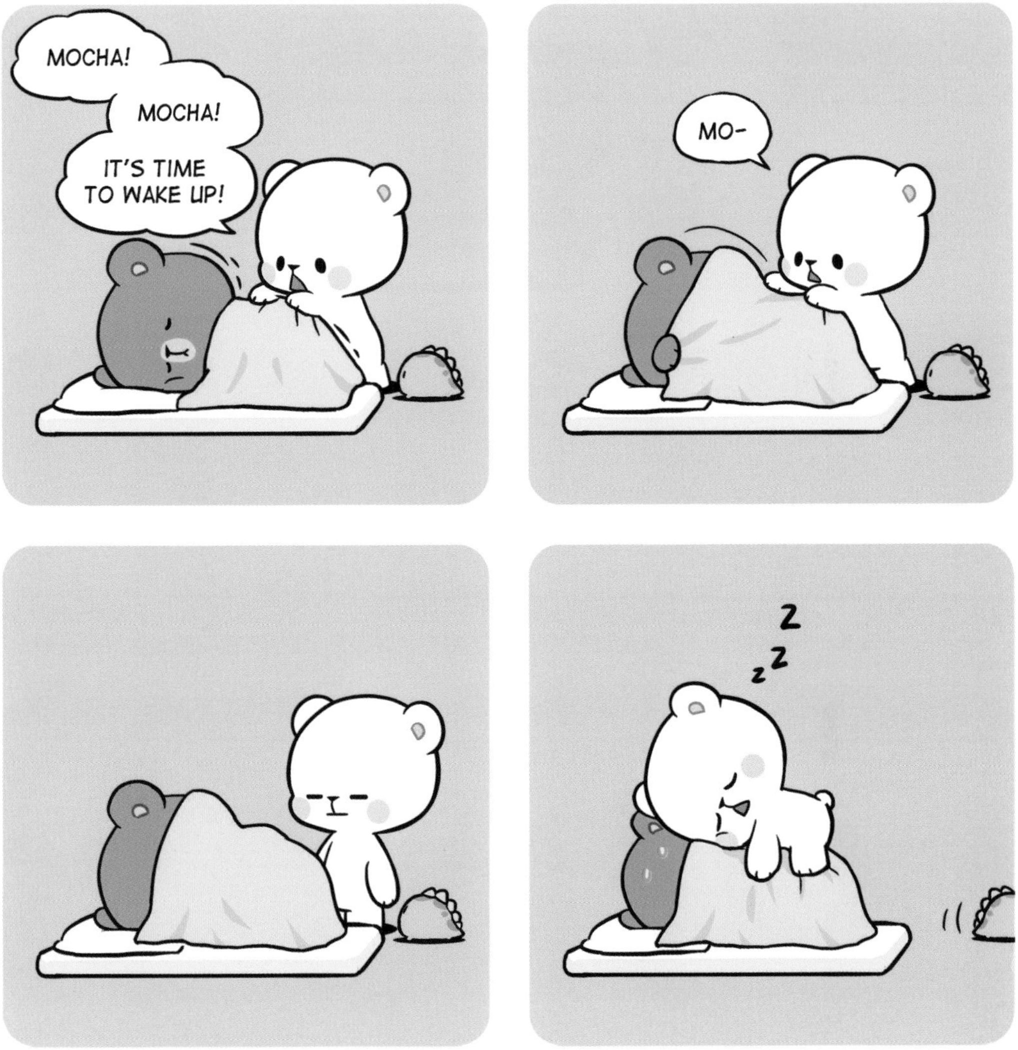
MOCHA!
MOCHA!
IT'S TIME TO WAKE UP!
MO-
Z
z Z

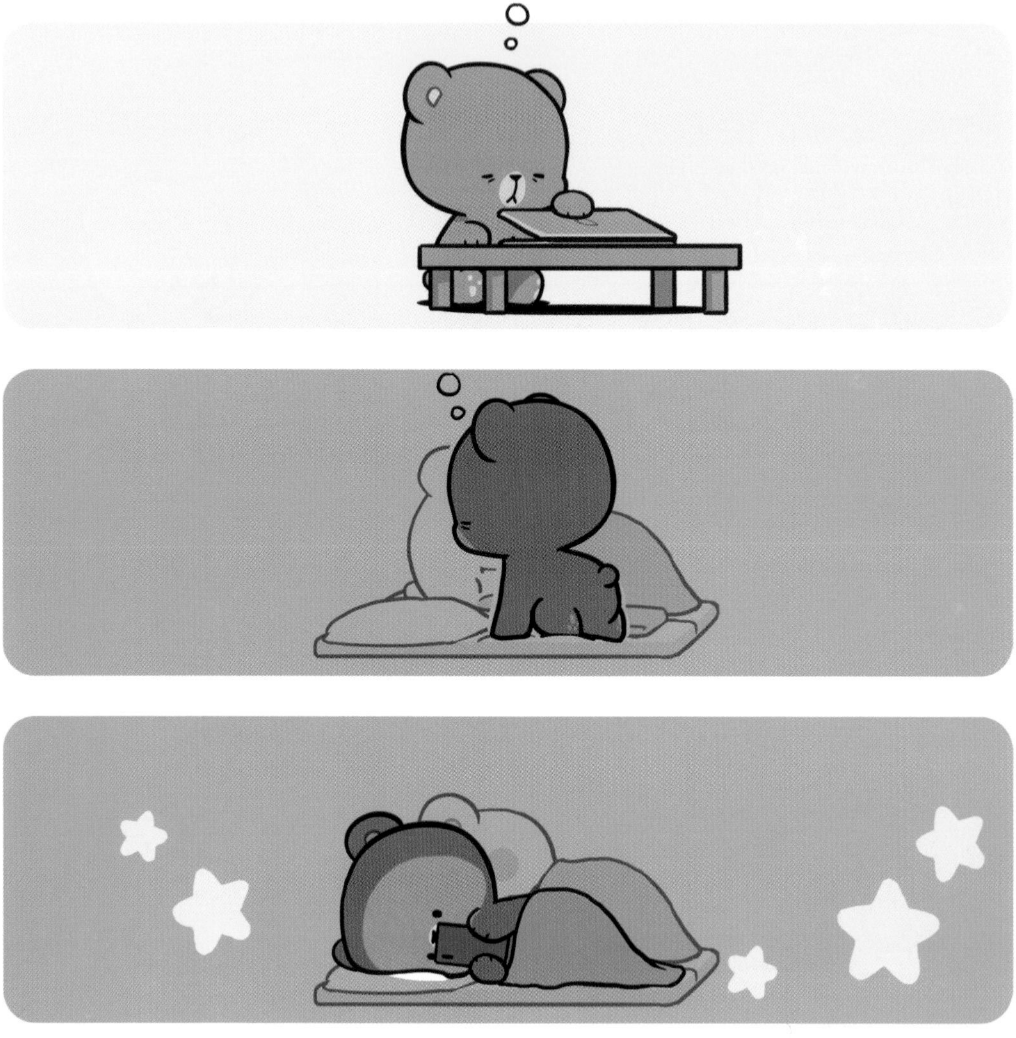

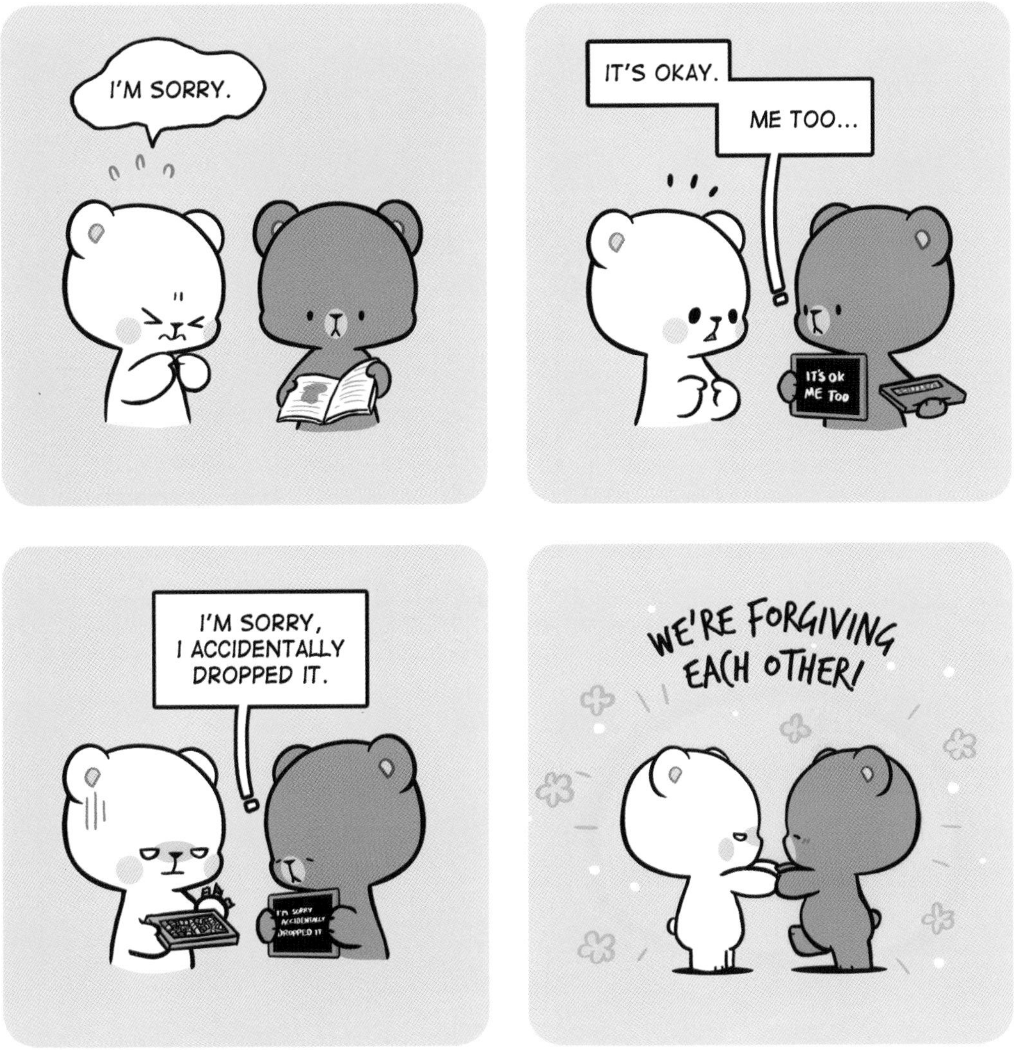
I'M SORRY.
IT'S OKAY.
ME TOO...
IT'S OK
ME TOO
I'M SORRY,
I ACCIDENTALLY
DROPPED IT.
I'M SORRY
ACCIDENTALLY
DROPPED IT
WE'RE FORGIVING
EACH OTHER!

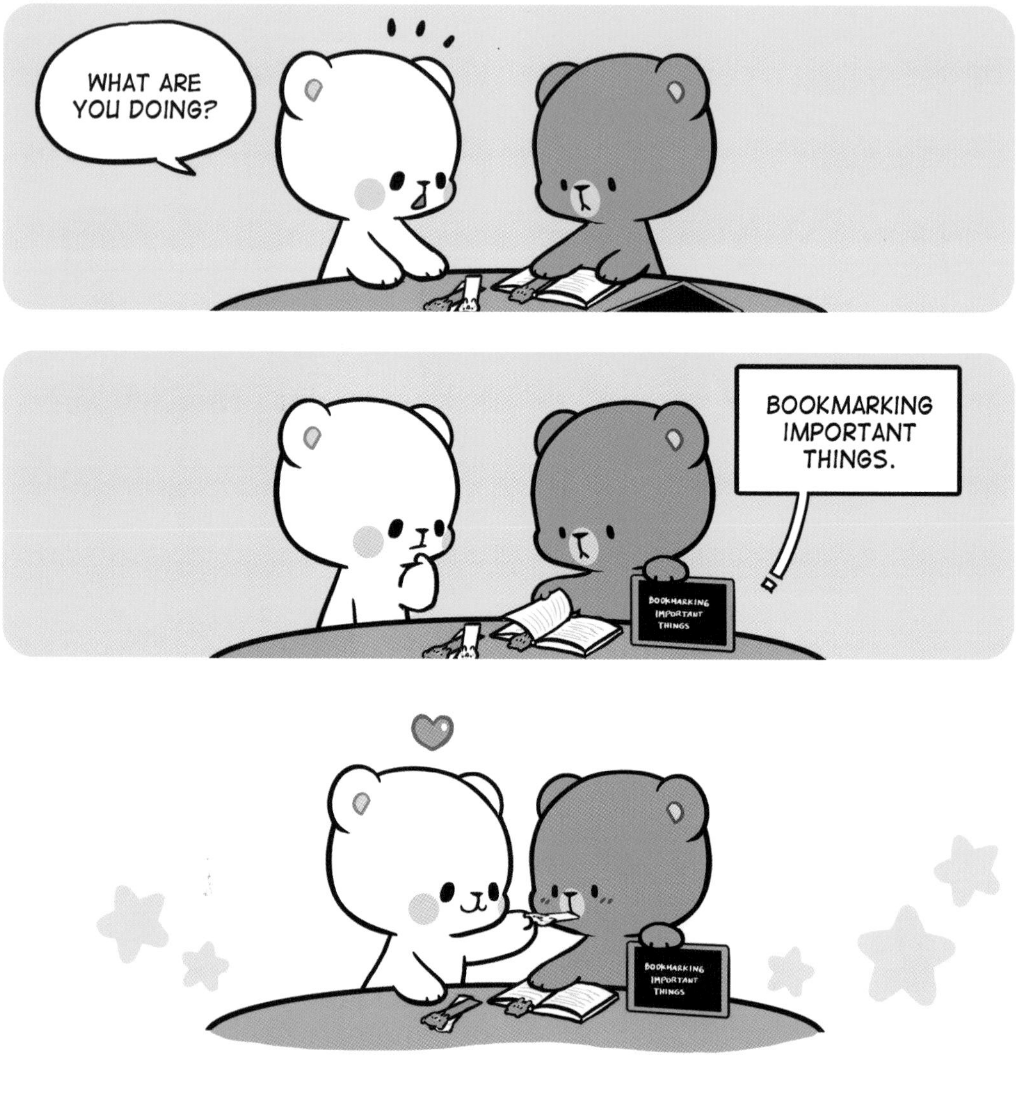
WHAT ARE YOU DOING?
BOOKMARKING IMPORTANT THINGS.
BOOKMARKING IMPORTANT THINGS
BOOKMARKING IMPORTANT THINGS

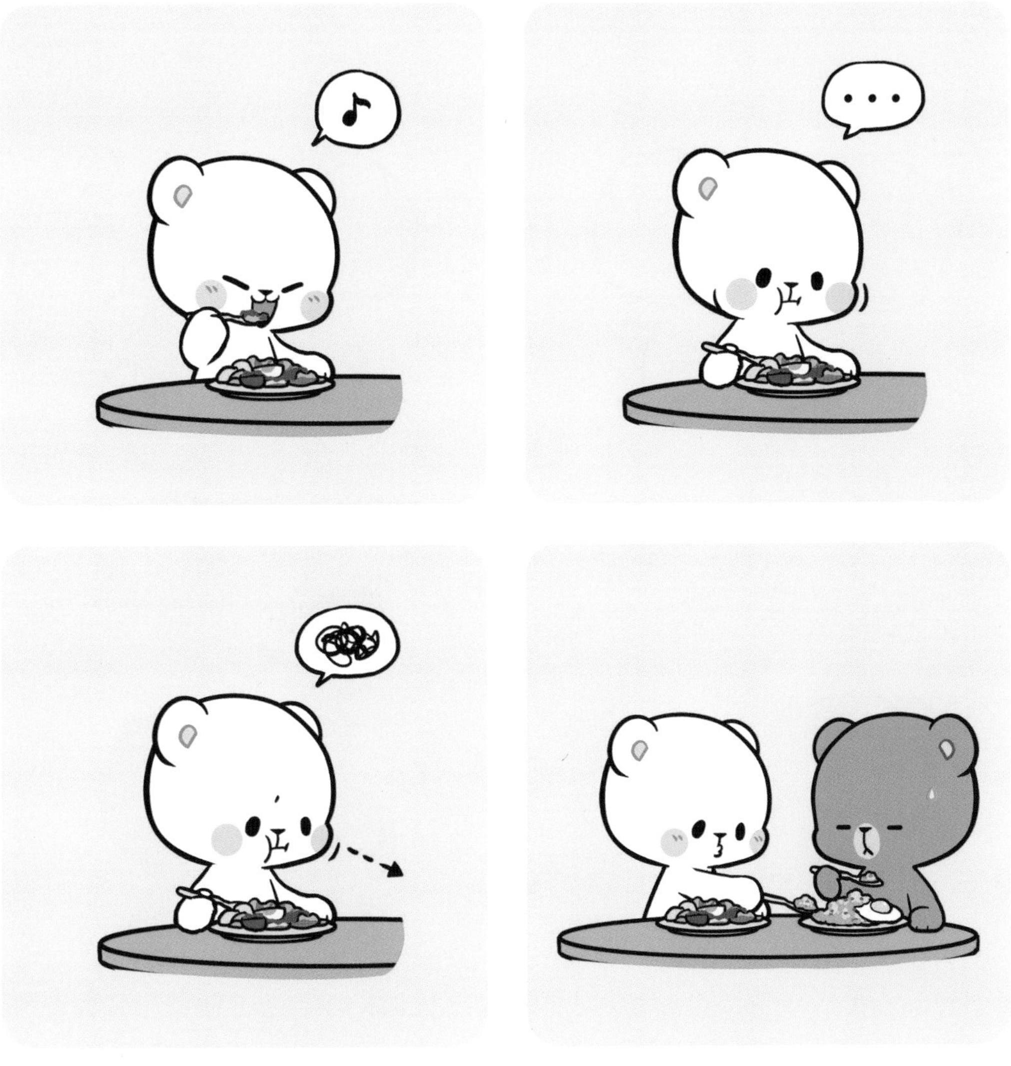
...

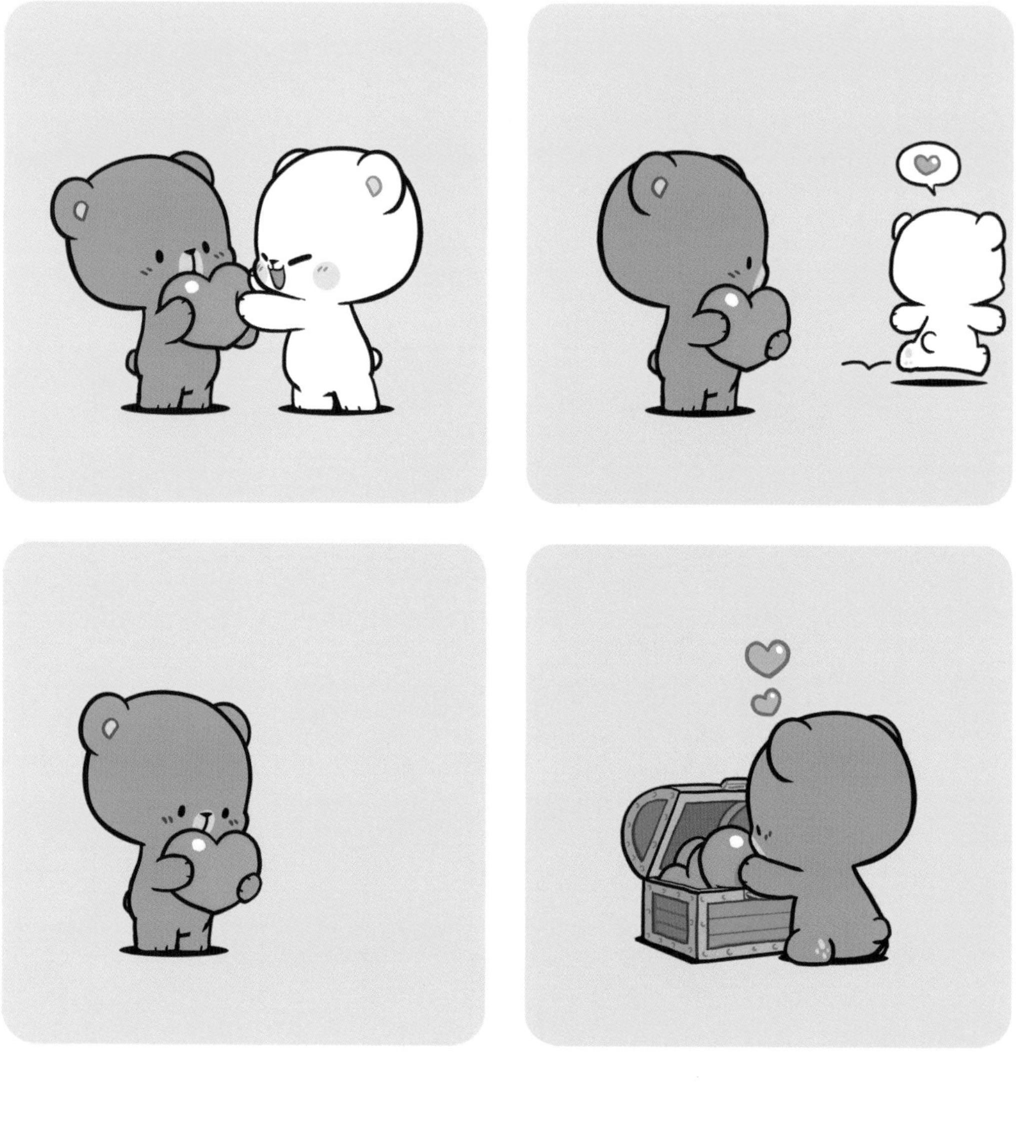

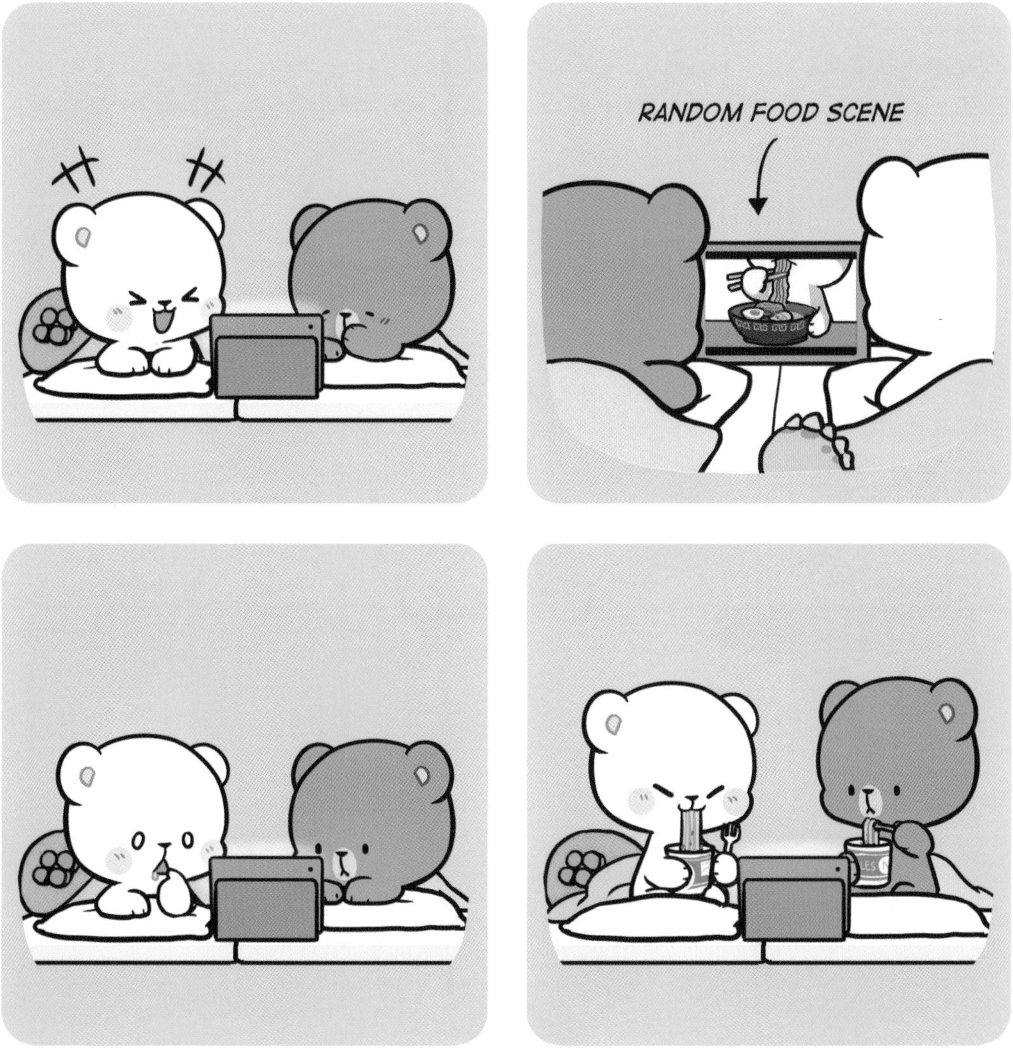
RANDOM FOOD SCENE

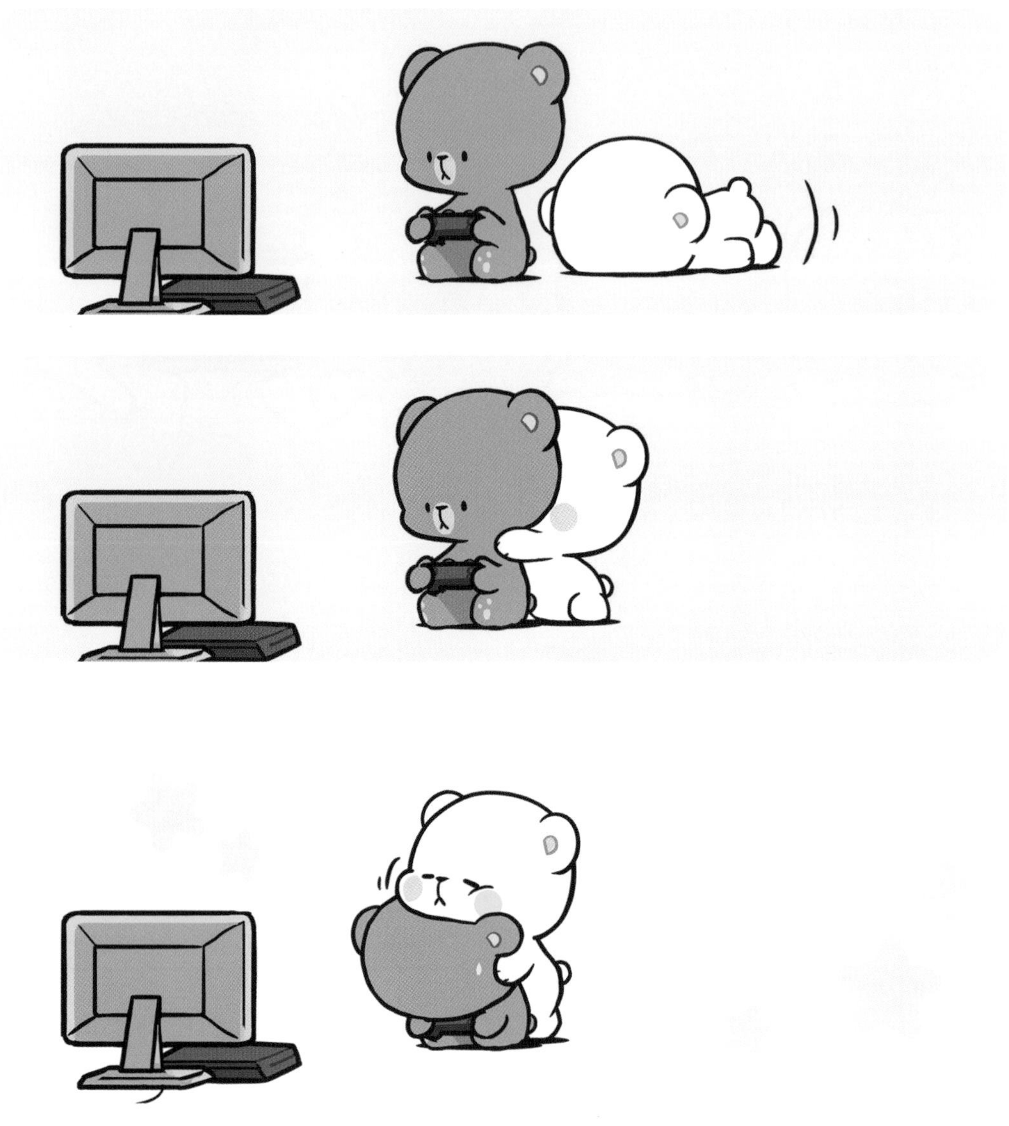

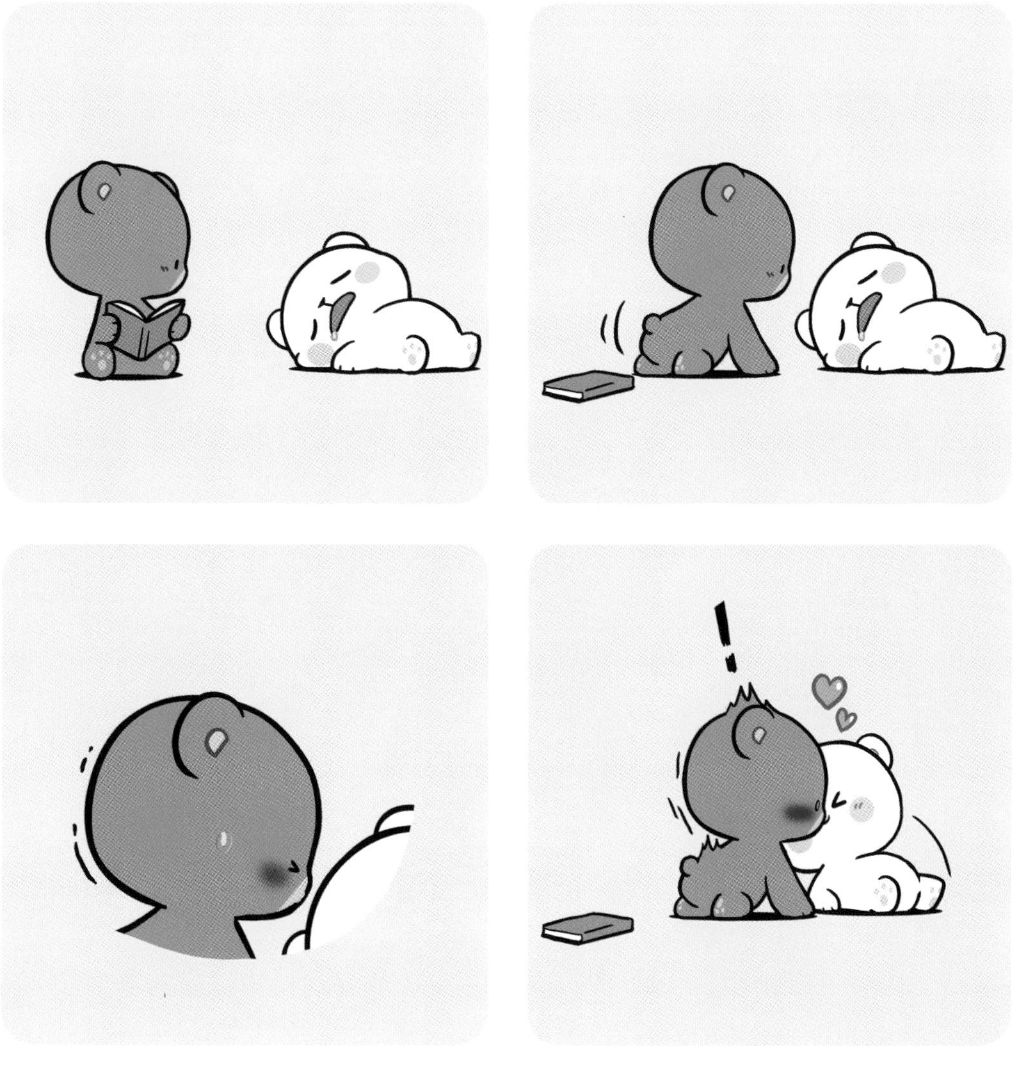

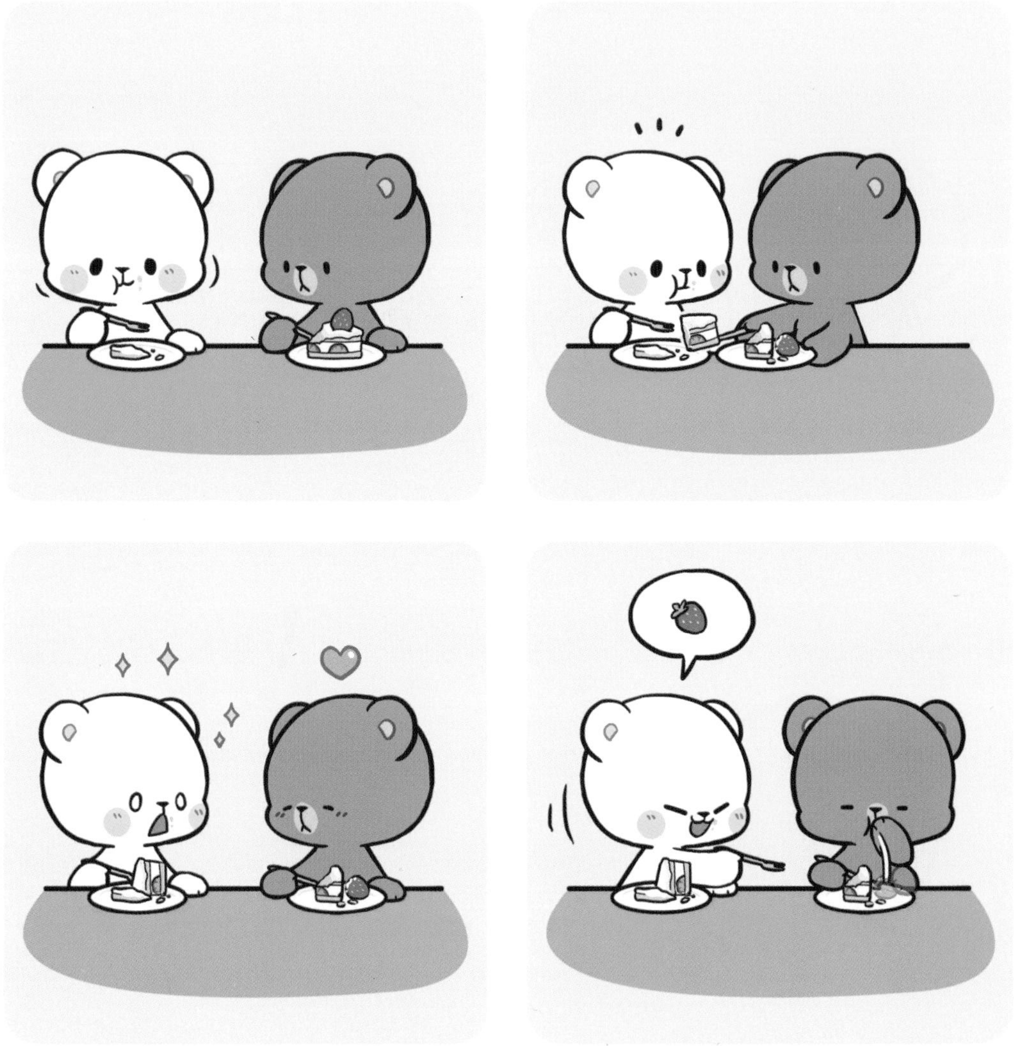

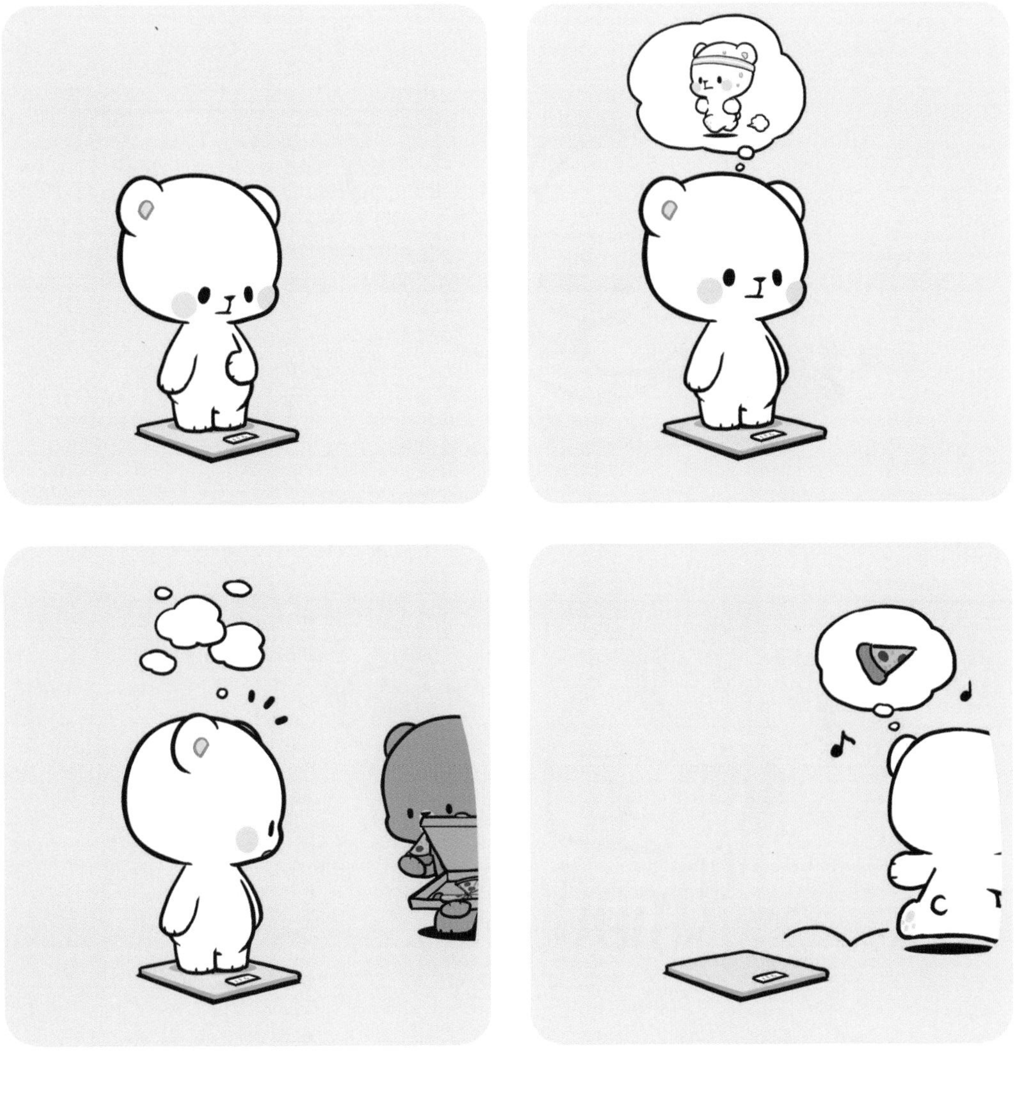

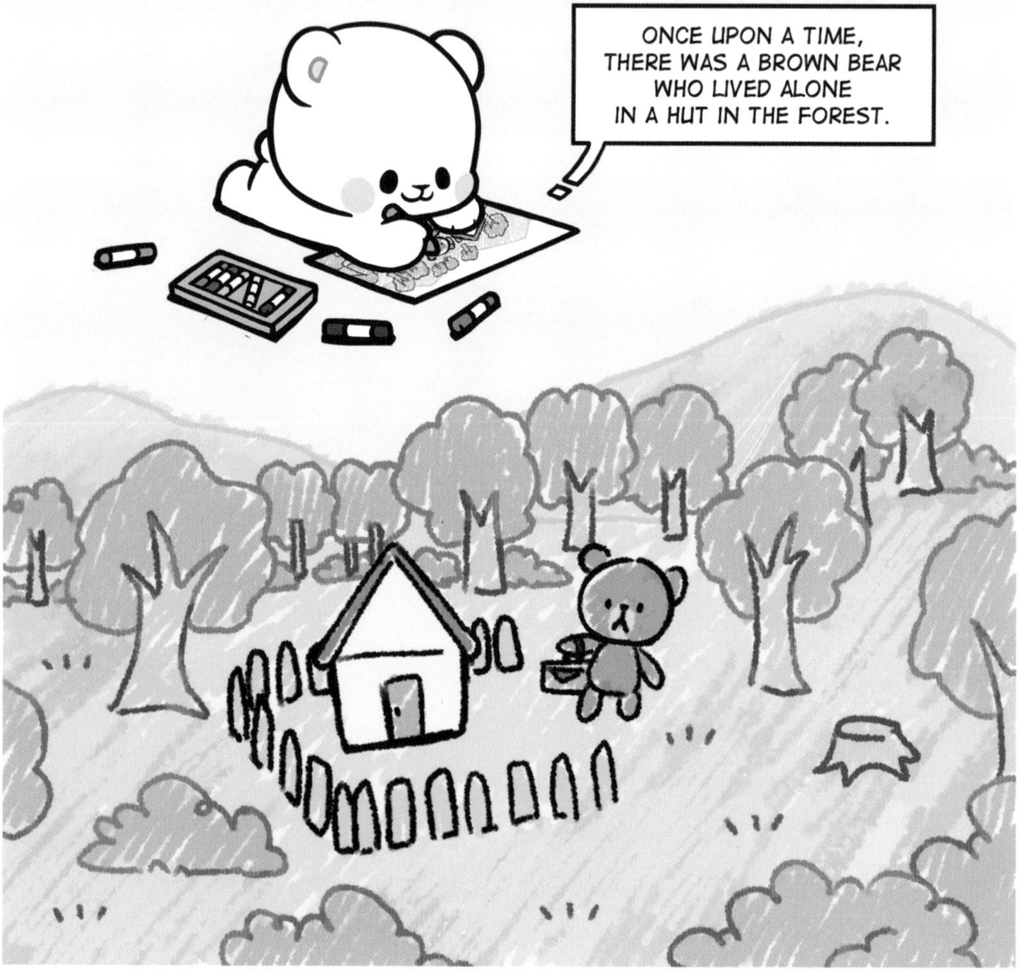
ONCE UPON A TIME,
THERE WAS A BROWN BEAR
WHO LIVED ALONE
IN A HUT IN THE FOREST.

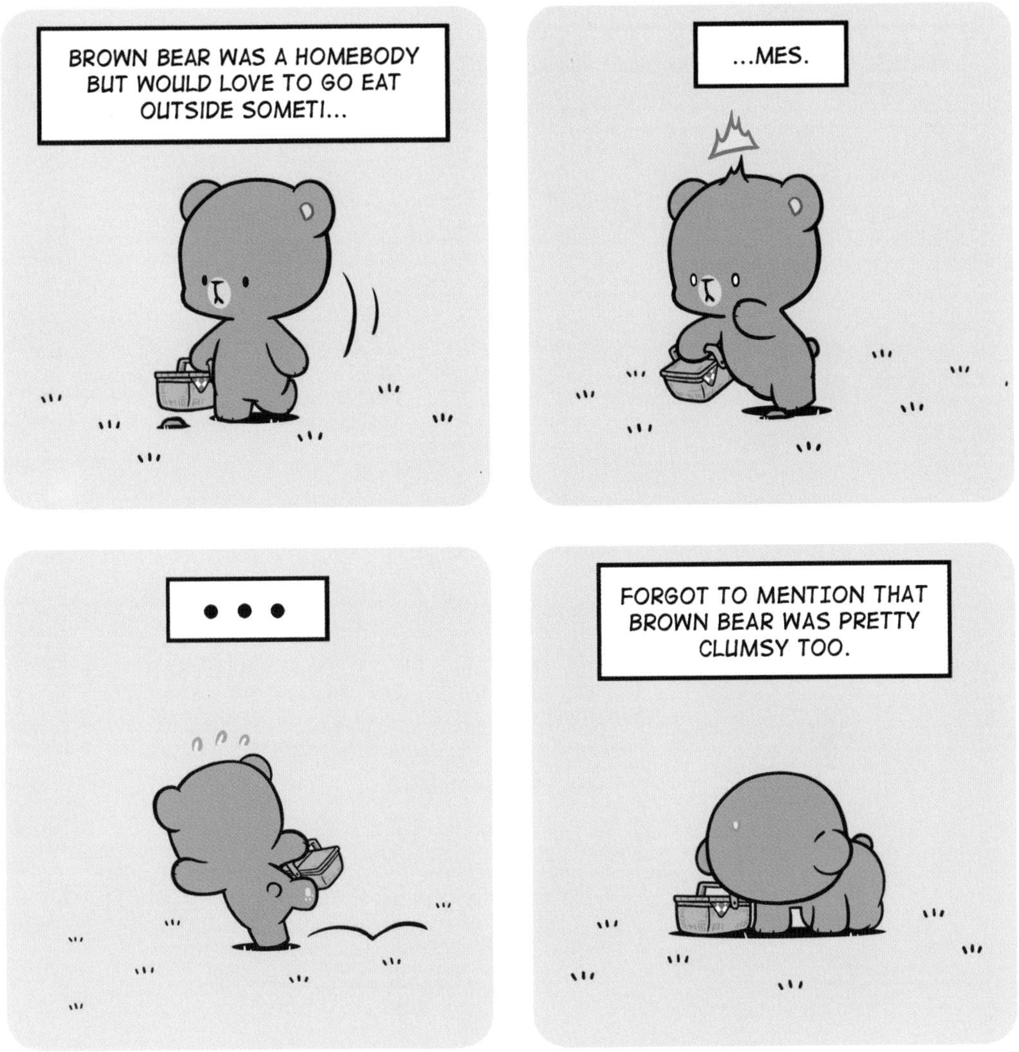
BROWN BEAR WAS A HOMEBODY BUT WOULD LOVE TO GO EAT OUTSIDE SOMETI...
...MES.
• • •
FORGOT TO MENTION THAT BROWN BEAR WAS PRETTY CLUMSY TOO.

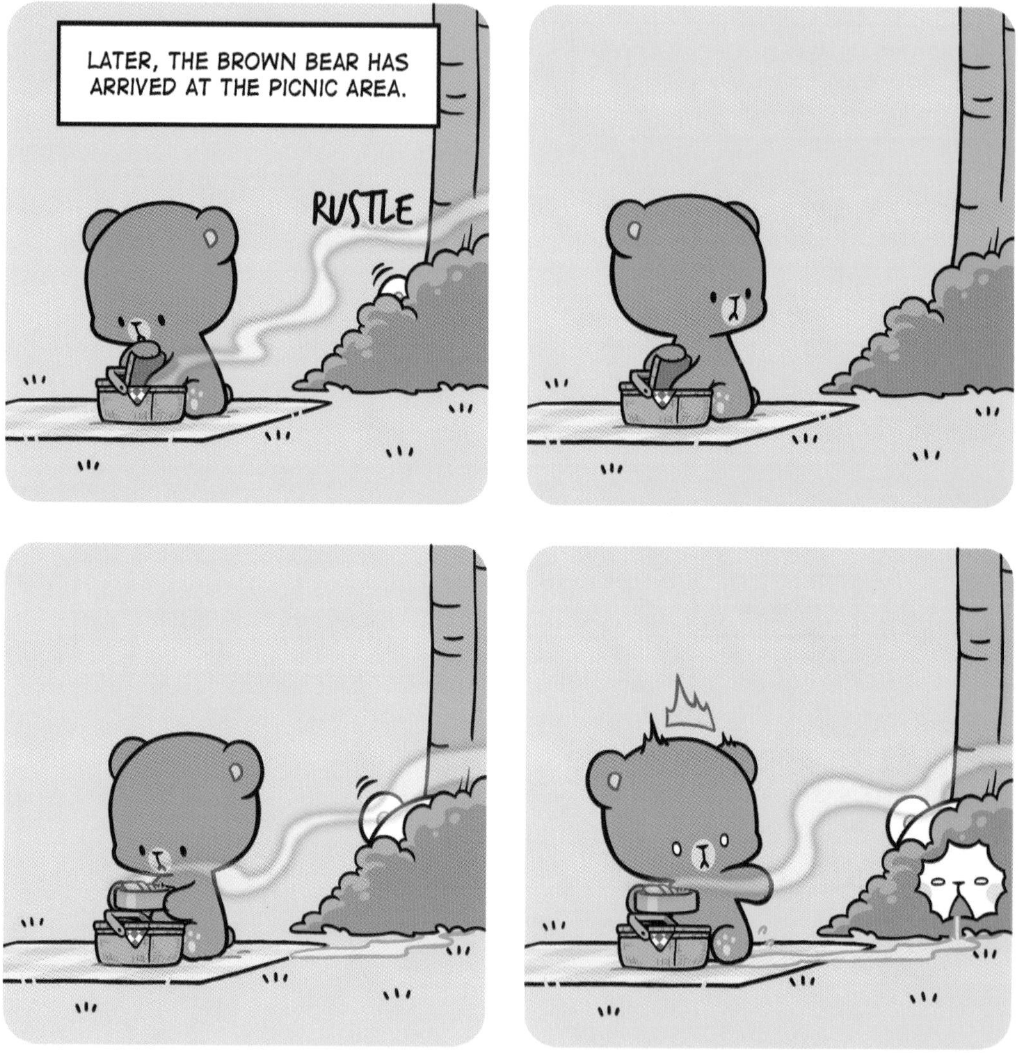
LATER, THE BROWN BEAR HAS ARRIVED AT THE PICNIC AREA.
RUSTLE

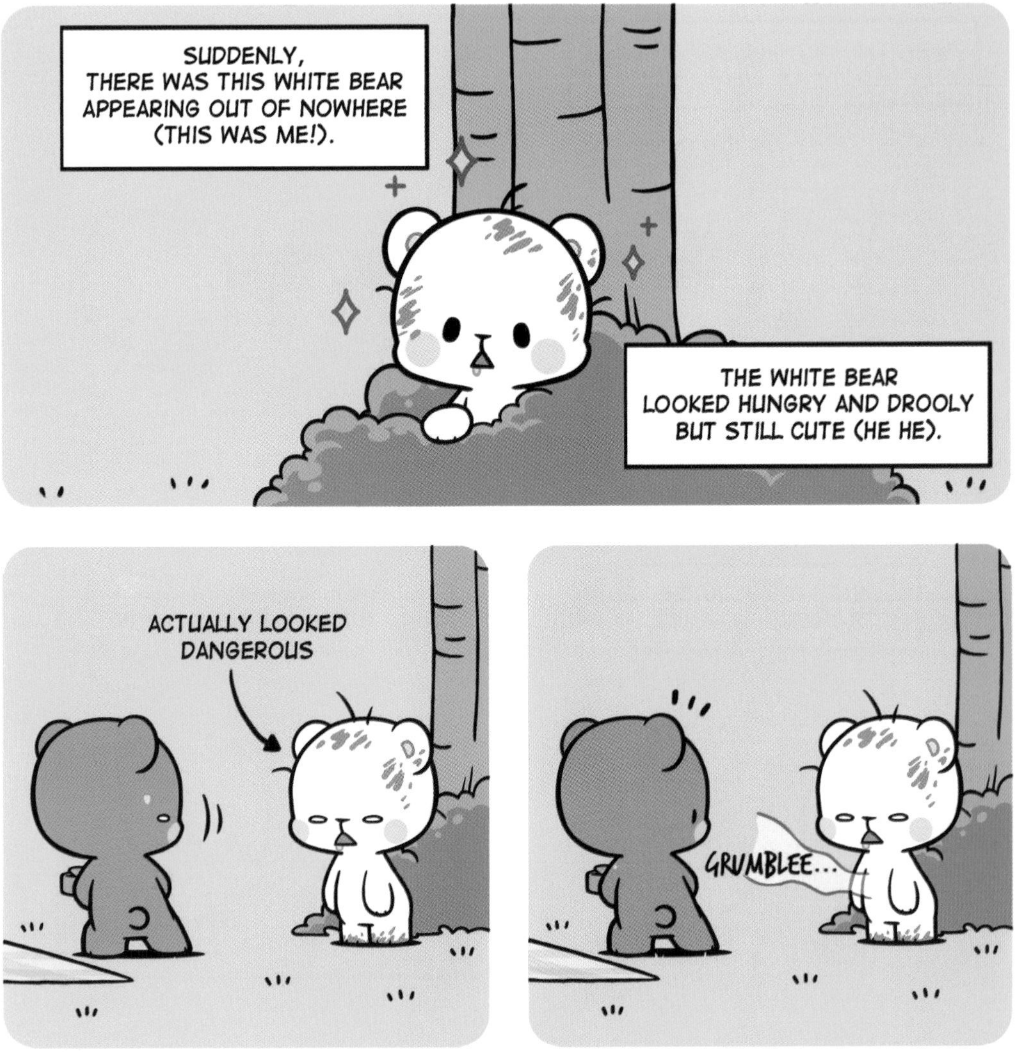
SUDDENLY, THERE WAS THIS WHITE BEAR APPEARING OUT OF NOWHERE (THIS WAS ME!).
THE WHITE BEAR LOOKED HUNGRY AND DROOLY BUT STILL CUTE (HE HE).
ACTUALLY LOOKED DANGEROUS
GRUMBLEE...

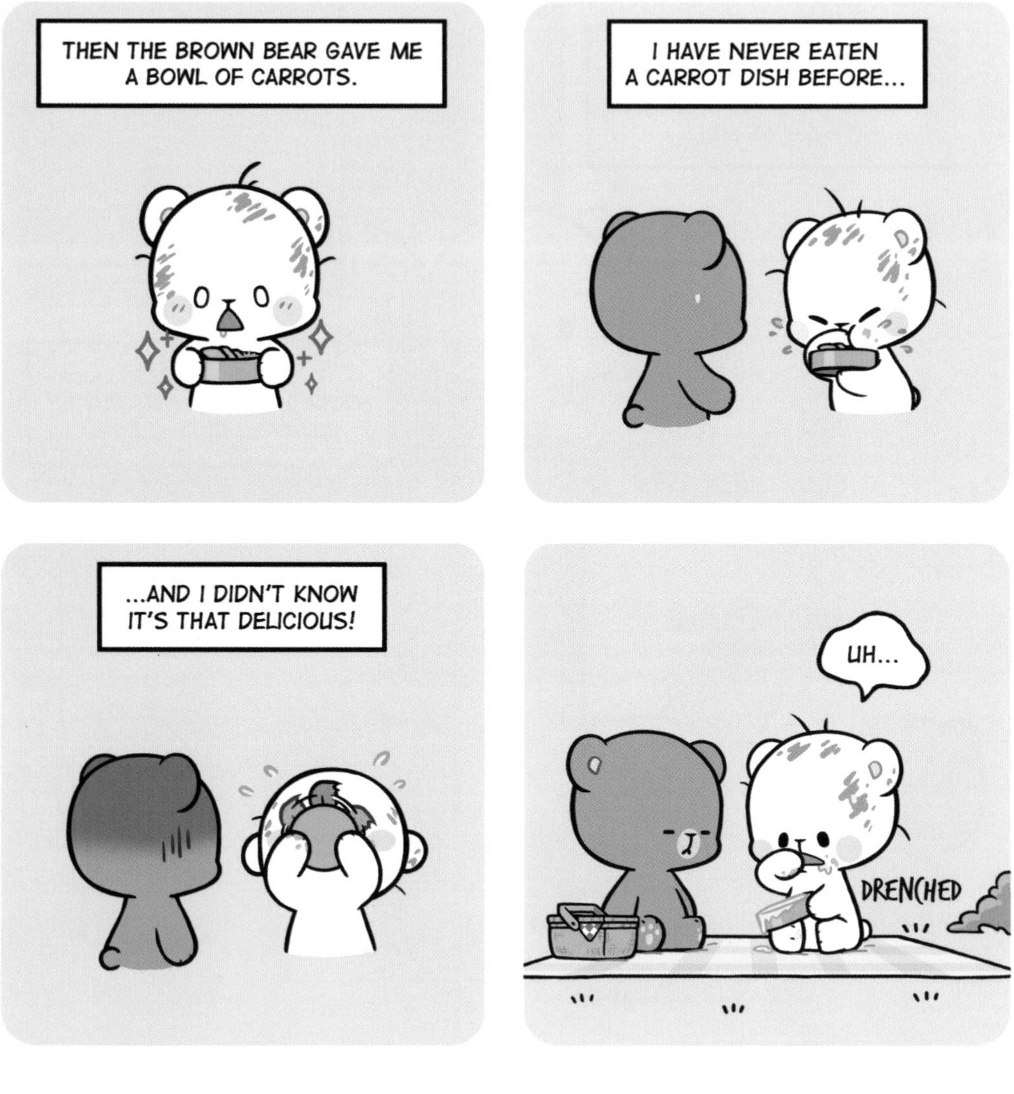
THEN THE BROWN BEAR GAVE ME A BOWL OF CARROTS.
I HAVE NEVER EATEN A CARROT DISH BEFORE...
...AND I DIDN'T KNOW IT'S THAT DELICIOUS!
UH...
DRENCHED

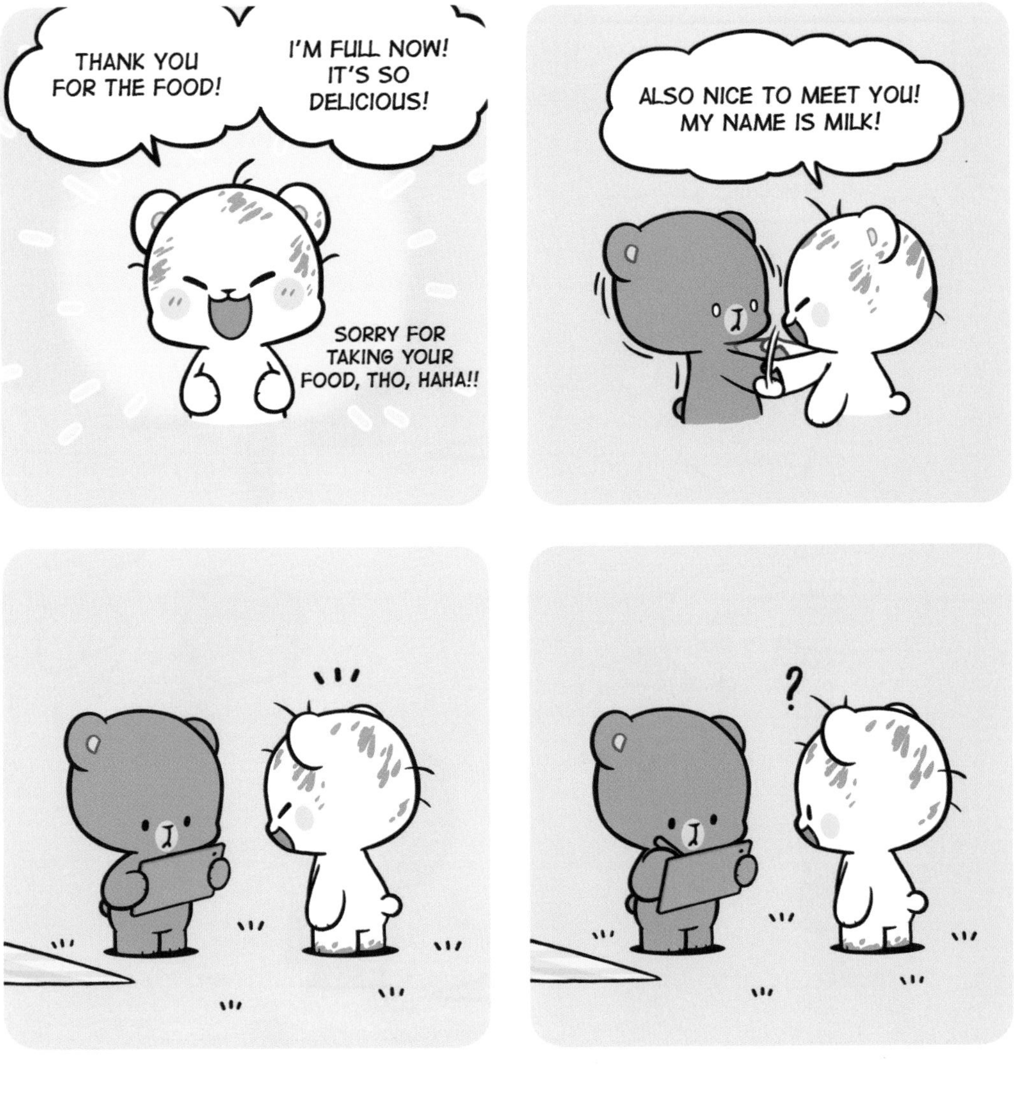
THANK YOU FOR THE FOOD!
I'M FULL NOW! IT'S SO DELICIOUS!
SORRY FOR TAKING YOUR FOOD, THO, HAHA!!
ALSO NICE TO MEET YOU! MY NAME IS MILK!
?

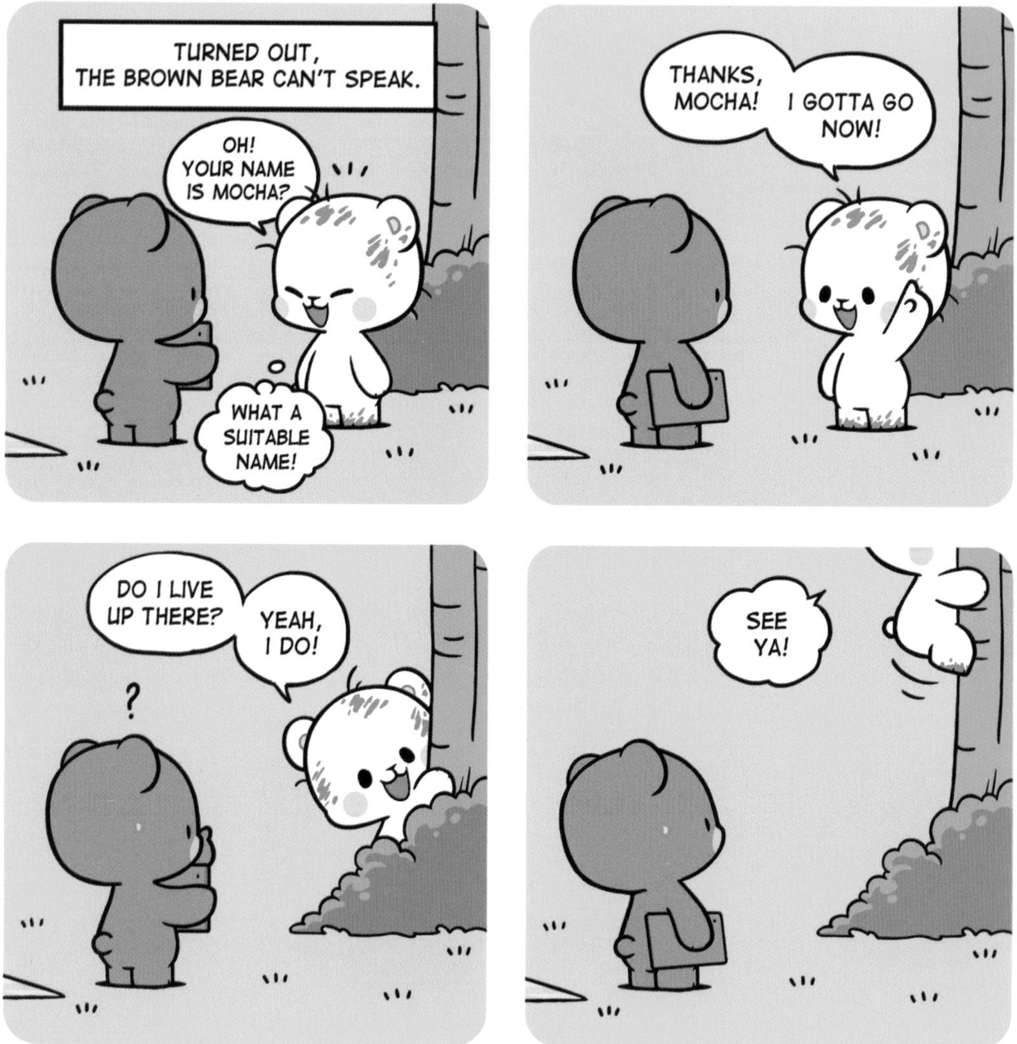
TURNED OUT, THE BROWN BEAR CAN'T SPEAK.
OH! YOUR NAME IS MOCHA?
WHAT A SUITABLE NAME!
THANKS, MOCHA!
I GOTTA GO NOW!
DO I LIVE UP THERE?
YEAH, I DO!
?
SEE YA!

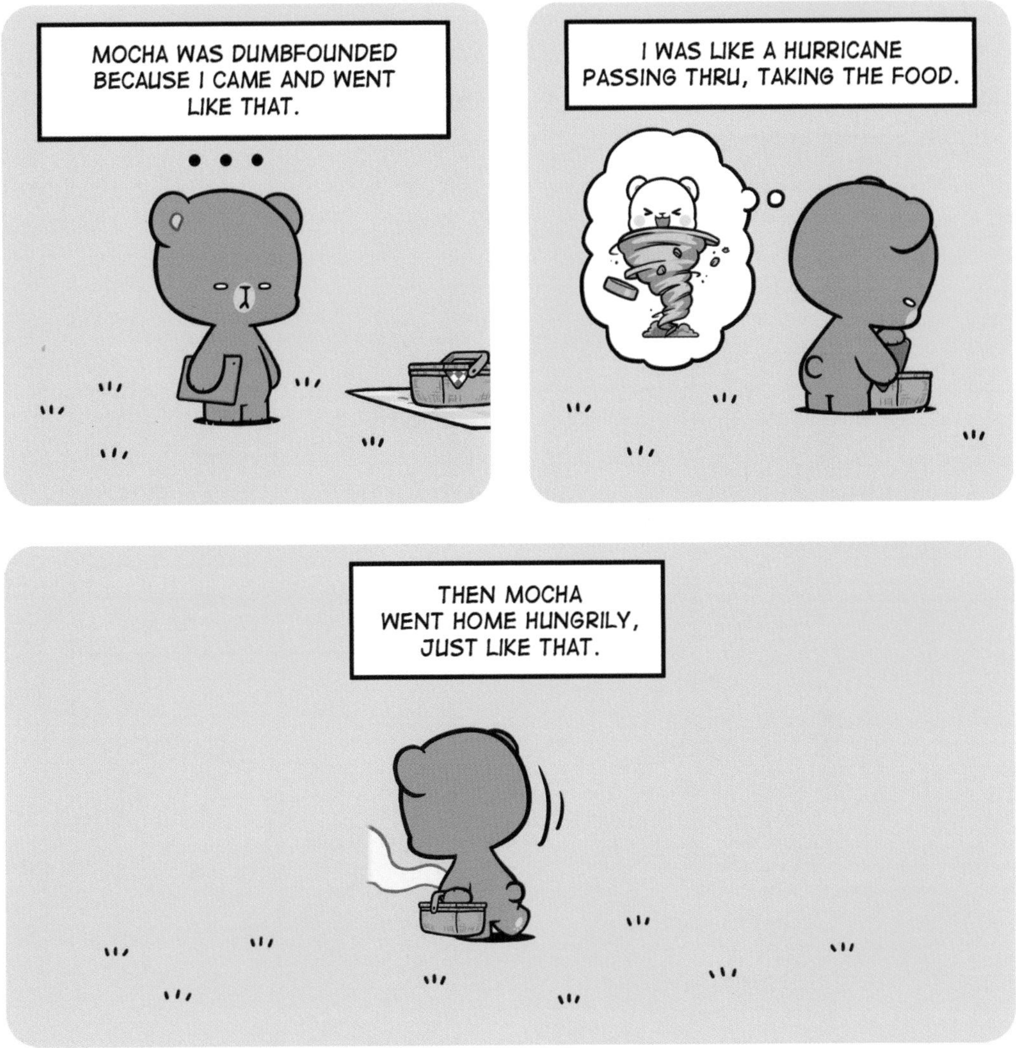
MOCHA WAS DUMBFOUNDED BECAUSE I CAME AND WENT LIKE THAT.
• • •
I WAS LIKE A HURRICANE PASSING THRU, TAKING THE FOOD.
THEN MOCHA WENT HOME HUNGRILY, JUST LIKE THAT.

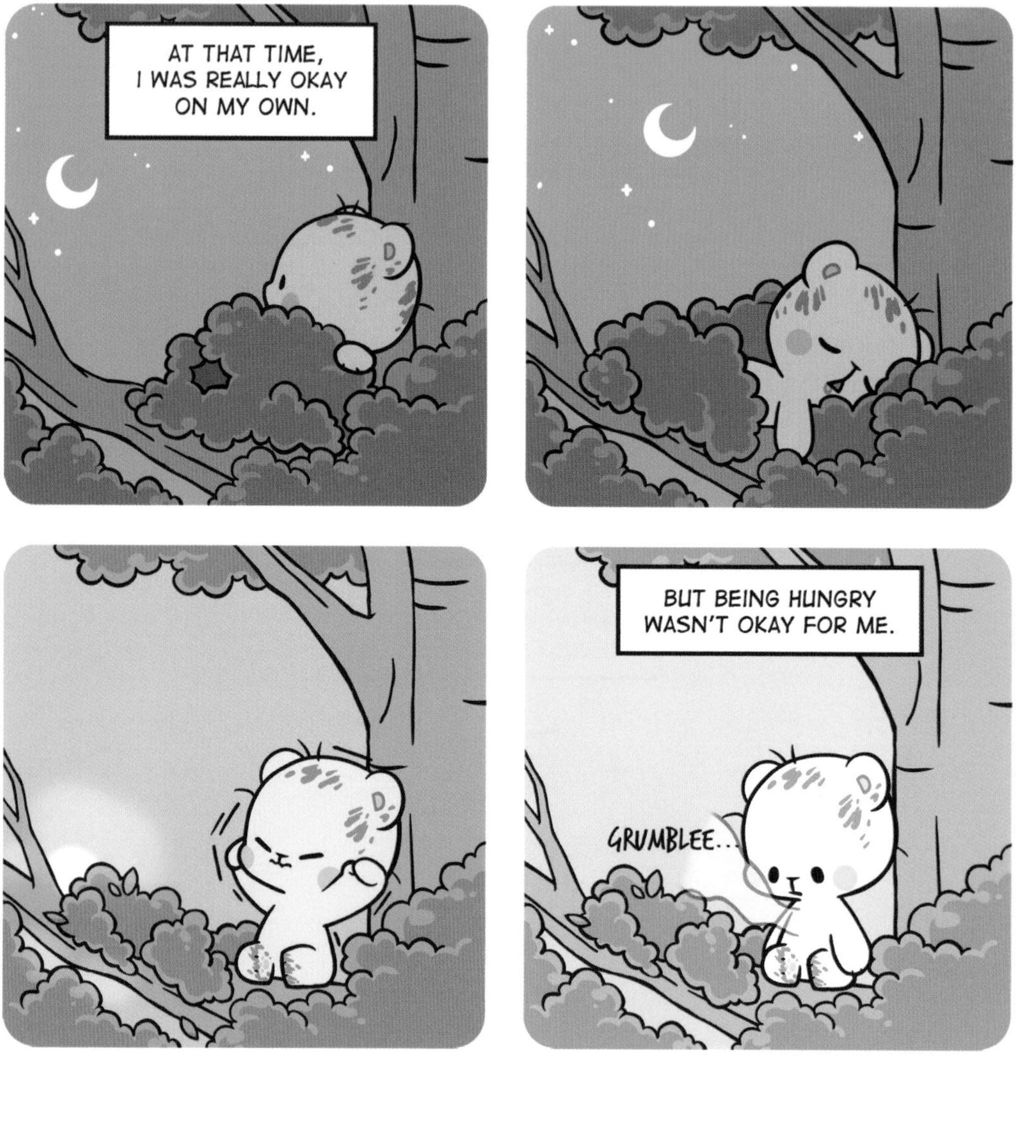
AT THAT TIME,
I WAS REALLY OKAY
ON MY OWN.
BUT BEING HUNGRY
WASN'T OKAY FOR ME.
GRUMBLEE...

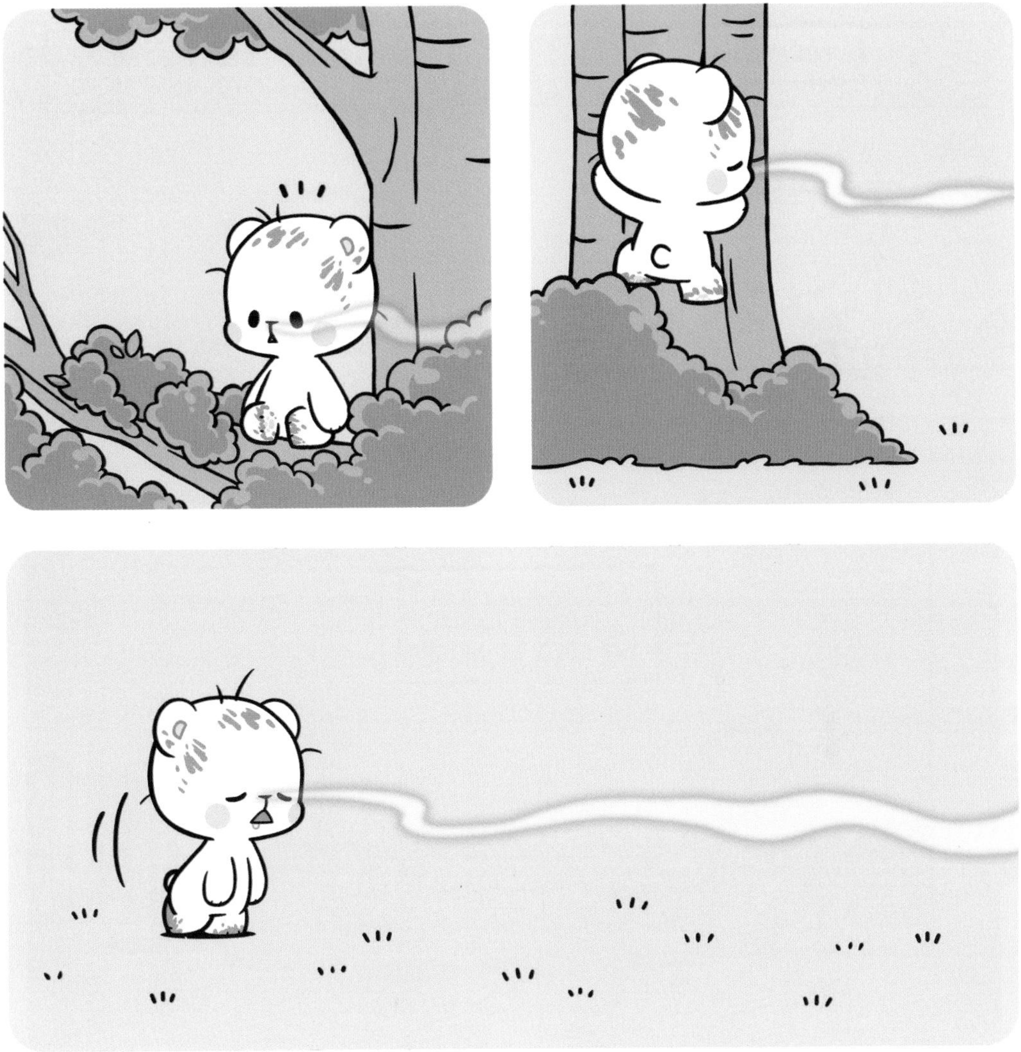

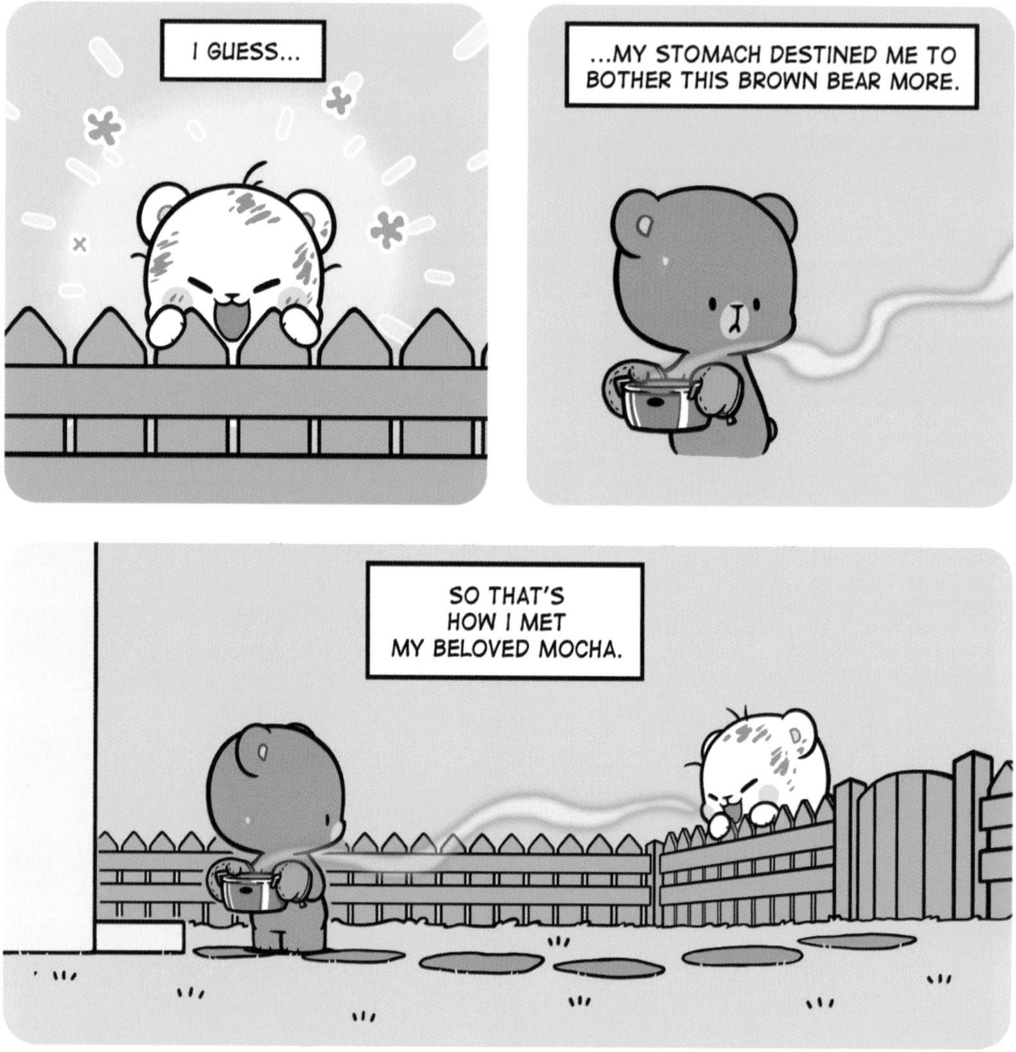
I GUESS...
...MY STOMACH DESTINED ME TO BOTHER THIS BROWN BEAR MORE.
SO THAT'S HOW I MET MY BELOVED MOCHA.

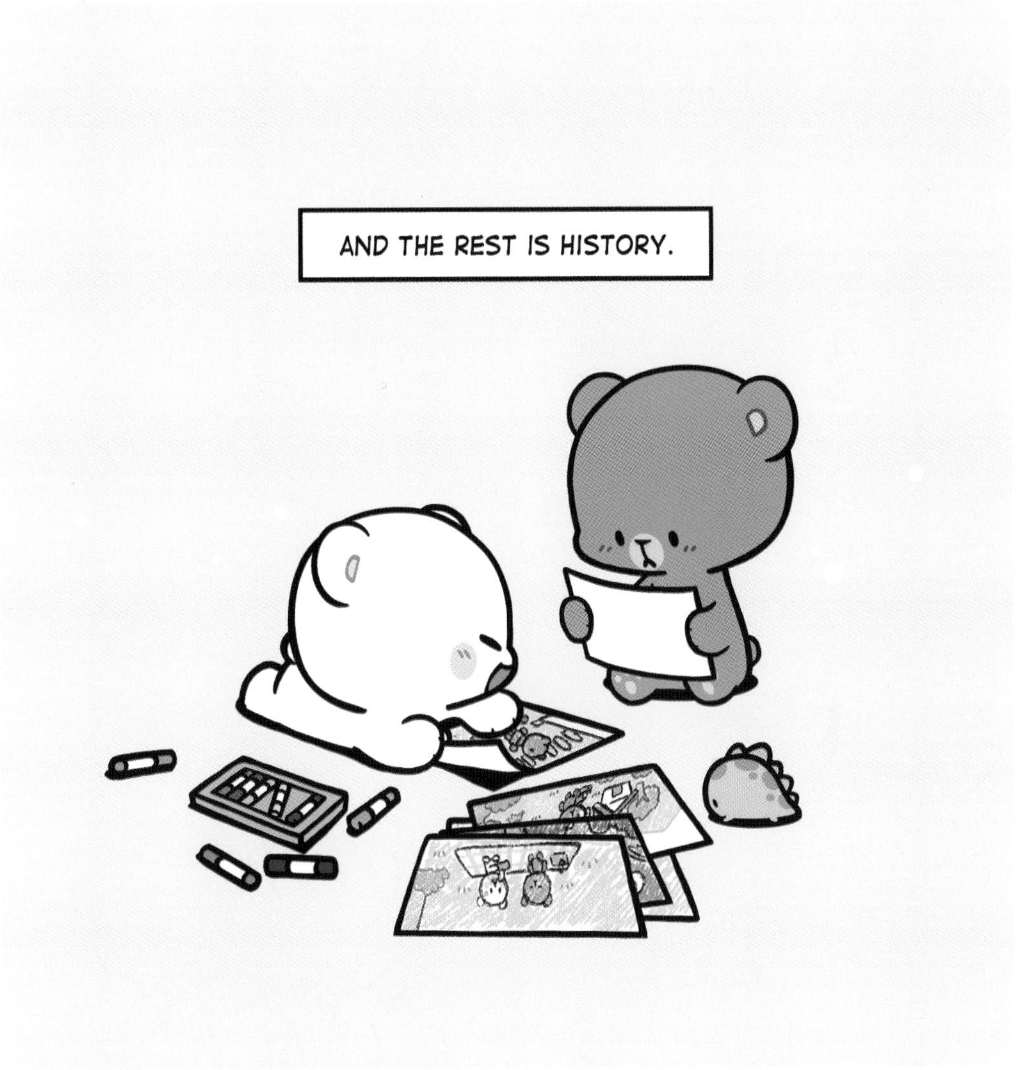
AND THE REST IS HISTORY.

ABOUT THE AUTHOR

Melani Sie is the creator and author behind the popular webcomic *Milk Mocha Bear,* which tells a story about the daily life of two bears and their dino pet. Melani loves to tell stories through her drawings. She lives in Indonesia and currently works to develop more Milk and Mocha stories while furthering their adventures with Klova Studios.

ABOUT KLOVA STUDIOS

Klova Studios manages several intellectual properties from Indonesia, and *Milk Mocha Bear* is one of them. Klova Studios started in 2019 with a vision to hallmark relatable characters and stories that will captivate and entertain a global audience.

Andrews McMeel Publishing
a division of Andrews McMeel Universal
1130 Walnut Street, Kansas City, Missouri 64106

www.andrewsmcmeel.com

23 24 25 26 27 LAK 10 9 8 7 6 5 4 3

ISBN: 978-1-5248-7969-3

Library of Congress Control Number: 2022948587

Editor: Hannah Dussold
Art Director: Julie Barnes
Production Editor: Elizabeth A. Garcia
Production Manager: Chuck Harper

ATTENTION: SCHOOLS AND BUSINESSES
Andrews McMeel books are available at quantity discounts
with bulk purchase for educational, business, or sales promotional use.
For information, please e-mail the Andrews McMeel Publishing
Special Sales Department: sales@amuniversal.com.

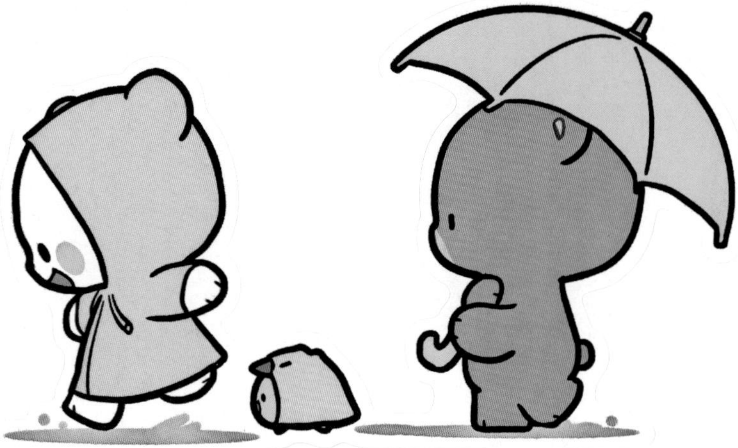
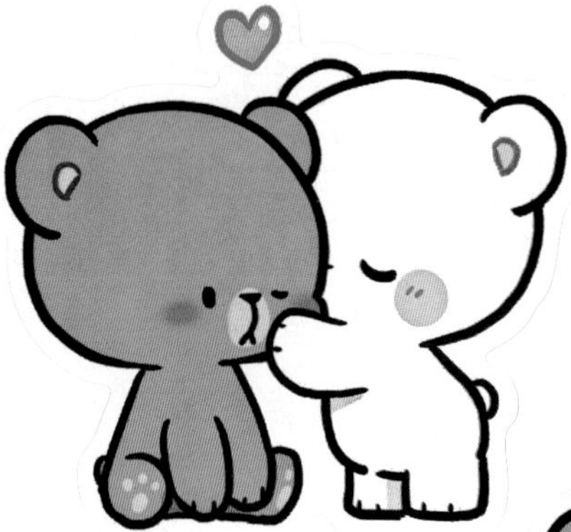
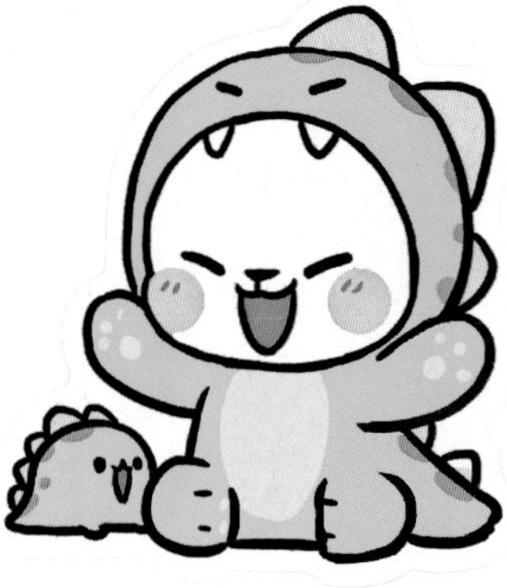
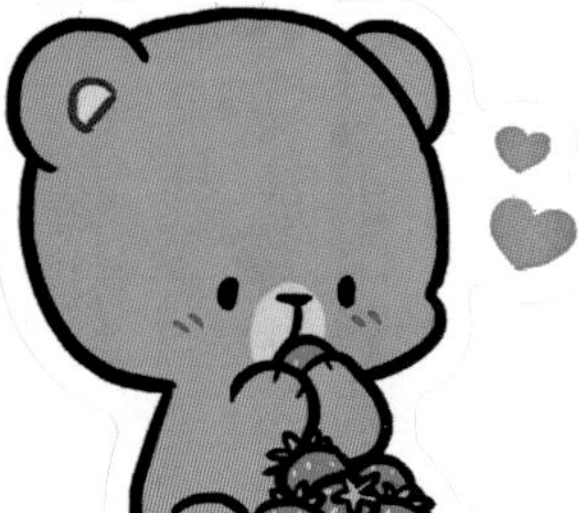
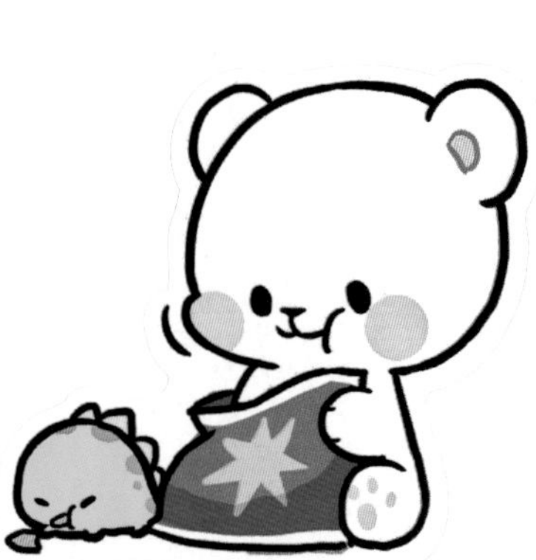
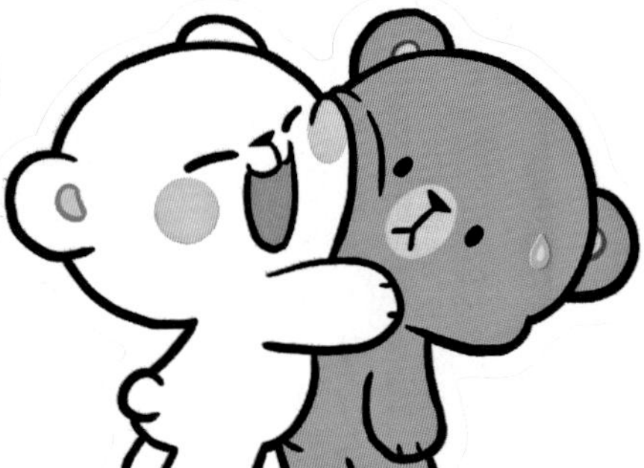

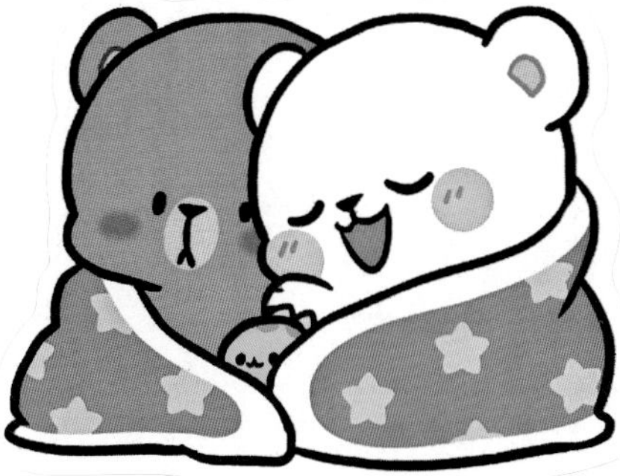

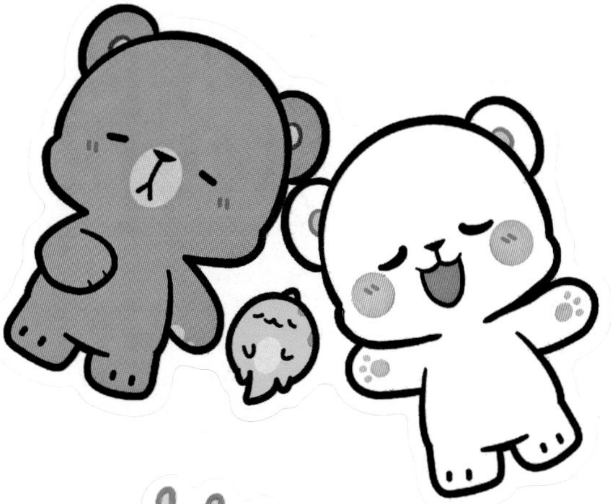

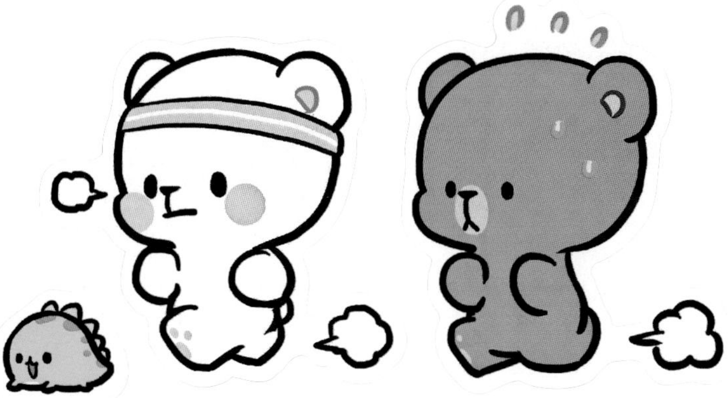

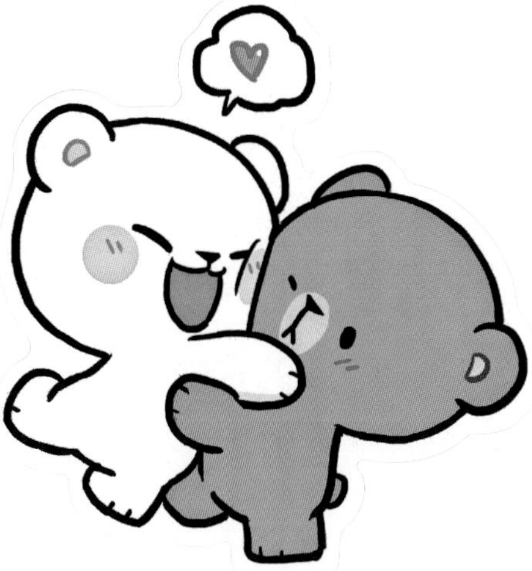

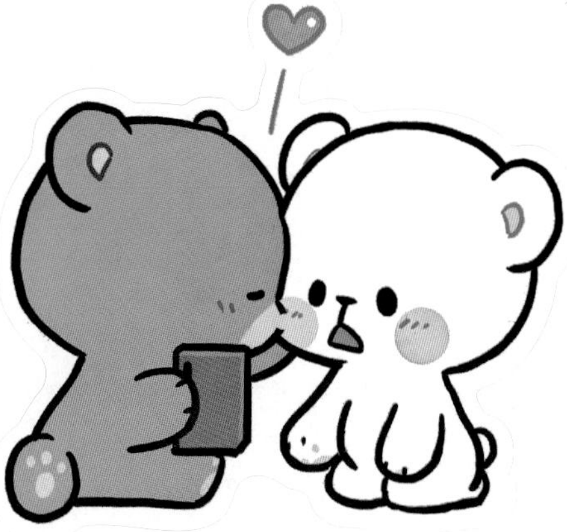